The Third Vision

The Third Vision

THE SCIENCE OF PERSONAL TRANSFORMATION

DR. FRANCIS H. VALA, MD

BALBOA.
PRESS

A DIVISION OF HAY HOUSE

Balboa Press books may be ordered through booksellers or by contacting:

Balboa Press
A Division of Hay House
1663 Liberty Drive
Bloomington, IN 47403
www.balboapress.com
1-(877) 407-4847

Because of the dynamic nature of the Internet, any web addresses or links contained in this book may have changed since publication and may no longer be valid. The views expressed in this work are solely those of the author and do not necessarily reflect the views of the publisher, and the publisher hereby disclaims any responsibility for them.

The author of this book does not dispense medical advice or prescribe the use of any technique as a form of treatment for physical, emotional, or medical problems without the advice of a physician, either directly or indirectly. The intent of the author is only to offer information of a general nature to help you in your quest for emotional and spiritual well-being. In the event you use any of the information in this book for yourself, which is your constitutional right, the author and the publisher assume no responsibility for your actions.

Certain stock imagery © Thinkstock.
Any people depicted in stock imagery provided by Thinkstock are models, and such images are being used for illustrative purposes only.

ISBN: 978-1-4525-6396-1 (e)
ISBN: 978-1-4525-6395-4 (sc)
ISBN: 978-1-4525-6397-8 (hc)

Library of Congress Control Number: 2012922299

Printed in the United States of America

Balboa Press rev. date: 12/12/2012

Dedicated to my adorable and supportive wife,
my angelic mother,
and my heroic father whose wisdom was my guide,
both in this life and afterlife.

CONTENTS

Preface   ix
Introduction   xi

PART 1.   Setting the Stage   1

CHAPTER 1.   Beyond Human Nature   3
CHAPTER 2.   Who Are You?   13

PART 2.   Biological Aspects: The Body   19

CHAPTER 3.   The Brain and the Nervous System   21
CHAPTER 4.   Neuroplasticity   30

PART 3.   Psychological Aspects: The Mind   49

CHAPTER 5.   The Human Psychology   51
CHAPTER 6.   Change Your Thoughts, Change Your Destiny   67
CHAPTER 7.   Human Psyche and the Ladder of Personal Growth   77
CHAPTER 8.   The Pain-Pleasure Principle   92
CHAPTER 9.   Defense Mechanisms of the Ego   109
CHAPTER 10.   Roots of Unhappiness   126

PART 4.   Spiritual Aspects: The Soul   135

CHAPTER 11.   The Science of Spirituality   137
CHAPTER 12.   Secrets of the Soul   155

PART 5.   Social Aspects: The Outer World   171

CHAPTER 13.   Social Aspects of Human Beings   173
CHAPTER 14.   Sexuality   184
CHAPTER 15.   Money and Mind   196
CHAPTER 16.   Mind and Conflict   203

PART 6.   Connecting the Dots   221

CHAPTER 17.   The Third Vision   223
CHAPTER 18.   Conclusion   235

Acknowledgments   255
Endnotes   257
About The Author   265

Why I wrote this book

The modern human being has been on this planet for two hundred thousand years. We experienced a major leap in civilization about six to seven thousand years ago. Despite tremendous advancements in science and technology, our collective problems are only growing. Today, signs of global crisis—economic, political, cultural, and moral—warn us of a threat to the existence of the human being, as well as thirty million other species belonging to this planet. The current civilization has failed to lead humanity to ultimate prosperity and happiness. The question is why? What are we collectively missing?

Mother Earth has been mistreated—as a fragmented body with numerous dysfunctional systems which do not collaborate to maintain its cohesiveness. We have failed to understand this heavenly body as a unified system. The cosmos as we observe it, the micro-cosmos, and the macro-cosmos are all in fact connected as part of a bigger picture—a fact that mankind has failed to understand with the current vision.

As an inquisitive teenager, I wanted to see a positive change. I wanted to make a difference at the highest level possible, but did not know how. Listening to a calling in me, I first became a physician to help others. After serving in underserviced areas in Iran for several years, I realized that I *can* and *must* do more. In pursuit of the dream of higher service, I immigrated to Canada in 1999. I did not exactly know what to do next, but one thing was clear—to follow my inner guidance. In 2002, after the sudden death of my beloved father, I realized my purpose—to write a book and contribute to global education and awareness.

I was determined to continue my journey in a more meaningful way, attempting to put together the pieces of the *puzzle of life*. I started an extensive research, accumulating evidence to some of the most unexplained concepts in humanity. Through this process of transformation, I became convinced of what Albert Einstein had concluded— that we cannot solve the challenging dilemmas of humanity with the same mind that created them!

A shift in paradigm—a new vision—is needed at this critical time of evolution. A new way of thinking from a higher perspective will enable us to perceive and observe Mother Earth as one unified system, connected to the rest of the universe. The book you are now holding in your hands, introducing a new mentality, was once only an idea somewhere in this universe, residing in the mind of this inquisitive young lad and waiting to be materialized into a physical form.

The Third Vision is a simple yet comprehensive approach to understanding different aspects of humanity, supported by a pile of science and evidence. It is intended to help the general population explain some of the most complex mysteries of the world and seemingly unsolvable problems created by mankind. Using a bio-psycho-socio-spiritual model, it provides a fast track for personal and global transformation. Once the truth about YOU is unveiled, the obstacles preventing you from achieving your highest potentials for personal growth will be removed, and your unlimited source of abundance can be accessed!

—*Dr. Francis H. Vala*
2012, Vancouver, Canada

INTRODUCTION

Imagine living in harmony and peace, in a much better world than the one we live in today—a place where geographic boundaries, racial varieties, and differences in opinions and beliefs are seen as possibilities and respected as every human's right. Instead of reasons for disputes and wars, these differences can be looked upon as the beauty and strength of creation and employed collectively to build a better future for generations to come. Commonalities of people can be highlighted, rather than varieties. Imagine a place where we care about the children of others, as we would for our own, and treat everyone the way we would like to be treated! Where poverty, hunger, and homelessness become obsolete! Where we come to realize that there is no true enemy but *ignorance*, and it is recognized as the root of almost all man-made problems, hence fought with through promoting **global education**! Where we realize that we are all connected as part of one unit! Where every non-human species on Earth is also considered as part of the equation in major global decision makings! Where we leave behind our shortsightedness and observe the bigger picture—the entire universe as a unit and a blessing of this creation—a creation that could have been non-existent today if matter was not formed in a split second 13.7 billion years ago!

How could we possibly make our world a better place to live in? What does it take for an individual or a society to contribute to this dream?

Curiosity has led mankind to seek answers to some of the most profound questions throughout history. Questions fascinating us with the mysteries of our astonishing universe, such as: Who am I? Why do people behave or think the way they do? Where do we come from?

Where do we end up? What is life all about? What is the meaning and purpose of life? Why do we have so many man-made problems today despite all the advancements in science and technology, and with all the religious and non-religious guides in the past and present? What is right or wrong, and who determines that? Who sets the normal or abnormal standards in a society? Is there a connection between our internal world and the external world around us, and if so, what is it? Does karma exist, and what is the science behind it? And probably most important, where can we find the answers to these questions?

These challenging questions have haunted me since age eighteen. Undoubtedly, millions of other people have similar questions at some point in their life. These are universal inquiries. It was the sudden death of my father in 2002 that instigated an urge to speed up the process of personal growth and transformation. Somehow, the deep emotional attachment to my father, who was also my best friend, and the withdrawal following his death created an immense connection to my inner soul and an enormous desire to find a way to be a better human!

In the quest to find answers, I realized that it is very unusual to find them where one would normally look—from family, friends, school, university, society, media, etc. In fact, it takes a lot more than the conventional, existing educational systems to deliver these life-skill answers. Wouldn't it be ideal to have a Life Skill Institution? Believe it or not, there is none. Unfortunately, some of the most basic skills are not being taught at schools and universities. Plus, most parents, who are the main guides of children during their most critical period of learning and development, are confused and lack the ability to pass on holistic knowledge because they never learned it in the first place. Thus, the snowball of ignorance continues, and this gap creates an opportunity for the media to lead societies in favor of a minority, at the cost of all inhabitants of this globe. This *partially* explains why we have so many problems today.

As a physician, I have learned, through my training and experience, to acquire a holistic approach to my patients' problems and to try to see beyond the apparent physical, mental, or behavioral presentation. In most cases, the presenting problem in a doctor's office is in fact a symptom of a much larger underlying distress in the person's present or past life. This may be dismissed or unexplored for various reasons, such as limitation of time, lack of expertise, lack of comfort of the practitioner in dealing with mental issues, and misrepresentation of the main problem by the patient due to confusion. This often results in a temporary "cure" or no cure at all, leading to frequent visits to different health care providers or other self-prescribed remedies; we turn to drinking or drugs, to fads or fetishes, or we import others' answers (philosophy, religion, politics, etc.).

In the last ten years, through extensive research, a pile of scientific evidence and philosophical explanations of some of these profound and unanswered inquiries has been accumulated. In the following chapters, some of the pieces of the *puzzle of life* will be shared with you, based on scientific facts and yet-to-be-proven opinions and theories, that you may find astoundingly pivotal in how you can change your path and take control of your life.

PART ONE

Setting the Stage

CHAPTER 1

"Where there is ruin, there is hope for a treasure."
—Rumi

Beyond Human Nature

For thousands of years, humanity has been suffering from illnesses at individual, societal, and international levels. Anxiety and depression, prostitution and crime, and worldwide wars are only a few of these examples. Despite hundreds of spiritual, religious, and non-religious leaders, and in spite of tremendous advancements in science and technology, our collective problems are only growing. *The question is why? Why do we still have so many problems today?*

The root of these problems points to one common element—not fully understanding the multidimensional human being. We cannot solve the challenging dilemmas of humanity with the same mind that created them! Of over thirty million species living on planet Earth, the two-legged human being is the only one changing the course and fate of this planet.

In order to make our dream of living in a better world come true, we must understand all aspects of the human being—biologically, psychologically, socially, and spiritually—especially how these are all interrelated. The following true, unrelated cases represent some of the most complex dilemmas endangering mankind at three levels— individual, social, and international. Although it may sound impossible to understand the root cause of these disorders, specific universal patterns and formulas explained in this book will unveil some of the mysteries of the mentality behind these scenarios.

Case 1

AK smiles, running his hands through his grey hair. He is a sixty-seven-year-old retired university professor. He had several visits to our Sexual Medicine Clinic at the Vancouver General Hospital. He appears intelligent, kind, and passionate about life. Had it not been for past experience in my career, it would have been very difficult to believe what he was there for.

AK presented with multiple forms of *paraphilia* (sexual deviations). Some of these included *transvestism* (feeling aroused when wearing the clothes of the opposite sex), *pedophilia* (engaging in any sexual activity with minors), *zoophilia* (engaging in any sexual activity with animals), *porn addiction*, *urophilia* (condition in which the person derives sexual excitement from urination), and more. However, he did not have *sadism* or *masochism*; he did not like to inflict physical pain on himself or others.

Without the knowledge and understanding of medicine and psychology, it would be easy to judge AK as a "bad person" with "evil" thoughts. But when I got to know him, he was actually a sincere, pleasant, and generous person who had lots of love for the world. AK had insight into his problems.

"The reason I'm here seeking help is that I have major problems in my mind and do not want to cause any physical or emotional harm to anyone. I just don't know how to stop these thoughts," he said. "Whenever I feel distressed about something, these thoughts continue to haunt me, and depending on my mood, I feel impulsive to act upon them, but then I would feel guilty and suffer even more." AK felt less guilty with acts that did not involve others, such as transvestism and porn addiction. He tried hard to avoid acts that involved others, such as zoophilia or pedophilia. He was fully aware of the legal consequences of these acts and hence sought help to get rid of these intensely provocative thoughts and feelings.

AK related his problems to childhood. He was a survivor of World War II and grew up in Germany in the post-war era. His father was killed in the war, so AK grew up with his harsh mother, who barely survived the war. He had few memories of early childhood (due to a defense mechanism called *repression*), but what he did remember was mostly negative.

Unfortunately, the treatment for these complex psychological disorders is very difficult. AK was referred to another psychiatrist with extensive experience in psychoanalysis, for psychotherapy, and my supervisor and I were following him on the side. At the time, I was training in my fellowship for Sexual Medicine. Over time, his condition improved as he gained more understanding of his thoughts and feelings. His life was less miserable but nowhere near satisfaction. We were thinking of starting him on medications to reduce sexual desire. These medications are generally used for the hypersexual criminals, and there was no clear evidence whether AK would benefit from them or not.

Case 2

I was approached by my supervisor in the corridor of the clinic. His eyes sparkled with excitement. "You don't want to miss the next case. I'll see you in half an hour," he said, smiling as he walked away. I was eager to see the next case. I rushed to finish my paperwork and grabbed the next patient's chart for preparation.

BT was a very interesting case from a psychological point of view. He was a middle-aged, Caucasian successful business owner. He had seen my supervisor over several visits and was happy to tell us that he *finally* found a surgeon to agree to amputate his hand.

BT had been struggling for a long time to find a surgeon to agree to amputate his healthy left hand. Initially, he sought help from his family physician and was referred for psychological assessment. He had seen multiple psychiatrists who formed a joint committee and approved his request, referring him to an orthopedic surgeon who agreed to comply unwillingly.

Who on earth would want to amputate a healthy part of the body? The condition is called *apotemnophilia*, also known as Amputee Identity Disorder. It is a rare psychiatric disorder where the person feels incomplete in the complete body, and feels complete in the incomplete body. There is a desire to amputate a *specific* part of the body to feel complete and healthy. In the absence of a surgeon to perform this procedure, some patients have gone as far as performing it spontaneously, leading to disaster and death. This condition is also referred to as Body Integrity Identity Disorder (BIID).

BT left the clinic that day enthusiastic about seeing the orthopedic surgeon and having his hand amputated. Apparently, the "extra" part of his body was his left hand, not the right one or any other part. This seems to be a common feature of the *apotemnophilia* patients; they are obsessed with eliminating one *specific* part of the body. I had never even heard about this disorder before that day. After interviewing the patient, my supervisor gave me a small book. The author had collected all the case reports and the latest expert opinions on how to deal with this disease.

How did two fairly successful individuals from a relatively high social class end up with these odd disorders?

These two cases are extraordinary. However, as you will see, they share some of the basic principles of human psychology, yet on a much exaggerated scale. By the end of this book, some of the most complex aspects of human behavior, including the ones above, can be understood in a more simplified approach.

Case 3

It was a hot summer day in 1997. I jumped out of my seat when the phone rang. It was my superior officer. "Mark your calendar for tomorrow for a special task," he said in a mysterious tone. "You cannot miss this."

Curious to know more, I asked, "Do you want to tell me anything more about it?"

He replied, "All I can tell you at this time is that this is a special situation."

I was serving my mandatory military service as a medical doctor in the police force in a small town in southern Iran. At the time, all men had a mandatory obligation to serve their country for two years at age eighteen or after graduation from university. As part of my duties in that specific area, I had to act as a forensic physician or "legal doctor" in criminal cases.

I was informed later in the day that, following a nine-month trial, two men were convicted of first-degree murder and were to be hanged as part of their death penalty the next day. They had hijacked a taxi and murdered the driver when he refused to give them the money they had demanded. My job as a medical police officer was to check their heartbeats and make sure they were dead, as part of the hanging ceremony, which was held in public! Unfortunately, I had no choice but to accept; otherwise I would be penalized for disobedience.

The death penalty is a routine practice in many countries, including Iran, for first-degree murderers and serial killers. In many cases, the task of executing the criminal offender is offered to the closest person to the victim. In this case, the victim's brother accepted the responsibility of completing the execution.

I cannot forget the scene. He kicked the chairs on which the offenders were standing with the rope around their necks, one at a time. After a little while, both villains were announced dead. There was chaos among the public. The relatives of the murderers were screaming in agony, while the friends and family of the victim were cheering and shouting words of justice.

Why do some people commit crimes regardless of the consequences? Why do others never commit a crime, no matter how desperate their circumstances may be? Why is the crime rate increasing throughout the world? What are the root causes of crime? How can it be reduced or prevented?

Case 4

It was 1948. Criminals who were prosecuted after World War II in international courts, for taking part in the Holocaust, were found guilty of crimes against humanity.

The term Holocaust is generally used to describe the killing of approximately six million Jews during World War II, a program of deliberate extermination planned and executed by the National Socialist German Workers Party in Germany, led by Adolf Hitler. This was accomplished in stages. Legislation to remove the Jews from civil society was enacted years before the outbreak of World War II. Concentration camps were established in which inmates were used for slave labor until they died of exhaustion or disease. Where the Third Reich

7

conquered new territory in Eastern Europe, specialized units murdered Jews and political opponents in mass shootings. Jews were packed into ghettos before being transported hundreds of miles by freight train to extermination camps. If they survived the journey, the majority of them were killed in gas chambers. Men were forced to dig their own graves before being shot by SS troops. Every arm of Germany's bureaucracy was involved in the logistics of the mass murder, turning the country into a "a genocidal nation."

Other targets of the Nazi mass murder, or "Nazi genocidal policy," included Slavs (Poles, Russians, Ukrainians, Belarusians, Serbs, Czechoslovaks, and others), Romani people, the mentally ill, homosexuals and "sexual deviants," Jehovah's Witnesses, and political opponents. R. Rummel estimates that over sixteen million people died as a result of genocide.

How is this sort of behavior even possible from the "intelligent being"? What could be some of the motives behind genocide? How could a criminal act to this extent become a national teamwork project?

The Big Question: Why?

Science and religion have somewhat failed to free humanity of its own-made problems. Politics and economics also play a major role in the process. This is partly justified by the complexity of our world and its inhabitants, and we may be thousands of years away from fully understanding the big picture. I wonder if the capacity for the big picture is even possible. Cognitive science seems to indicate that we are restricted by the capacity of our senses, and if phenomena are not perceptible by these limited means (or with their extensions, such as microscopes, telescopes, satellites, etc.), we will always have only part of the picture. Yet, truly, there is a bigger scheme that is humanly possible. However, one question is crucial to answer in order to reach our final desired destination: *Are we on the right track?* In other words, are we moving toward or away from who or where we want to be?

Some of the reasons for relative failures are outlined below.

1. *Connecting the dots.* While each path in life has helped identify pieces of the puzzle, the big picture is missing. In order to have a better sense of the big picture, we need to understand the **connection**s

between these pieces. Imagine a jigsaw puzzle, where you have all the pieces, and your task is to complete it to the best of your ability. How would that be possible without paying attention to the lines and connections in between?

2. *Lack of unity.* In general, humanity has failed to envision the entire universe—or at least Mother Earth—as a single unit. The lack of understanding of our ecosystem and its crucial role in our survival leads humans, organizations, and governments to behave in a destructive manner to achieve short-term gains, resulting in long-term consequences. One example is global warming, which is moving us closer to climate instability and the extinction of our own species. Similarly, our selfishness—and not necessarily our *ego*—may eliminate specific nations, people, races, religions, and other living creatures from the global benefits that belong to all inhabitants of the world. We can easily forget that humans are only one of the thirty million species that inhabit Mother Earth. This is predominantly based on our lack of understanding of the most complex phenomena in the world—the human brain, mind, and psyche!

3. *Inadequacy of the scientific approach.* Despite all our scientific achievements, what we know today is only a fraction of what is unknown to humanity. Furthermore, it is problematic to rely on science as the sole way to reach the ultimate truth and explain the big picture. Accessibility to science is limited, either due to the simple fact of illiteracy, or for other reasons, such as poverty, lack of technology and information, and politics. For most scientific literature, there seems to be a need for translation of information into simple and understandable language, in order to make it useful for the majority of the population. It seems like most specialists become enamored with their own jargon and create the illusion that specialized naming makes something real.

4. *The class effect.* When one is highly educated, there is a sense of belonging to a higher social class, limiting connection to other people from various backgrounds and social levels. This disconnection may limit the real purpose for which education was designed, restricting accessibility for many underserved populations in the world. The level of education is only one of the ways in which classes are determined, formally or informally. Wealth, race, nationality, etc. are all gradations

that we choose to make distinctions about, assigning worth or importance.

5. *The iceberg analogy.* As mental health practitioners, those we see seeking medical help as the "ill" or "unhealthy" represent only the tip of the iceberg (which some believe reflects only about 10 percent of this population). The majority of "normal" people have hidden issues that may surface at some point. While millions of psychiatrists, psychologists, counselors, and other mental health practitioners primarily target the "cure of illness," the vast majority of the population—the rest of the iceberg—is missing out, with a significant proportion of them becoming ill at some point later in life. In fact, the supply simply does not match the demand! *Mental health is much more than just the absence of mental illness!*

Our existing models of mental health care delivery simply do not work efficiently, and it is time to change our approach and look at new ways to enhance access to the entire world. As we all know, the "global village" is significantly interconnected and needs to be treated as one "body," as opposed to separate organs or systems. Current educational and health care systems—at community, national, and international levels—are deficient in programs and resources that focus on the **prevention** of mental illness and **promotion** of mental wellness. Instead, they are focused on *curative* programs. We need more proactive and preventive programs to teach individuals at very early stages of development and personal growth, to self-manage their issues and distresses. "One ounce of prevention is better than a pound of cure!"

6. *What is the weakness of religion?* While religions may have been very powerful and possibly the best approach to help people with their personal growth thousands of years ago, they do not seem to meet the needs of generations today. Human beings today have a different mentality, brain structure, and view of the world. Thus, a different language with more scientific explanation is needed. With the advancement in science and our understanding of the world, blind faith is not the best solution for personal growth anymore. In fact, being restricted to one discipline or path with a limited view of the world, and having a lack of skepticism, criticism, and creativity, is *incompatible* with the very fundamental nature of humanity—**a free spirit with unlimited potential**! It also creates the opportunity for being manipulated and abused by irresponsible

individuals who mimic the role of a religious leader. Examples like the sex scandals in the Catholic church crisis, or the extremists in different religions are testimonies to this deficiency.

7. *Political and economic failures.* The world's economy is led by major gigantic corporations that are in control of the media and capable of using it to their advantage. They tremendously benefit from ordinary people's consumerism. What these corporations may not realize is that they are a subset of a larger resource provider—the Earth's biosphere. The end goal for these corporations is unlimited growth, which is not possible with our limited resources, not without detrimental consequences to all life on Earth. Today, there is no doubt about the effect of fossil fuels and greenhouse gases on climate changes. Despite many other sustainable forms of energy, such as solar, wind, and other green fuels, we continue to drain the oil-based fuels for economic gains. *Human greed and consumerism is the number-one threat to climate change, jeopardizing the existence of millions of species, including humanity.* The two-legged, intelligent creature has become the worst poison to the global "body," acting like cancer cells and utilizing all the resources in an exponential way without respecting nature's rights. In the context of "lifestyle," we have come to believe that "nature" is property belonging to humans, and we have the right to use it any way we want. Yet, we use the phrase *human nature* to excuse a host of failings. We seem to have forgotten that we *are* part of nature, and each of the fifty trillion cells in our body is made up of **natural** elements. What is it about being human that causes us to see ourselves as separate and apart? This exponential surge in consumerism and misuse of the planet's resources will inevitably lead to self-destruction. No one and no species is immune from disaster. After all, we're all in the same boat! The only hope is that we humans respond to the wake-up alarm and **act now**, before it's too late. We need to think and act *globally. We need a change of global culture and lifestyle!*

8. *Do we truly understand the ego?* Finally, one of the most profound and fundamental dilemmas is lack of understanding of the ego and its defense mechanisms. In most philosophies, the message is to suppress the ego if you want to achieve happiness and freedom. In the following chapters though, it will be clarified why it is not the best idea to suppress your ego—simply because it is equipped with extremely powerful defense mechanisms that will not allow you to do so without detrimental

consequences! The best strategy is to learn about it in an attempt to understand it, and to simply live with it in harmony and peace!

I believe a global change in our mentality is necessary—change in our lifestyle, culture, and educational systems. *Unless we change the way we look at things, things will not change!* Maybe it is time for a **Psychological Revolution**! What is holding us back, as a species, from moving toward a better future? What are the obstacles, and how can they be removed?

In this book, you will find several features designed to address some of the most mysterious inquiries humanity has been struggling with for thousands of years.

- Scientific explanations of some of the most complex philosophical questions are unveiled using a holistic **bio-psycho-socio-spiritual** approach to understand humans. Evidence is based on numerous sciences, including biology, medicine, genetics, psychology and psychiatry, neuroscience, sociology, anthropology, history, astrology, cosmology, physics and mechanics, chemistry, mathematics, etc.
- Existing theories, models, and ideas borrowed from other intellectuals, as well as those of my own, are proposed to tackle some of the most challenging dilemmas.
- Scientific evidence will be referenced for those skeptical minds that seek further evidence and supportive material.
- Significant emphasis is placed on the connections between what we have learned to date, trying to understand the big picture.
- By emphasizing proactive prevention, this material is designed to help individuals acquire self-management skills at any stage of their personal growth.
- It will demonstrate a new vision—the **Third Vision**—to observe the world from a higher perspective and move toward making it a better **global nation**!

Let us now begin this exhilarating journey with one of the most fundamental questions posed by mankind: Who am I?

CHAPTER 2

*"Do not be satisfied with the stories that come
before you. Unfold your own myth."*
—Rumi

Who Are You?

Truth versus Reality

Ancient people believed that the Earth was flat. The prevailing theory
of the universe included a flat Earth around which the sun, moon, and
stars all revolved. The ancient Greeks began to speculate that the Earth
is spherical as far back as 570 BC. Plato, a Greek philosopher, put forth
the theory of a spherical earth. Pythagoras, a Greek mathematician,
later confirmed the theory through mathematical calculations: the earth
was round. In the sixteenth century, an ambitious sea expedition was
made by the Portuguese Ferdinand Magellan. By navigating around
the earth in 1522, he proved it to be round, once and for all. Ferdinand
Magellan provided firsthand proof by being the first person to sail all
the way around the Earth.

Every judgment about our "reality" should be defined in the context
of *Time, Person, and Place (TPP)*. Before this concept was officially
proven and widely accepted, many people in different parts of the world
had their own theories, including, "The world is flat," or, "The world
is sitting on the back of a turtle." Now, the myth has been solved, and
there is no argument in any part of the world!

So what is the reality of the shape of Earth? Is reality the same as truth?

No. There is a major difference between truth and reality. While the truth has *always* been that the world is spherical since its birth 4.6 billion years ago, this was not discovered and validated until 1522. Before then, the reality of different people was *what they believed to be true*. Their reality was a flat Earth, or something sitting on the back of a huge turtle! Once proven, the truth and reality became one!

This exemplifies the difference between a fact and an opinion. For every concept, there is only one truth, but there may be multiple realities. The truth is the fact (objective)! Reality is an opinion—an observer's **perception** and understanding of that truth (subjective). It is what they **believe** to be the truth!

So, what is the point?

With this introductory explanation about the difference between truth and reality, let us unveil one of the most fundamental misunderstandings about who we are—our *identity*.

A universal dilemma: The Mask

Twelve-year-old CH is the recipient of a treatment that cured his congenital blindness. CH was able to navigate his way through school and identify people across a crowded room by only the sounds of their voices, but he now has full vision. Scientists are able to cure certain forms of congenital blindness through gene replacement therapy. Doctors introduce a replacement gene via a virus into the eye, and it can cure a type of congenital blindness called Leber's Congenital Amaurosis (LCA).

As soon as I read this news, my mind started wandering. Hmm ... it would be interesting to try an experiment on CH, who was born blind. Imagine he is placed in front of three different mirrors—a concave, a convex, and a plane mirror. He has never seen himself before and has no point of reference to compare to! He sees three different figures: short and fat, tall and thin, and the third image in between. Which one is CH? Which one is the "real" image from his perspective?

The answer is: he does not know. He may have an intuitive understanding of his image, but he would not know for sure until someone else told him or he saw himself in other mirrors. The first image that CH perceives or believes to be the real self becomes his reality. *This is what I look like—this is me!* If someone decides to play a trick on CH and shows him only one mirror—let's say the concave one—repeatedly, how would CH view himself? The answer is: short and fat. Although he may soon discover the misperception when he compares himself to other people, the point here is that *we tend to believe what we see, even though it may be an illusion.* This is a common mistake of the human mind, which has caused us a lot of problems!

Suppose CH never received the treatment and remained blind. How did he see himself before his cure? How did he observe his self—his identity?

The human subconscious mind, which will be explained in detail in later chapters, creates an illusion of who we truly are. The *reality* of "you"—what you appear to be or who you think you are—is different from the *truth* about "YOU."

From a psychological point of view, every human being has two identities.

1. The true identity, hereon expressed as "YOU" with capital letters, is your unconditioned divine self that came with you since birth, and even before birth with the consummation of the sperm and egg.

2. The false identity, hereon expressed as "you," becomes your reality. It is nothing but a perceived image of your true identity. This illusionary self, which is falsely believed to be the real you, is conditioned over time based on learned experiences and exposures.

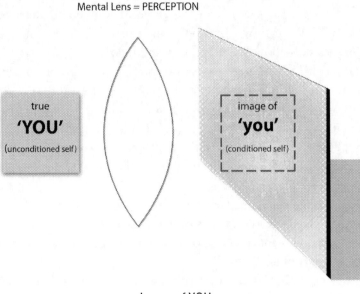

Image of YOU

As demonstrated in the diagram, the fundamentally critical point is this: the image of your identity shaping your reality—the real you—is in fact, a **reflection** of your true identity—the true YOU—filtered through the observer's lens, called **perception**. The type of lens you wear determines how you view yourself, create your reality, and shape your destiny. What is observed and defined as your identity is nothing but a mask.

Suppose we wish to unveil this mask and understand these two identities in depth and in relation to each other. Let us take this concept to our imaginary body shop, break it apart, and rebuild it. What do we want this renovated identity to look like? How would our wishful life and dream planet look like if we had the opportunity to discover the truth about our self?

My intention is to help the general population explore some of the most complex mysteries of the world and seemingly unsolvable problems created by mankind. In the following chapters, I will introduce a different perspective to view the big picture of life—a new lens called the **Third Vision.** The first few chapters will expand on the basic science of the nervous system (the hardware) in an oversimplified way.

The next chapters will reveal its relevance to how humans function in their thoughts, feelings, and behaviors (the software). Part five explains complex aspects of how an individual relates to the outside world. In the final part of the book, the dots will be connected, and practical solutions will be summarized.

PART TWO

Biological Aspects:
The Body

CHAPTER 3

"Science knows no country, because knowledge belongs to humanity, and is the torch which illuminates the world. Science is the highest personification of the nation because that nation will remain the first which carries the furthest the works of thought and intelligence."
—Louis Pasteur

The Brain and the Nervous System

While visiting the Kennedy Space Center in Florida in 2007, something caught my eye. In one of the crowded visitor areas, the following was written in bold print: *Someday in the near future, our children or grandchildren will be born on Mars—the first Martians!*

That same night, I heard a heartbreaking news on TV. A young teenager was arrested and sentenced to three consecutive lifetimes in prison after a prolonged trial in Seattle, Washington. He was convicted of first-degree murder of his parents and disabled sister, together with his best friend. His motive seemed to be greed—access to $350,000 in life insurance!

Hmmm … I thought. How far has humanity gone in technology and science to explore the wonders of the universe? In the near future, the first spacecraft, possibly manned, will have the ability to travel beyond our galaxy. At the same time, how far can humans descend in cruelty? There seems to be no limit in some individuals. Crime and other social diseases are growing despite the significant advancements in science and technology.

How is this possible? What are we collectively missing? How can we utilize the knowledge, expertise, and technology acquired in the past and present to make this world a better place to live?

I believe we are missing the connections between the dots. Without understanding humanity with a comprehensive view as a multidimensional being, it is impossible to resolve fundamental problems created by mankind!

Extraordinary Structure of the Human Brain

I remember traveling by bus from one city to another about fifteen years ago. "Mom, do crocodiles feel bad after eating somebody?" asked a sweet, inquisitive, young boy in the seat behind me. Giggling, I turned around and looked at the boy with a smile, and then looked at his mom, who was also giggling. He was about six years old and had a round face with cute little glasses. I thought to myself, *Hmm ... how come I never thought of that? Do they really have any feelings?* Indeed, I didn't think they would feel remorse, simply because they were hungry! But I didn't know if they ever had any kind of feelings at all! What do *you* think? Well ... you'll find out.

Trying to understand how the human thinks, feels, behaves, and runs his daily activities without exploring the brain and the nervous system in further detail is irrational. Undoubtedly, the brain is the master of mind and body. Through a complex network of electrochemical activities, the **nervous system** can receive and deliver signals to different parts of the body. The endocrine system also plays a significant role in controlling various organs and tissues. It consists of organs that produce and secrete hormones (proteins that regulate the biochemical function of tissues, organs, and cells, either locally or through the bloodstream).

The Brain Evolution

The brain is *the most complex* phenomenon in the world! Weighing about three pounds (with 85 percent of that being water), it accounts for only 2 percent of the body weight, while consuming 20 percent of our energy. Despite remarkable discoveries about the brain in the last few centuries, the unknowns about this miraculous phenomenon are so significant that we are only beginning to understand some of its mysteries. Thanks to modern technology, we are now much more capable of obtaining objective measurements and assessments of the brain functions. The use of PET scans, SPECT scans, brain mapping, functional MRI (fMRI), etc., each with their weaknesses and strengths, has set a new foundation, enabling us to conduct scientific research to prove or disprove theories about the brain.

Science will eventually unveil myths about our brain, mind, and body, and we will progressively have a better understanding of the connection between our internal and external worlds. This may have both negative and positive impacts on our society and us. The complexity of our brain, with its unlimited unknowns, is an opportunity for us as humans to have a significant leap forward in understanding the connections between our brain, mind, body, and the rest of the world. Thus, I believe we are in the verge of a scientific revolution in the coming decades. *It is an opportunity for humanity to shape the future direction of the world!*

For the purpose of this book, the three virtual levels of the brain will be briefly described in an oversimplified manner.

1. *Hindbrain*—consisting mainly of the **brainstem**
2. *Midbrain*—composed mainly of the **limbic system**
3. *Forebrain*—which holds one of the most critical parts, the **prefrontal cortex (PFC)**

The Ice Cream Analogy

Throughout evolution, the human brain has acquired three components that progressively appeared and became superimposed, just like in an archeological site: the oldest, located underneath and to the back; the next one, resting on an intermediate position, and the most recent, situated on top and to the front. They are, respectively:

1) The **archipallium** or **primitive** (reptilian) brain, comprising the structures of the brainstem (1). It corresponds to the reptile brain, also called the *R-complex* by the famous neuroscientist Paul MacLean.

2) The **paleopallium** or **intermediate** (old or inferior mammalian) brain, comprising the structures of the limbic system. It corresponds to the brain of the inferior mammals.

3) The **neopallium**, also known as the **superior** or **rational** (new mammalian) brain, comprises almost the entire hemispheres (made up of a more recent type of cortex, called **neocortex**) and some subcortical neuronal groups. It corresponds to the brain of the superior mammals, thus including the primates and, consequently, the human species.

Ice cream analogy of the brain

Actually, we have three units in a single brain. These three layers appeared, one after the other, during the development of the fetus, restating chronologically, the evolution of animal species, from lizards up to homo sapiens. According to Maclean, they are three biological computers, and although they are interconnected, each one retains "their peculiar types of intelligence, subjectivity, sense of time and space, memory, and other less specific functions."

Three layers of the brain evolved over millions of years

The Brainstem (Hindbrain)

The brainstem is the lower extension of the brain where it connects to the spinal cord. It is part of the primitive (reptilian) brain, which is responsible for *self-preservation*. It is in the primitive brain that the instinctive reactions of the so-called reflex arcs occur, and the commands that allow some involuntary actions such as functions of the heart, lung, and the gastrointestinal system. Neurological functions located in the brainstem include those necessary for *survival* (breathing, digestion, heart rate, blood pressure, etc.) and for *arousal* (being awake and alert). *The key component to this system is **survival**, meaning that the entire system is designed biologically to sustain and preserve life!*

The brainstem is involved in the following critical functions:

- Alertness (level of consciousness)
- Arousal
- Breathing
- Blood pressure
- Contains most of the cranial nerves
- Digestion
- Heart rate
- Other autonomic functions
- Relays information between the peripheral nerves and spinal cord to the upper parts of the brain

Thus, brainstem damage is very serious and often life-threatening. Diseases of the brainstem can also result in abnormalities in the function of cranial nerves, which may lead to visual disturbances, pupil abnormalities, changes in sensation, muscle weakness, hearing problems, vertigo, swallowing and speech difficulty, voice change, and coordination problems.

The Limbic System (Midbrain)

In 1878, the French physician Paul Broca first called this part of the brain *"le grand lobe limbique,"* but most of its crucial role in emotion was unveiled only in 1937 when the American physician, James Papez, described his anatomical model of emotion, the Papez circuit (2). It was initially recognized as the *"emotional center"* of the brain, but we now know that this area serves other purposes as well. Many scientists have suggested the use of *"limbic system"'* and abandoning "center." This system commands certain behaviors that are necessary for the survival of all mammals. Emotions and feelings like fright, passion, love, hate, joy, and sadness are mammalian inventions, originated in the limbic system. This system is also responsible for some aspects of personal identity and for important functions related to memory. Similar structures can be found in almost all mammals, such as dogs, cats, and mice. Reptiles, however, only possess a brainstem, and this answers the six-year-old child's question!

The limbic system consists of a number of anatomical structures, but the four most recognized ones are (HHAT):

- *Hypothalamus.* Known as the brain's **pharmacy** or drug factory. Critical in homeostasis and involved in many endocrine functions (3).
- *Hippocampus.* Required for the formation of long-term memories and implicated in maintenance of cognitive maps for navigation. It converts short-term to long-term memories (4).
- *Amygdala.* Involved in **emotional memory** and social functions, such as mating. Also known by many neuroscientists as the **stress center** (5).

- *Thalamus.* A large double-lobed structure, known as the **relay center**. Involved in relaying sensation and motor signals to the cerebral cortex, along with the regulation of consciousness, sleep, and alertness.

Other important components of the limbic system are:

- *Pituitary Gland.* Known as the **master gland**. Involved in hormonal regulation of vital functions, such as growth and metabolism.
- *Mammillary Bodies.* Important for the formation of memory and **memory recognition**.
- *Cingulate Gyrus.* Also known as the brain's **shifting gear**. Involved in autonomic functions regulating heart rate, blood pressure, and cognitive and attentional processing.
- *Dentate Gyrus.* Thought to contribute to new memories and to regulate happiness.
- *Nucleus Accumbens.* Known as the brain's famous **pleasure or reward center**. Also involved in addiction.

Prefrontal Cortex (Part of the Forebrain)

When the superior mammals arrived on the Earth (the primates and descendants up to the homo sapiens or modern human beings), the third cerebral unit was developed: the neopallium or rational brain, a highly complex net of neural cells capable of producing a symbolic language, thus enabling man to exercise skillful, intellectual tasks, such as reading, writing, and performing mathematical calculations. This part of the brain is the great generator of ideas or, as expressed by Paul MacLean, *"it is the mother of invention and the father of abstractive thought."*

The prefrontal cortex **(PFC)** is the very front of the brain, located right beneath the forehead. It is fairly large in man and some species of dolphins. It underwent a great deal of development and expanded greatly in size throughout the hominid evolution, turning into the homo sapiens. In the past seven million years of human evolution, the size of the PFC has increased six-fold. The size of the PFC relative to the rest of the brain has also increased. Throughout these seven million years, the brain itself has only increased in size about three-fold.

The PFC is involved and responsible for planning complex cognitive behaviors and executive functions, which include mediating conflicting thoughts, making choices between right and wrong or good and bad, predicting future events, and governing social control, such as suppressing emotional or sexual urges. The prefrontal cortex is the brain center most strongly implicated in qualities like sentience, human intelligence, and personality. It is reasonable to say that the PFC is the neurological basis of the **conscience**, and the main center of our **conscious thinking**, which will be explained in detail in later chapters. Weak interconnections between the PFC and the rest of the brain have been observed in criminals, sociopaths, drug addicts, and schizophrenics.

The PFC does not belong to the traditional limbic circuit, but its intense bi-directional connections with thalamus, amygdala, and other subcortical structures account for the important role it plays in the formation and, specially, in the expression of affective states. When the pathways between the PFC and the rest of the brain are damaged due to head injury, massive personality changes can result. The prototypical example is Phineas Gage, a railway worker whose neocortex was destroyed by a railroad accident. He survived, but exhibited shocking behavior, getting into fights and choosing the pleasurable and the easy over longer-term satisfaction. His personality changed rapidly! Unfortunately, the PFC, one of the most important areas in the brain, is also one of the most susceptible to injury. For this reason, it is always important to wear your helmet when biking!

Interestingly, as the prefrontal cortex evolves and develops with aging, a child becomes more mature and conscientious, exhibiting more "grown up" types of behaviors. However, this center evolves very slowly in most individuals, compared to other centers that are involved with emotional or immature behaviors—the more primitive brain structures. This explains why we usually act like a child first, before we grow up and act like an adult!

The big question worth pondering is: although the human brain today is well equipped with different levels of sophistication, how much of the more rational or intellectual parts do we actually use as a species? In other words, what percentage of people actually thinks and behaves thoughtfully, as opposed to emotionally and reactively? How many people and how much of the time do people act at a superior mammal versus at an inferior mammal level? And why is that? Why are we humans so complicated? This has a lot to do with our psychology, which will be further explored and explained in the following chapters.

CHAPTER 4

"I am one of those who think like Nobel, that humanity will draw more good than evil from new discoveries."
—*Marie Curie*

Neuroplasticity

For 400 years, mainstream medicine and science believed that the brain anatomy and the nervous system were essentially fixed and unchangeable after a critical period during early childhood. This applied to brain functions, and it was thought to be impossible for new neurons to develop after birth. The common understanding was that when brain cells failed to develop properly, or died due to injury, they could not be replaced. Nor could the brain ever change its structure and find a new way to function if part of it was damaged. Based on this notion, scientists believed for centuries that people with mental limitations or structural brain damage would be impaired and "incurable" for life. If the brain could not be changed, nor could the character be changed … or could it?

In the 1970s, the prevailing sense of hopelessness and helplessness in the field of neuroscience was slowly replaced by a sense of hope after a series of discoveries in this field. *Neuroplasticity* is a non-specific neuroscience term referring to the ability of the brain and nervous system in all species to *change* structurally and functionally as a result of input from the environment (6). The most widely recognized forms of plasticity are learning, memory, and recovery from brain damage.

This idea was first proposed in 1890 by William James in *The Principles of Psychology*, though the idea was largely neglected for the next fifty years. The first person to use the term *neural plasticity* appears to have been the Polish neuroscientist Jerzy Konorski.

One of the fundamental principles of how neuroplasticity functions is linked to the concept of *synaptic pruning*, the idea that individual connections within the brain are constantly being removed or recreated, largely dependent upon how they are used. This is best described as *"neurons that fire together, wire together"* and *"neurons that fire apart, wire apart."* If there are two nearby neurons that often produce an impulse simultaneously, their cortical maps may become one. This idea also works in the opposite way; neurons that do not regularly produce simultaneous impulses will form different maps.

Norman Doidge, MD, is a Canadian psychiatrist, psychoanalyst, researcher, author, poet, and author of *The Brain That Changes Itself* (2007). This book describes some of the latest developments in neuroscience and became a *New York Times* and international bestseller. In it, Doidge illustrates and explains the revolutionary discovery that the brain's structure and function can **change** itself, under natural conditions, by mental experience. As told through the stories of scientists, doctors, and patients, the following cases characterized in his book demonstrate the astonishing adaptability and plasticity of the human brain.

Case 5

TS was a seventeen-year-old amputee who lost his arm in a car accident. Within a month, he developed what is known as "phantom pain" in the amputated limb. Also quite irritating was a symptom of itching in the same arm, but there was nothing to be scratched!

Phantom limbs give rise to a "phantom pain" in 95 percent of amputees. This devastating condition can persist for a lifetime and is often extremely difficult to treat. How do you remove an organ or limb that isn't there?

Born in India, Dr. Vilayanur S. Ramachandran is a Hindu neurologist with a PhD in psychology. He is the inventor of *mirror therapy*, used with high success to tackle phantom pain. He uses neuroplasticity to reconfigure the content of the mind and brain. Using imagination and perception, he can treat the phantom symptoms and alter the wiring in the brain.

He worked with TS to help cure his phantom pain. While blindfolded, TS was stroked gently with a Q-tip, moving from the upper body slowly toward the face. When his cheek was stroked, TS felt the touch there, as well as in his phantom arm. When his upper lip was touched, he felt it in his index finger as well. Hmm? *What's going on?* he thought. Using magnetoencephalography (MEG), Ramachandran confirmed that his hand map was being used to process facial sensations. In other words, his face and hand maps in the brain had somehow blurred together. After some experiments, Ramachandran helped TS finally scratch the un-scratchable itch that had devastated him for years!

Ramachandran believes that when a body part is physically or functionally lost, there are no more signals to its specific brain map any longer. Then the surviving brain map "hungers" for incoming stimulations. *Depending on the type of stimulation,* specific nerve growth factors are released, inviting neurons from nearby maps to form new connections. In other words, rewiring and **neurogenesis**—formation of new brain cells—happens due to incoming signals and stimuli. He creatively used this fundamental neuroplasticity principle to treat phantom pains. What if he could send false signals to the brain by using something like a "mirror box" to make the patient *think* that the phantom limb is moving?

Ramachandran used his invention on PM, who had lost the function of his left arm in a motorcycle accident. With it completely paralyzed and useless, PM decided to amputate his arm and was left with a terrible phantom elbow pain. When he put his good arm into the mirror box, PM felt his phantom arm move for the first time. This only happened when his eyes were open though. After practicing for ten minutes a day for four weeks, using imagination and perception, his phantom pain was completely gone, even without using the box. Hence, Ramachandran became the first physician to successfully cure a seemingly impossible problem—to amputate a phantom limb!

Case 6

Born in 1961, Alvaro Pascual-Leone was a young Spanish physician and physiologist, the first to use Trancranial Magnetic Stimulation (TMS) to map the brain. TMS has different applications in neuroscience; it may be used to turn on a brain area or to block it from functioning. One of his greatest heroes, the famous Spanish neuroanatomist and Nobel laureate, Ramon y Cajal, had argued in 1904 that "through mental practice, repeated thoughts must strengthen the existing neuronal connections and create new ones." Using his imagination, he had envisioned and described what we know today as neuroplasticity, but he did not have the tools to prove it at the time. Pascual-Leone went on to prove his role model right. Using TMS, he wanted to test whether mental practice and imagination can actually induce physical changes in the brain.

He taught two groups of people who never knew how to play the piano a sequence of notes, showing them which fingers to move while allowing them to hear the specific notes as they were played. The two groups were divided into the "physical practice" and "mental practice" groups. The physical practice group actually played the piano two hours a day for five days. The mental practice group instead *imagined* playing the piano for two hours a day for five days. Both groups had their brains mapped before and after the experiment, and during each of the five days. Then both groups were asked to play the sequence, while the computer measured their performance accuracy, and TMS was used to map their brains.

Remarkably, mental practice alone produced the same physical changes in the motor system and the brain as physical practice! At the end of fifth day, however, the level of improvement was slightly better in the physical practice. This minimal discrepancy was compensated by a single, extra two-hour training after the fifth day, and the overall performance quality of the two groups was equal!

Case 7

Born in 1931, Edward Taub is a behavioral neuroscientist at the University of Alabama at Birmingham. He is best known for his involvement in the Silver Spring monkeys case and for making major breakthroughs in the area of neuroplasticity and developing the *constraint-induced therapy (CIT)*—a powerful technique used in the rehabilitation of people who have suffered neurological injuries from a stroke or other cause. Taub's techniques have helped survivors regain the use of paralyzed limbs and have been acknowledged by the American Stroke Association as "at the forefront of a revolution." By constraining the good limb and forcing patients to use the affected limb, new brain circuits can be called into service to replace lost brain tissue and restore movement and sensation.

In CIT, Taub uses an old technique known as *deafferentation,* which was used by Nobel Prize winner Sir Charles Sherrington in 1895. An afferent nerve is a sensory nerve that sends electrochemical messages from a limb to the spine, and then to the brain. Deafferentation is a surgical procedure in which the sensory nerve is cut, interrupting the transmission of these signals. A deafferentated monkey cannot sense where its affected limb is in space, or feel any sensation or pain when touched.

In one experiment, Taub tests his theory and lays the foundation of his stroke treatment by deafferentating a monkey. As expected, when one arm was deafferentated, the monkey could not use it. Paradoxically however, when *both* arms were deafferentated, the monkey started using both after a while! Then Taub deafferentated the whole spinal cord, so there were no signals going up to the brain, and the monkey could not receive any inputs from the limbs. Still it used both limbs after some time. How is that possible?

Taub's explanation transformed the treatment of strokes. He proposed that the monkey did not use its arm after a single limb deafferentation because it had *learned* not to use it in the period after surgery, when the spinal cord was still in "spinal shock." This is a period when the weakened neurons have trouble firing. After several failed attempts, the monkey gives up and chooses the easier way—simply not to use them anymore. Instead, the good arm is used to feed itself and survive. Taub called this *learned nonuse,* a phenomenon based on the fundamental principle of *use it or lose it*, leading to *disuse atrophy* of the affected limb. On the contrary, monkeys that had both arms deafferentated had no opportunity to learn *nonuse* because they had no other option but to use them to survive!

Case 8

MM was born in 1973, with only half her brain. Her left hemisphere never developed through gestation for unknown reasons. She must be crippled in her wheelchair, surviving on life support ... or is she?

MM is a young lady who speaks fairly normally, holds a part-time job, and enjoys what most other people do, such as reading and watching movies. How is all this possible with only half the brain?

This is an incredible testimony that neuroplasticity has allowed massive brain reorganization and *rewiring*. Essential functions like speech and language (usually a left-brain function) have been reassigned to the right hemisphere, which not only fulfills its own duties, but also carries on new responsibilities. MM has some extraordinary mathematical skills, while she suffers from some disabilities and weaknesses. She has trouble with abstract thinking.

Jordan Grafman is a research scientist at the National Institutes of Health (NIH), and a captain in the US Air Force, who tests the upper limits of neuroplasticity. He is trying to figure out how MM is able to function and further develop her brain.

Grafman's own life is an inspiring story of transformation. When he was a child, his father experienced a massive stroke, leading to frontal lobe damage and resulting in remarkable personality changes. He had emotional, aggressive, and sexual impulses, a condition referred to as *social disinhibition* at the time. His mother left his father, who ended up in a hotel in Chicago for the rest of his life and ultimately died due to a second stroke.

As Grafman explains, the brain is divided into sectors. Each of these sectors acquires a primary responsibility for a specific type of mental activity during development. In complex activities, several sectors must interact. In any sector, the neurons at the center are the most committed ones to each task. Those on the border are less committed, so nearby brain areas compete with each other to recruit these less busy neurons.

Grafman's theory explains how MM's brain is capable of handling such extraordinary tasks. The loss of brain tissue in the left hemisphere occurred at very early stages of brain development, before there was any major commitment from the right side! Since plasticity is at its peak at very young ages, this phenomenon is probably what saved MM from certain death. When her brain was still forming, her right hemisphere was less specialized and had the time and ability to adjust in the womb!

Case 9

Paul Bach-y-Rita is known as the "father of sensory substitution and brain plasticity." In the 1960s, he invented a device that allowed blind people to read, perceive shadows, and distinguish between close and distant objects. Bach-y-Rita believed in *sensory substitution*—if one sense is damaged, other senses can sometimes take over. He thought skin and its touch receptors could act as a retina (part of the eye apparatus and necessary for vision), using one sense for another. In order for the brain to interpret tactile information and convert it into visual ones, it had to learn something new and adapt to the new signals. The brain's capacity to adapt implied that it possessed plasticity. He thought, *We see with our brains, not with our eyes.*

A tragic stroke that left his father paralyzed inspired Bach-y-Rita to study brain rehabilitation. His brother, a physician, worked tirelessly to develop therapeutic measures. Those measures were so successful that the father recovered complete functionality by age sixty-eight and was able to live a normal, active life that even included mountain climbing. His father's story was firsthand evidence that a 'late recovery' could occur even with a massive lesion in an elderly person.

In working with another patient whose vestibular system had been damaged, Bach-y-Rita developed the *BrainPort*, a machine that would replace her vestibular apparatus (involved in balance regulation) and send signals to her brain from her tongue. After she had used this machine for some time, it was no longer necessary, as she had regained the ability to function normally. Her brain had acquired new skills.

This can be explained by neuroplasticity. Because her vestibular system was "disorganized" and sending random rather than coherent signals, the apparatus found new pathways *around* the damaged or blocked neural pathways, helping to reinforce the signals that were sent by remaining healthy tissues. Bach-y-Rita explained plasticity as such: "*If you are driving from here to Milwaukee, and the main bridge goes out, first you are paralyzed. Then you take old secondary roads through the farmland. Then you use these roads more; you find shorter paths to use to get where you want to go, and you start to get there faster. These 'secondary' neural pathways are 'unmasked' or exposed and strengthened as they are used. The 'unmasking' process is generally thought to be one of the principal ways in which the plastic brain reorganizes itself."*

Case 10

Michael Merzenich is a neuroscientist who has been one of the pioneers of brain plasticity for over thirty years. He has made some of the most ambitious claims for the field:

- That brain exercises may be as useful as drugs to treat diseases as severe as schizophrenia;
- That plasticity exists from cradle to the grave;
- That radical improvements in cognitive functioning—how we learn, think, perceive, and remember—are possible even in the elderly.

Merzenich's work was affected by a crucial discovery made by David Hubel and Torsten Wiesel in their work with kittens. The experiment involved sewing one eye shut and recording the cortical brain maps. Hubel and Wiesel saw that the portion of the kitten's brain associated with the shut eye was not idle, as expected. Instead, it processed visual information from the open eye. It was *as though the brain didn't want to waste any 'cortical real estate' and had found a way to rewire itself.*

This implied brain plasticity during the *critical period*. However, Merzenich argued that brain plasticity could occur *beyond* the critical period, based on an experiment conducted with another scientist, Clinton Woosley. They cut a peripheral nerve in a group of monkeys and observed what occurred in the brain with subsequent regeneration of the nerve. The two scientists micromapped the hand maps of monkey brains before and after cutting a peripheral nerve and sewing the ends together. Afterwards, the hand map in the brain that was expected to be weakened was nearly normal. This was a substantial breakthrough. Merzenich asserted that *"if the brain map could normalize its structure in response to abnormal input, the prevailing view that we are born with a hardwired system had to be wrong. The brain had to be plastic."*

So, how are these cases relevant?

Today, it is widely accepted in the worldwide neuroscientific community that the adult brain is not hard-wired with fixed and immutable neuronal circuits. There are many instances of the rewiring of neuronal circuits in response to training or injury. There is solid evidence that *neurogenesis* occurs in the adult mammalian brain, and such changes can persist well into old age. Most of the evidence for neurogenesis is mainly restricted to the hippocampus and olfactory bulb, but current research has revealed that other parts of the brain, including the cerebellum and cortex, may be involved as well (7).

These cases are extraordinary examples of real-life situations where the brain adapted to preserve life and maximize neurological rehabilitation. We will now explore the extraordinary potentials of the brain and its ability to rewire as a result of internal and external stimuli, which has a revolutionary impact on how we can shape our destiny!

Miraculous Functions of the Brain

The brain is the control center of the entire body. It works very closely with the rest of the body, specifically the endocrine (hormonal) system, to run your daily life. The nervous system is, on a small scale, primarily made up of **neurons** (nerve cells) and **glial cells** (supporting cells). Neurons are sensors that send electric messages to the brain, which then sends them back to the neurons, telling them how to react. Glial cells are non-neuronal cells that provide support and nutrition, maintain homeostasis, form myelin (the nerve sheath), and participate in signal transmission in the **nervous system.** These cells provide support and protection for neurons. They are thus known as the *glue* of the nervous system, while the neurons are the wires embedded in them.

The four main functions of glial cells are: 1) to surround neurons and hold them in place; 2) to supply nutrients and oxygen to neurons; 3) to insulate one neuron from another; 4) to destroy pathogens and remove dead neurons.

In the human brain, glial cells are estimated to outnumber neurons by about ten to one. There is a lot more unknown about the glial cells compared to neurons. This is where the misconception comes from that *only one tenth of the brain is explored.*

Different parts of the brain talk to one another in unique ways, which makes humans superior and far more capable and intelligent than any other species on this planet.

How Does the Brain Communicate?

The brain is a communications center consisting of about a hundred billion (100,000,000,000) nerve cells, more than the total number of stars in the Milky Way galaxy! What makes this even more fascinating is the number of connections between neurons—about 164 trillion (164,000,000,000,000) in adults. Can you imagine this? The junction between two consecutive neurons is called a **synapse**. There is a very narrow gap (about 20nm in width) between the neurons—the synaptic cleft—where an electrical impulse is transmitted from one neuron to a neighboring one. They relay this message with the use of neurotransmitters, which are protein substances called **neuropeptides**, produced and secreted by the neuronal axons. The next neuron then receives the electrical signal. It is then determined by the neurotransmitter to carry the message to its appropriate destination. Electrical impulses travel at a speed of *a hundred meters per second* across the axon. A single nerve can send up to *a thousand impulses per second.* These are called brainwaves.

Networks of neurons pass messages back and forth to different structures within the brain, the spinal cord, and the peripheral nervous system. These nerve networks coordinate and regulate everything we feel, think, and do. These neurons transmit information in four fundamental ways:

1. **Neuron to Neuron**—*The Brain's Electrical System*
   Each nerve cell in the brain sends and receives messages in the form of electrical impulses. Once a cell receives and processes a message, it sends it on to other neurons.

2. **Neurotransmitters**—*The Brain's Chemical Messengers*
   Messages are also carried between neurons by chemicals

called neurotransmitters. In 1921, an Austrian scientist named Otto Loewi discovered the first neurotransmitter in an experiment with frogs. This was called **acetylcholine.**

3. **Receptors**—*The Brain's Chemical Receivers*
   The neurotransmitter attaches to a specialized site on the receiving cell called a *receptor*. A neurotransmitter and its receptor operate like a "key and lock," a very specific mechanism that ensures each receptor will forward the appropriate message *only* after interacting with the right kind of neurotransmitter.

4. **Transporters**—*The Brain's Chemical Recyclers*
   Located on the cell that releases the neurotransmitter, transporters recycle these substances (i.e., bringing them back into the cell that released them), thereby shutting off the signal between neurons.

The dual mechanism in which the neurons talk to each other (electro-chemical) makes this system extremely fast, which is necessary to acknowledge the presence of danger—for example, a hand touching a hot stove. If the nervous system was comprised only of chemical signals, the body would not tell the arm to move fast enough to escape dangerous burns. So the speed of the nervous system is a necessity for life!

How Does the Brain Register and Record Things?

Another important component of communication, other than transmission of information, is the *memory*. Without memory, cognitive and executive capabilities significantly decline. Memory is essentially comprised of three virtual parts: sensory, short-term, and long-term memory. These will be explained further in this chapter.

Where Does the Brain Interpret Events and Situations?

The *cerebrum,* or *neocortex*, is the largest part of the human brain located on the outer surface, associated with higher functions such as thoughts and actions. It demonstrates the highest level of sophistication and evolution in humans. It is basically the *evaluation center* of the brain. The neocortex, holding also the prefrontal cortex, is involved and responsible for interpreting situations, planning complex cognitive behaviors and executive functions, such as mediating conflicting thoughts, making choices between right and wrong or good and bad, predicting future events, governing social control, and suppressing emotional or sexual urges.

The cerebral cortex is divided into four sections, called "lobes" (see diagram): the **frontal lobe, parietal lobe, occipital lobe,** and **temporal lobe.** Here is a visual representation of the cortex (the cerebellum demonstrated is not part of the cortex):

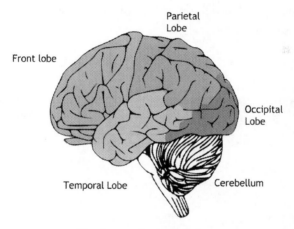

The four major brain lobes

- Frontal Lobe—associated with reasoning, planning, parts of speech, movement, emotions, and problem solving
- Parietal Lobe—associated with movement, orientation, recognition, and perception of stimuli
- Occipital Lobe—associated with visual processing
- Temporal Lobe—associated with perception and recognition of auditory stimuli, memory, and speech, and feelings

The Brain as One Unit

The functions and characteristics of neurons and other brain units have been mentioned. In the following simple example, the physiological aspects of this master organ and its overall systematic function as a team will be demonstrated.

Intending to get some exercise, SM decides to walk to work. He reaches a busy street where there is no pedestrian line and decides to jay walk to the other side. Cars are passing by in both directions, and SM has to take extra caution while doing this task. How many times have you come across this scenario? Let us see what is going on in SM's mind and body as he completes this task.

The following diagram demonstrates what is actually happening in his brain in *a split second*.

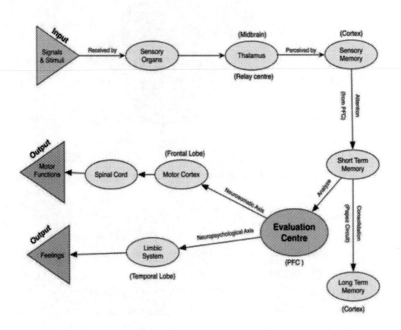

Thought process in the brain

1. Signals are **received** by the brain. These signals consist of both **external** and **internal** ones. External signals are numerous, received by the special sensory organs in the brain; images of the cars passing by, people walking by, stores around, trees close by, and many other things happening around him in that moment are observed by the eyes. The ears hear the sounds of cars passing, people walking and talking, and birds chanting. The ground SM is standing on is felt through *proprioceptors* in his feet (touch sensation). The taste of his chewing gum is received by the tongue, and the smell of spring flowers is received by the nose. These are the five specialized sensory organs—eye, ear, nose, tongue, and the skin.

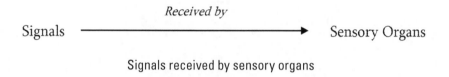

Received by

Signals ⟶ Sensory Organs

Signals received by sensory organs

2. These signals are relayed to the **thalamus** in the limbic system. As described earlier, this paired structure functions as the relay center. Its function includes *relaying sensation, spatial sense, and motor signals* to the cerebral cortex. In this station, signals await further instructions from the higher cognitive function centers, the master control headquarters, which is the **prefrontal cortex (PFC)** in the frontal lobe. The PFC chooses and prioritizes which signals need to be amplified, and which ones need to be ignored or diminished, *based on the mission to be accomplished.* That is why, while the chanting of the birds are heard, and the signs on the stores are observed, they are not as important as the image of the cars approaching. Only the selective, important ones *pertinent to the task* are **perceived.** *This selection of electrochemical signals is extremely important and has a major association with spiritual philosophies,* a concept that will be explained in further detail in later chapters.

3. The selected signals are perceived and registered in the **sensory memory.** This is the first component of memory, able to store information for *less than one second.* The actual physical storage for

this task is in the **sensory cortex** (see figure). Visual signals are stored in the occipital lobe, auditory (hearing) and olfactory (smell) signals are stored in the temporal lobe, tactile (touch) signals are stored in the parietal lobe (somatosensory and vestibular cortex), and gustatory (taste) signals are stored in both the parietal and frontal lobes.

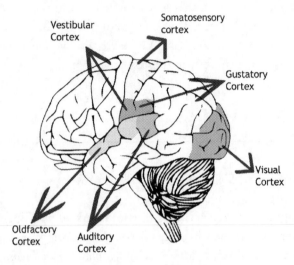

Sensory cortical regions in the brain

4. The task of choosing which parts of information to be stored in the sensory memory requires **attention** and **focus** from higher cortical centers. The virtual "attention center" is composed of sophisticated areas in the cortex. However, the PFC plays a key role in this task.

5. Selected signals from the sensory cortex are then drawn into the second component of memory, the **short-term** memory. This is mainly where **interpretation** of the data takes place. Information can stay in this virtual part for *less than one minute*. At any given time, about two thousand bits of information can be received by the brain, but only seven, plus or minus two bits can be stored and processed in the short-term memory. This is the *working memory*, acting like the RAM of a computer. It has less than a minute to decide what to

do with the information received and pass it on to the next station. It is also important to mention that **internal** signals can bypass the sensory memory and directly enter the working memory from other parts of the brain. These signals can be *memories from the past* or *imaginations from the future.*

6. So far, the information is received, perceived, and interpreted. It is then processed into one of three options: either: a) deleted; b) consolidated and transferred into long-term memory; or c) analyzed in higher evaluating centers in the frontal lobe (PFC).

7. There is controversy about the fate of information that is not mandatory for a specific task. Some experts believe these are entirely deleted, and others propose that nothing is deleted, but sent off to remote memory stores in deeper parts of our mind. While no one really knows the answer, I think there is some truth in both theories. Generally speaking, a recycling mechanism makes sense in any dynamic balanced system. Meanwhile, I believe some of the undesired data is stored in remote parts of our memory. The memory itself can be considered as a complex system, consisting of the *conscious, subconscious, and unconscious memory.* The conscious memory helps us retrieve information that we are aware of. The subconscious stores remote data that come to us in situations where we are not fully aware (such as **déjà vu**). The unconscious memory plays a significant role in our unconscious thinking, such as dreams, or when we are under general anesthesia.

8. Consolidation and transfer of information to **long-term memory** is mainly done through the **hippocampus** and **Papez circuit** in the brain. Also, data from the long term-memory is retrieved mainly through the hippocampus, and the **mammillary bodies**. Multiple cortical structures are part of the long-term memory, and data can be stored there for days, months, years, or even indefinitely.

9. Information can also be transferred to *higher evaluating centers,* which mainly consists of the PFC (as well as other higher cortical areas). As mentioned, this is where planning complex cognitive behaviors and

45

executive functions is accomplished. The distances, directions, and timing of the cars approaching are analyzed. The speed at which SM has to move to avoid any collision is calculated precisely. In a split second, a series of sophisticated executive and cognitive functions is accomplished, requiring *focus* and *awareness*.

10. After analysis in the final evaluation center, information takes one of two separate pathways (or both): either a) what I would call the **neurosomatic axis**; or b) the **neuropsychological axis**.

11. The neurosomatic axis is a virtual path of neuronal network responsible for different voluntary and involuntary functions of the motor (movement) system. Multiple motor areas, including the motor cortex, cerebellum, basal ganglia, etc., are involved, conveying their message through the spinal cord to the arms and legs and other body parts. They give the order to move or stop, speed up or slow down, or change directions where necessary. In this scenario, after complex calculations and analyses, the motor system transmits messages through the neurosomatic axis and spinal cord to the legs, the heart, and other body parts, to cross the street at a specific pace and in a well-coordinated way to avoid any catastrophe!

12. The neuropsychological axis is another virtual pathway connecting to mainly the *limbic system* and regulates mood and psychological effects. In this scenario, suppose SM observes a dead animal's body run over by passing cars. The feeling of sadness is a function of the neuropsychological axis.

In summary, in any task in life, the brain plays a vital role and masters it in extraordinary ways that we may take for granted. The simple illustration below shows a summary of what was mentioned above.

Evaluation and control center in the brain

So, as you can see, the brain is an extremely fast and intelligent part of the body and mind, capable of completing the most extraordinary tasks in a fraction of a second. This is why the two-legged, small creature has been able to outpace the fastest cougars, the strongest elephants, and largest whales in the world!

In the following chapters of this book, you will see why it is important to understand how the brain and mind work together. It will make sense as you realize how we shape our destiny and connect to the rest of the world. This takes us to the next chapter, which unveils some of the most profound mysteries of the *human psychology*!

PART THREE

Psychological Aspects: The Mind

CHAPTER 5

*"Education is the most powerful weapon which
you can use to change the world."*
—*Nelson Mandela*

The Human Psychology

Basic Principles of Human Behavior

MN is having a bad day at work. He stays later than usual to catch up on paperwork and make a few extra phone calls. Upon arrival at home, his wife is disappointed and complains that he is late. MN loses it and furiously objects to her concern. She gets upset and stops communicating, not giving him the opportunity to explain why he was late in the first place. Instead, she starts thinking, *Maybe he doesn't love me anymore the way he used to. Perhaps that's why he's spending more time at work or with his friends—to avoid spending time with me,* and so on. Even worse is when MN stops talking about this "little" issue and allows it to escalate, leading to more distance and problems in their relationship.

Does this scenario sound familiar to you? In relationship counseling, this is a common observation—that problems escalate based on mistaken assumptions and miscommunications.

Here's the point: *how you feel and how you act is based on what you think is going on, not what is actually happening.*

Every situation observed around us on a daily basis is interpreted in a unique way, which may sometimes not be quite the same as what is truly happening. This usually occurs automatically at the *subconscious* level of mind, and we may not even be aware of what we are doing or how we're thinking. The fact is that *each of us lives in our own mental world, the "reality" we construct in our minds based on our interpretations of the world.*

This is a profound concept that may be poorly understood. As explained previously, there is a fundamental difference between *truth* and *reality*. Truth is what is actually happening every moment without any interpretation or judgment, whereas reality is what we **think** is happening. Reality is *our conceptual image of the world*. It is the difference between a fact and opinion.

Let us go back to the example of the couple having miscommunications.

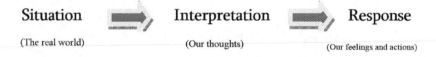

Situation	Interpretation	Response
(The real world)	(Our thoughts)	(Our feelings and actions)

Fortunately, our interpretations are correct most of the time. However, we can sometimes get it wrong, and when we do, we may suffer the emotional and behavioral consequences if there's no room for a second thought.

Consider this example: You are tired and upset because you had a bad day **(situation)**. ---> Your wife takes this personally and assumes you don't love her as much anymore **(interpretation/thought)**. ---> She feels hurt and sad **(feeling)**. ---> She stops communicating with you **(action)**.

This process is universal in mankind. It happens in a split of a second repeatedly on a daily basis, zillions of times, without us noticing it. As we allow it to occur repeatedly, a pattern develops, forming a **habitual** neuronal network in our brain. This solidifies over time, and the entire process becomes second nature and automatic (subconscious)—similar to learning to play the piano! With practice and repetition of the same finger movements, automatic learning occurs. Over time, the pianist does not need to actively think where to place the next finger. The automatic mind (subconscious) will do the job, and the process becomes very smooth and skillful.

The key points to highlight about this universal process are the following:

- A situation has to go through several stages to reach an action (and hence a result). It cannot skip the brain.
- *If we learn how to control our thoughts and feelings, we can change the actions and achieve the desired results.*
- In order to establish a habitual pattern (whether playing the piano or making regular assumptions in a certain way), similar processes need to occur repeatedly, solidifying the neuronal network in the brain. If the electrophysiological bonds between the brain neurons are loose, the habit can also break easily. But once it becomes *solidified* due to repetition, the pattern becomes much more difficult to undo. This is an extremely important concept to understand in addictive behaviors.

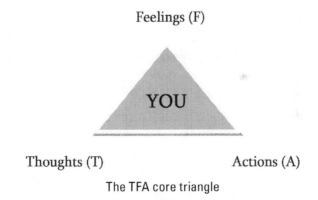

The TFA core triangle

The **TFA model** has been widely accepted in modern psychology as a principle of human behavior. These three factors are connected to one another. It means that *if one point of the triangle changes, the others will follow.* So if you wish to change one of these elements and have difficulty doing that directly, you can *indirectly* change one of the other two factors. Change your feelings, and your thoughts and actions will change, and so on. Some of these are easier than others to change. *Actions are easier to change than thoughts, and thoughts are easier than feelings.*

For example, suppose you feel sad and depressed because you are overweight. Sadness will reduce your motivation and energy to exercise—the very thing you need to do to change results! If you work the triangle backward, and push yourself to become more active—despite lack of motivation, you will start to feel better. Exercise can increase certain hormones in your brain (endorphins) to increase energy, induce a state of euphoria, and reduce anxiety and depression. The other key note to realize is that:

Negative thoughts ⟶ Negative feelings ⟶ Negative actions

Positive thoughts ⟶ Positive feelings ⟶ Positive actions

The key to changing a negative cycle is to *break the cycle* by changing *any one of the arms.* It is usually the *feeling* that bothers us and needs to be changed to a positive one. It is easier to change the *action* or the *thought* related to that feeling.

The TFA demonstrates what is going on within the individual—our internal world. Now for a better understanding of how our mind and body connect with the environment, the external world, I have modified the TFA concept to the following model. Let us call this **the modified core triangle** or the **STFAR(P) model.**

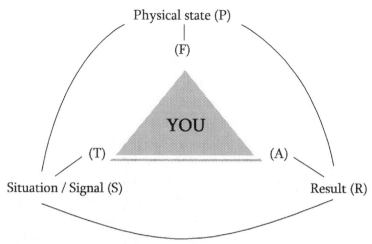

Signal (S) <--> Thought (T) <--> Feeling (F) <--> Action (A) <--> Result (R)
Feeling (F) <--> Physical state (P)

Proposed STFAR(P) model

External or internal signals (S) can trigger a thought (T) and provoke a feeling (F), which may lead to an action (A), ultimately leading to a specific result (R). At the same time, feelings (F) can directly change your physical state (P), such as muscle tension or headaches. The outer arms—**(S), (P), and (R)**—can also occasionally interact directly. For example, drinking lots of coffee **(S)** will directly increase your heartbeat **(P)** through change of brain neurotransmitters.

Let's go back to the couple's example.

You are tired and upset because you had a bad day **(S)**. ---> Your wife takes this personally and assumes you don't love her as much anymore **(interpretation or T)**. ---> She feels hurt and sad **(F)**. ---> She stops communicating with you **(A)**. ---> The result is no more communication **(R)**, and more anger and frustration build up. At the same time, the wife may feel tension headaches, muscle aches, and stiffness **(P)**. So she has to take pain killers and muscle relaxants for the physical symptoms and/or antidepressants and mood stabilizers for the emotional symptoms. Hmm ... does that sound typical these days?

So, how can we help this couple break the cycle? There are generally two approaches: medicational and/or non-medicational. Most people chose the easier route—medications that temporarily alter their state of distress. While this approach has its own place and benefits, it is not the fundamental cure in most cases. Medications generally treat the symptoms and feelings (anxiety, depression, physical or emotional pain, etc.) temporarily, and one must understand their potential consequences. This explains why medications have to be taken for long durations, and yet the root of the problem is rarely addressed. Evidence-based research suggests a compounded benefit from *both* medicational *and* non-medicational therapies. Our focus is on the latter in this chapter. I will show you how to get control over your mind and body in a fundamental and natural way.

1. **TFA**. The first step is to *understand* and *acknowledge* what is actually happening in the mind and body. Often, all we have to do in relationship counseling is to educate the partners about this principle, and upon reflection of these thoughts and feelings, they usually manage to figure out how to reverse the cycle. Remember, in the modified model, the outside arms—situation (S), physical state (P), and result (R)—are all secondary results of the inside arms, thought (T), feeling (F), action (A). The center of focus is the core triangle (TFA). Now, let us break this triangle backwards.

2. **A ...** Change your actions. Often, the apparent area that one *would want* to change in the STFAR(P) model is the **situation (S), feeling (F),** or end **result (R).** The **thoughts (T)** and **actions (A)** usually remain unnoticed, and those are exactly what the focus should be on.

    This is why: the **situation** is an external factor and is often out of our control. The **feeling** is the most difficult part to change and may not be the best area to put all our efforts into. A **result** which *can* be changed, is often a consequence of a series of events happening internally. And externally driven **results** usually *cannot* be changed at all (e.g., damage caused by an earthquake). As a reminder, in order to change the **result**, we need to focus on the three main arms of the core triangle (TFA). One of the simplest ways is to change the **action.** In the earlier example, despite the challenge, just break the loop and initiate conversation with your partner when you are both in a better mood. Things will usually fall into place, and the knot will unwind. After some time has elapsed, communication about your thoughts and feelings about this specific situation is highly encouraged to avoid accumulation of negative feelings toward each other.

Techniques like deep abdominal breathing when you're feeling anxious or having a panic attack, or relaxation techniques when you feel tense, are other examples of modifying your action. Practical strategies to change actions are the cornerstone in **behavioral therapy**.

3. **F ...** Changing your feelings. It is often very difficult to alter our negative feelings directly. This requires an exceptional level of self-control, significant training, and continuous practice. Minority groups across the globe have learned these skills through vigorous trainings, such as meditation, religious trainings, self-disciplinary approaches, etc. However, for the ordinary population, it is much easier to achieve the desired results *indirectly* through modifying the other arms of the triangle.

4. **T ...** Understand and take over your thoughts. This is one of the most sophisticated and poorly understood areas in human psychology. Unveiling this area provides the basis for explaining some of the most bizarre behaviors in human beings. Upon learning the knowledge and skills of how to observe and manage thoughts, we can favorably modify our feelings and results. This profound, fundamental concept in the **psychology of change** will be expanded on in detail.

States of the Mind: Understanding Thoughts

In the Oxford dictionary, "thought" is defined as "an idea or opinion produced by thinking." As you notice, "thought," "idea," and "thinking" are all abstract concepts. So, where exactly in the brain are the thoughts located?

The more concrete concept can be described at the cellular and electrochemical level. As mentioned earlier, the brain consists of about a hundred billion nerve cells (neurons) with 164 trillion synapses or connections. In a more physical description, thinking is the process of electrochemical charges that travel across the surface of the axon of one neuron to the body of the next, through one of the four mechanisms of neuronal communication, as described in previous chapters.

Of extreme importance is to notice that thoughts are brainwaves, a form of energy with physical properties, such as frequencies and wavelengths. In this and future chapters, novel theories based on physical and metaphysical principles will be explored in further detail to unveil mysteries that have astounded humanity for thousands of years, such as karma, telepathy, unexplainable dreams, and so on!

While our knowledge of the brain and its functions is extremely limited, **thoughts** will be explained in an oversimplified fashion in order to understand our mind–body connection.

What many people may not know is that there are **three** different levels of thoughts:

1. **Unconscious** thinking
2. **Subconscious** thinking
3. **Conscious** thinking

For simplicity, let us refer to the ice cream analogy described in chapter 3.

Ice cream analogy of the brain

Unconscious Thinking

Unconscious thinking develops in the most primitive part of the brain, the reptilian (or primitive) brain (the first layer in the ice cream metaphor). This part was the first to form in the process of the nervous system evolution in the animal kingdom. Other parts superimposed later on as the mammals became more intelligent and sophisticated.

This kind of thinking happens at the level of the spinal cord and brainstem, which is the lower extension of the brain where it connects to the spinal cord. Neurological functions located in the brainstem include those necessary for survival (breathing, digestion, heart rate, blood pressure, and other vital functions), and for arousal (being awake and alert). These thoughts occur automatically as a reflex.

When you are anesthetized for a surgical operation, only this part of the brain is working. It is extremely intelligent and has the ability to automatically adjust to maintain homeostasis—the balanced state of cells, organs, and body systems necessary for survival. For example, if the anesthesiologist introduces a 500 ml bolus of fluid, the blood pressure will initially increase. Instantly and *unconsciously*, the brainstem will respond by reducing the heart rate in order to maintain the normal blood pressure—a reaction that is crucial for life.

Another simple example is the well-known knee-jerk reflex. Signals from the knee are transmitted to the spinal cord through sensory nerves from the skin and knee tendon, exchange information with the motor neurons through synapses at the spinal cord level, and order the leg to respond to the stimulus via a jerky movement. This is also critical to avoid potentially dangerous hazards.

It is important to realize that this part of the brain functions completely on a physiological basis, and no interpretation or judgment from the upper brain parts are involved.

Subconscious Thinking

At times of severe distress in life, we may not be able to tolerate our reality. This creates significant amount of emotional pain, and we need a way to avoid, minimize, or cope with it. This is when the mind plays tricks on us, distorting the inner or outer world in such a way that the pain becomes tolerable, and we can survive. Our mental defense mechanisms creatively rearrange the sources of conflict to make them manageable, and we can carry on with life. From a mental health standpoint, such emotional and intellectual dishonesty is not only creative, but also healthy and necessary for mental survival. However, from a behavioral and social perspective, some defense mechanisms are *constructive* while others are *destructive*. Therefore, one may appear or behave in a neurotic, psychotic, or odd manner to the outside observer. This will be explained in depth in the following chapters. This concept forms the basis of behavioral sciences and can explain *why humans behave the way they do*!

Subconscious thinking developed in the next stage of brain evolution. Shown as the second layer in the ice cream analogy, the paleopallium or intermediate (inferior mammalian) brain, comprising the structures of the limbic system, is the main center of the subconscious thoughts and feelings. This is the most complex and undiscovered part of the brain; there is much to be learned about it.

An iceberg can serve as a useful metaphor to understand the subconscious mind. As it floats in the water, the huge mass of the iceberg remains below the surface. Only a small percentage of the iceberg is visible above the surface. This represents the conscious mind, while the subconscious mind, the largest and most powerful part, remains unseen below. All memories, feelings, and thoughts that are out of conscious awareness are by definition in the "non-conscious" part of the brain (subconscious plus unconscious). This is the part of brain we use in our dreams.

In this part of the brain, interpretation of situations, judgments, and analyses are carried out by the mind, without you being aware of them.

According to classical Freudian psychoanalysis, the subconscious mind (also mistakenly referred to as the "unconscious" mind by numerous psychologists), is a "part" of the mind that stores repressed memories. To avoid confusion and clarify terminology, the "non-conscious" mind under the water is composed of the subconscious part closer to the surface, and the unconscious part deeper in the water.

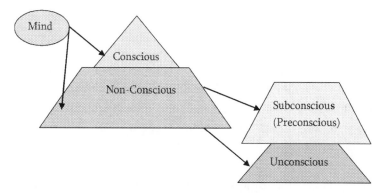

The three levels of the mind

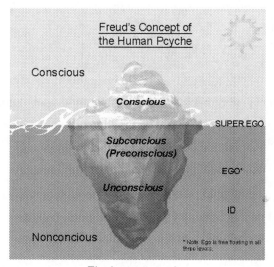

The human psyche

Sigmund Freud (1856–1939), an Austrian psychiatrist, was the main founder of the psychoanalytical school of psychology, later on accompanied by Alfred Adler (8) and Carl Jung (9). Freud is best known for his theories of the unconscious mind (more appropriately referred to as the subconscious mind) and the defense mechanism of repression. His theory of repression suggests that some experiences are too painful to be reminded of, so the tricky mind stores them in the "cellar" of the brain. These painful, repressed memories manifest themselves in neurotic or psychotic behavior and in dreams. While of significant historical interest, there is no obvious scientific evidence for the subconscious repression of traumatic experiences in neurotic or psychotic behavior, and many of Freud's ideas have fallen out of favor or have been modified by Neo-Freudians. However, in the past ten years, advances in the field of neurology and neuroscience have shown some evidence for many of his theories. Freud's methods and ideas remain important in clinical psychodynamic therapies. Along with Freud, Carl Jung and Alfred Adler are considered to be the principle founding fathers of modern psychology.

The subconscious mind is also thought by some, such as Jung and Tart and many modern spiritual leaders, to be a reservoir of transcendent truths. This forms the scientific basis of **transcendental meditation (TM),** established by Maharishi Mahesh Yogi in India about fifty years ago. Similar techniques have been used in the Eastern world for thousands of years. Today, over five million people in thirty-three countries across the globe use this technique to achieve inner peace and tranquility. There are over 600 published articles in reputable scientific journals about TM, with more than 350 of them being peer reviewed.

In simple words, this is the part of the brain that connects to the unlimited source of energy and intelligence—the *universal matrix.* What are often blocking this connection are the overlying, obstructing layers of the mind and soul. My favorite metaphor to explain this is Dr. Wayne Dyer's example of the glowing light bulb covered by layers of dirt, attached through an invisible wire to the source of universal energy. Although it is connected to the source and has the potential to glow, this will not happen unless the layers of dirt are removed. In my opinion, these layers of dirt are the "negative" or "destructive" parts of the subconscious mind that "blind" us to our own souls and interfere with the connection to the source of universal intelligence and abundance. **The ideal scenario for ultimate personal growth is to achieve one's peak potential by removing the obstructing layers. This will automatically result in transcendence of Truth and a revolutionary change in the state of consciousness. This is the highest purpose of human life!**

At the water line of our metaphoric iceberg is where we imagine. Imagination is a two-way communication medium between the non-conscious and conscious mind. It functions as the membrane through which processes happening in the non-conscious mind come into conscious awareness. The conscious can also communicate by sending messages about what it wants, through the imagination phenomenon. *It imagines things, and the non-conscious intelligence works to make them happen! Bingo!*

New ideas, hunches, daydreams, and intuitions come from the non-conscious to the conscious mind through the medium of imagination and memory. This partially explains the mystery of **karma** and the rationale of our connection to the source of universal intelligence. This may happen in a positive or negative way. Have you ever wondered why some people regularly complain of being "unlucky," while others constantly feel blessed with "luck"? This is because of how they think and connect to the universal intelligence through their non-conscious mind. *A negative collective state of mind attracts the negative energies of the universal matrix, and a positive state attracts the positive energies.* Remember, a thought is a form of energy with its physical properties, of the same nature and essence as that of the rest of the universe. *Quantum physics and quantum mechanics provide plenty of evidence that matter does not truly exist as we observe it, and at the subatomic level, everything is nothing but pure energy, just like everything else in the universe.*

Another fabulous example of the power in the lower part of the iceberg is dreaming. Dream images, visions, sounds, and feelings come from the non-conscious. Although some dreams may not be meaningful, we all have likely experienced extraordinary and unexplainable dreams that have come true.

Psychologist Carl Jung has named this realm the **Collective Unconscious**. For clarification, I'd like to call it the **Collective Non-conscious** (subconscious plus unconscious mind). This is the area of mind where all humanity shares experience, and from there we draw on the energies and symbols that are common to us all. Past-life memories are drawn from this level of non-conscious. The deeper we get in the iceberg, this commonality becomes even more apparent.

Another, even deeper level can be termed the **Universal Non-conscious**, where experiences beyond just humans can also be accessed. This is where human beings can connect as a single unit to the rest of the world. Understanding this phenomenon is key to being able to see the world through the **Third Vision**, as will be explained in future chapters. This paradigm shift will enable you not only to change your life and destiny forever, but also to make an unimaginable difference to the world!

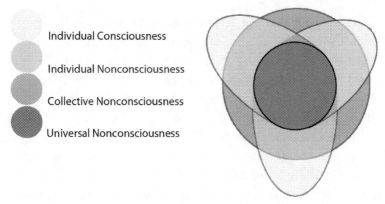

Individual Consciousness

Individual Nonconsciousness

Collective Nonconsciousness

Universal Nonconsciousness

The human psyche and collective states of awareness

It is also at this level that many core issues of mental disorders begin, and where their healing needs to be accomplished. The non-conscious connection between people is often more potent than the conscious level connection, and it is an important consideration in healing. Many traditional healers who have applied their skills for thousands of years draw their healing energy from this part of the human brain. Some day in the future, as our collective scientific knowledge matures, we may be able to explain the mysterious, unexplainable phenomena through pure scientific language. But until then, we can change our view of how to see the world through a different perspective, one that does not try to explain everything through limited experimental science, but rather through the **art of being** (present). "Sounds right but feels wrong" is an example of information from under the iceberg surfacing in the consciousness, but conflicting with what the conscious mind is able to receive. This kind of awareness is also called "sentience," the realm of **"intuition,"** or "gut feelings." *"Consciousness in the service of sentience" is the key to healing at the deepest levels and tapping unto the extraordinary powers of the universal energy.*

Unfortunately, our culture has discouraged us from giving this information credibility. The reason, some may argue, is that "there is not enough scientific evidence," as if we even had the capacity to explain the world scientifically! We seem to forget that humanity as a whole is just learning the alphabets of the universal language! "It's just your imagination" or "just a dream" is a commonly heard dismissal of information coming from the deep mind. This kind of conditioning has kept us disconnected from the deep richness of our vast nonconscious resources. *One of the most profound reasons why we all try to "fit in" to society and seek approval from others in the external world is this disconnection to the wonders of our inner world. If we were aware of such powers and capabilities, there would be no need to feel anxious about "fitting in."* All you have to do to access these resources and achieve your peak potential is to *undo* the obstacles and misunderstandings (layers of dirt covering your light bulb)!

Conscious Thinking

The conscious mind is what most people mistakenly refer to when they talk about "my mind." Whereas, if you pay close attention, the predominantly governing part of most people's brain in today's modern societies is the subconscious mind, not the conscious one. This is the part of mind above the surface of water in the iceberg analogy. *It is within the realm of our mental awareness. Of significance, is that the conscious mind speaks a different language from that of the subconscious mind.*

It is also the part of our brain that we use when thinking actively and rationally. The conscious mind is actively sorting and filtering its perceptions because only so much information can reside in consciousness at once. Everything else falls back below the water line, into non-consciousness. Only seven, plus or minus two bits of information (maximum forty) can be held consciously at one time in the short-term memory. Everything else we are thinking, feeling, or perceiving now, along with all our memories, remains subconscious.

The conscious mind is *logic based*, as opposed to *emotion based*. It takes into consideration our needs and desires within the context of social circumstances, meanings, and values. One of my favorite analogies is Dr. Daniel Amen's example of the "cop in the rear mirror of the car."

It represents the "watching eye" that controls our behavior in a socially acceptable manner.

The **neopallium**, also known as the **superior** or **rational** brain, comprises almost the entire hemispheres (**neocortex**) and some subcortical neuronal groups (shown as the top layer in the ice cream analogy). It corresponds to the brain of the superior mammals, thus including the primates and, consequently, the human species. The most important part of the brain responsible for conscious thinking is the **prefrontal cortex (PFC),** explained earlier. The PFC is the brain center most strongly implicated in qualities like sentience, human general intelligence, and personality. It is reasonable to say that the prefrontal cortex is the neurological basis of the **conscience**.

CHAPTER 6

"From thoughts come words. From words come actions. Actions form habits. Habits form character. Character shapes your destiny."
—*Margaret Thatcher*

Change Your Thoughts, Change Your Destiny

Conscious versus Subconscious Thinking

Consider this experiment. Place five monkeys in a cage with a banana hanging on a string and a set of stairs underneath it. Before long, a monkey will go up the stairs toward the banana. As soon as he touches the stairs, spray all of the *other* monkeys with cold water. After a while, another monkey makes an attempt with the same result—all the other monkeys are sprayed with cold water. Pretty soon, when one monkey tries to climb the stairs, the other monkeys will try to prevent it. Now, put away the cold water. Remove one monkey from the cage and replace it with a new one. The new monkey sees the banana and wants to climb the stairs. To his surprise and horror, all of the other monkeys attack him. After another attempt and attack, he knows that if he tries to climb the stairs, he will be assaulted, *without knowing the reason*. Next, remove another of the original five monkeys and replace it with a new one. The newcomer goes to the stairs and is attacked. The previous newcomer takes part in the punishment with enthusiasm! Likewise, replace a third original monkey with a new one, then a fourth, then the fifth. Every time the newest monkey takes to the stairs, he is attacked. *Most of the monkeys that are beating him have no idea why they were not permitted to climb the stairs or why they are participating in the beating of the newest monkey.* After replacing all the original monkeys, none of the remaining has ever been sprayed with cold water. Nevertheless, no monkey ever again approaches the stairs to try for the banana. Why not? Because as far as they know, that's the way it's always been done—that is the *standard*. Does this type of behavior sound familiar to you? Look around … there are plenty of similar social behaviors being copied without anyone questioning the purpose behind it!

This was a typical example of the subconscious versus conscious thinking. As discussed previously, the unconscious mind (first level) is designed to sustain homeostasis and survival. It is based on fundamental physiological reactions and is out of our control. Hence, our main discussion and focus will be on comparing the subconscious (second level) versus conscious thinking (third level). This is extremely important, as it forms the basis of how one can take control of his/her life, as opposed to being driven by the "automatic" mind that drives our lives.

As you may have noticed, we are often driven by unknown sources, originating thoughts, feelings, and behaviors, sometimes very painful, and we have no idea where they're coming from. As a result, more painful feelings such as guilt or self-resentment may follow, leading to the activation of more destructive defense mechanisms (to be described in detail in the following chapters). Once these actions and reactions are sustained long enough, or are repeated frequently, specific neuronal network patterns establish in the brain. Depending on how well these networks are solidified, certain types of negative personality traits or even disorders will develop, ultimately ruining one's life. AK and BT mentioned in chapter 1 are extreme examples, but if you look around, there are millions of real-life cases with milder forms of negative traits.

For better understanding, some of the characteristics of these two types of thinking will be described in an oversimplified manner.

- The subconscious is exemplified as the immature inner child, whereas the conscious is the mature adult in you.

68

- The subconscious can also be exemplified as the military soldier designed to ensure **survival**. *It does not guarantee happiness.* On the other hand, the conscious is like the inquisitive, skeptical student who asks many questions, designed for personal growth. This is what can lead you to happiness.
- The subconscious mind is *reactive*. It instantly reacts to situations to sustain survival, based on the exposures and experiences learned throughout life. This often leads to irrational feelings and behaviors. On the contrary, the conscious mind is *proactive*. It takes its time to think rationally and to make the best choice for you, not only to sustain homeostasis, but also to bring happiness.
- The subconscious is often focused on short-term gain (sometimes leading to long-term pain). The conscious ensures the opposite.
- The subconscious thinking often leads to destructive attitudes and behaviors, whereas the conscious is usually constructive.

These characteristics are outlined in summary below:

Subconscious Mind	Conscious Mind
Consider as the immature inner child	Consider as the mature grownup in you
Designed to sustain survival	Designed to bring happiness
Reactive thinking (often irrational)	Proactive thinking (often rational)
Focus on short-term gain	Short-term and long-term benefits
Irresponsible and self-centered	Responsible and conscientious
Usually destructive	Often constructive

Characteristics of the subconcsious and conscious minds

As you notice, these two may be in conflict and opposing each other at the same time. This is one of the most common sources of anxiety in a person (the concept of **cognitive dissonance** will be expanded upon in the following chapters). The more these two minds are in discordance, the higher level of anxiety and depression. Whereas, concordance of these two sides of you results in inner peace and happiness. Remember, this is only one reason for anxiety and depression, but a very mysterious and profound one. One of the most powerful but challenging skills is to learn how to bring these two minds together. One way is to gradually let the conscious mind take over the lead by default, instead of the subconscious (which is the current situation in most people). This, of course, is not an easy task, though it is simple!

Learning how to switch from the S mode (subconscious) to C mode (conscious) not only provides you with the fastest vehicle to your happiness, but also enables a much better connection to the external world. This leads to better relationships with other humans and much improved contribution to the other thirty million species in the world!

But this is easier said than done!

How do we know when the brain is in S mode as opposed to C mode? How do we switch gears when desired? How do we sustain this and set the C mode as the default mind state?

Imagine driving along the beach from one city to another. You have driven this route many times before and are quite familiar with the roads. As you are driving, the music is playing, you are looking at the beautiful scenery, and also thinking about your bills! How can the brain do so many things simultaneously? Well, the brain can intake a significant amount of information, while only processing and understanding seven, plus or minus two bits of information at a time consciously. At any given time, you are only aware of certain thoughts (conscious thoughts). The rest of it would be at the subconscious level, which is able to function more than a million times faster than the conscious mind (up to forty million bits of information). If you're focusing on your bills, that is the thought in your conscious awareness. If you focus on the scenery, the rest of the thoughts remain subconscious. If suddenly a dog crosses the road, and you have to step on the brake, your thoughts have automatically shifted, and the dog becomes the main focus in your conscious (aware) mind. The rest of the thoughts are subdued!

It is critical to realize the thoughts you are aware of (C mode), and even more critical to see the ones that are under the surface (S mode).

Psychology of Change

In simple words, there are two main steps involved in the concept of change; the first is **knowledge**, and the second is **practice.** We know that the human body has the capacity to do almost anything, once you put your mind into it. By learning the fundamental principles, and through practice, the mind and body can accomplish the unimaginable! The same rule applies here.

1. **Knowledge.** The key is to understand that the true YOU is not always what you think is YOU! As discussed in chapter 2, there are in fact two identities in you: the true self, which we will exhibit as **YOU**, and your false self, shown as **you**—your illusionary image and perception of self.

    Try to see YOU through the eyes of an outside observer! Instead of taking immediate action and reacting to external situations or internal feelings, take a moment to question your thoughts, feelings, and actions (TFA core triangle). The key word that makes a significant difference in life is **why?** (or other interrogative words). Why am I feeling sad? What am I afraid of? Why am I acting in a passive-aggressive manner toward my family? Are my current thoughts rational, and is there supporting evidence to back it up? Why am I working so hard and spending so little time with my loved ones? Why do I need to be approved by society? What am I looking for in life? Why? Why? Why?

    Most people are so caught up in life that they do not question themselves. They spend the majority of their lifetime under the water in the iceberg analogy without being fully aware of it—in the subconscious! We often repeat habitual patterns day and night, over and over again, without questioning whether it is the best path we have chosen. We often wake up in the morning, get ready for work, repeat the same work pattern, and do the same things repeatedly for a long time. One day, we wake up and realize this may not have been the right thing for us.

    The key point in living a conscious life (as opposed to subconscious) is to question our patterns of life constantly and self-assess them by breaking down these patterns to the core TFA triangle. Then write down the answers to *"observe" your thoughts. This is the fundamental principle of cognitive and behavioral therapy (CBT).* What I'm emphasizing here is to learn the skills of **Self-Cognitive Behavioral Therapy (SCBT)!**

2. **Practice.** After a prolonged pursuit of happiness since the age of eighteen, my profound understanding of the TFA core triangle was intensified in 2002 (right after the sudden death of my father). The sudden shock and deep emotional state likely had something to do with it. Since then, I started applying this principle to any ordinary or extraordinary event in life. What I found was that **it applies to every single situation. It is a universal phenomenon!** The modified TFA model or STFAR(P) applies to examples as uneventful as pounding your fist on the desk when you're angry, or large global events like wars and mega crimes. Let's consider two scenarios in detail.

   - Scenario one: A serious argument has been sparked between you and your girlfriend **(S)**. You disagree with her and think, *This situation is not acceptable to me* **(T)**. You feel upset, which escalates to anger **(F)**. You start pounding your fist on the table **(A)**. The table breaks **(R)**. Then the doorbell rings. You open the door, and it's your neighbor who brought you some homemade food with a smile **(change in S)**. You are distracted from the argument and think, *Wow, this is nice of my neighbor* **(new T)**. You feel appreciative **(new F)**. You lower your tone, smile back, and thank her **(new A)**. Your mood changes, and you realize what just happened. You apologize to your girlfriend for breaking the table **(new A)**. Your girlfriend accepts your apology, and the dispute is resolved in a more mature way **(new R)**.

   - Scenario two: In general, there are two categories of believers. One group believes the global resources are limited **(T)**. This creates a sense of insecurity **(F)**. Therefore we need to compete in order to survive **(A)**. This may mean destroying other humans or species, hence one main reason for wars throughout history **(R)**. Another group believes that the resources in this universe are not limited, but abundant **(alternative T)**. There is plenty of room, food, and energy for every single one of the thirty million species that inhabit this planet. We just need to see the big picture through the right lens! Rather than fighting over fossil fuels, the global village may collectively focus on other green sources of energy, such as wind, solar, nuclear (with caution!), water, electric, etc. There is abundant food in the world, and there's no need for anyone to die from starvation. The agricultural revolution is a testimony to this. About ten thousand years ago, it resulted in an exponential increase in food supply— hence the rapid population growth on the planet. This belief and understanding can immediately put us at ease and reduce our "survival anxiety" **(alternative F)**. We focus on global collaboration and teamwork rather than destructive competition **(alternative A)**. There will be fewer wars in the world, newer technologies will be created, and the Earth will become a friendlier place to live in **(alternative R)!**

In the examples above and in every single situation in your life, you can find the application of the STFAR(P) formula.

Here is a chart used in cognitive therapy that helps us control and manage our thoughts and feelings in a more desired manner. Continuous practice will enable us to develop a "self-critical view" as an outside observer and in a more constructive way. My recommendation is to place this chart in view (e.g., on your fridge), and practice it every night before going to bed, focusing on a specific situation during that day. Imagine yourself sitting in a plane to Europe, ready for takeoff, and feel the flight anxiety that numerous people experience:

Situation	Feeling (score 0–100)	Thought (subconscious)	Evidence supporting thought	Evidence *not* supporting thought	Alternate Thought	Alternate Feeling (0–100)	Improved? (Y/N/no change)
Sunday evening in the plane, on the runway, waiting for the plane to take off.	Feeling sick, anxious, afraid. (98%)	My heart is beating faster and harder. I'm having a heart attack. I'll never make it to the hospital. I'll die here.	My heart is racing. I'm sweating. These are two symptoms of a heart attack.	Rapid heartbeat can be caused by anxiety or other reasons. Rapid heartbeat is not always dangerous. This happened before during flights, and I did not die in similar situations.	Could be symptoms of anxiety. My MD assured me that a rapid heartbeat is not always dangerous. It will return to normal in a few minutes. This happens to many, and they don't die.	Less fearful and anxious. (30%)	Yes.

An example of self-cognitive therapy

In the example above, the thoughts **(T)** and feelings **(F)** in a common situation **(S)** are demonstrated. This condition is very common and is known as "flight phobia" or "flight anxiety," which is due to fear of altitude or fear of flight itself. Many people resort to anxiolytic agents, such as lorazepam, prior to their flight to calm them down. This can directly and physiologically alter the physical state **(P)** of the person by altering the neurotransmitters in the brain and causing a temporary relaxation (see **STFAR(P)** model). While medication is a reasonable option, it does not address the underlying phobia and never cures the problem. Whereas, long–term cognitive therapy not only addresses the anxiety during each experience, but will also cause the subconscious fear to dissipate over time.

Q: Is it really this simple to change our pattern of thinking?
A: Yes, it's simple, but not easy. It requires continuous practice.

Q: So why are most people (probably more than 95 percent) in the habit of subconscious thinking?

A: Because most of us have been conditioned with the "standard living" (the monkey experiment). Most have not learned the skills of continuously monitoring our thoughts, feelings, and actions. Even once you have, it is difficult to remember to apply it in daily events. It requires energy and a high level of responsibility toward yourself and the rest of the world. By nature, we tend to choose the path of least resistance and like to stay in the comfort zone, which means shifting back to the "automatic" or "subconscious" mentality. However, through knowledge and practice, it is possible to make the new "conscious" thinking "automatic" and "second nature," once enough neuronal network has been solidified.

Q: *In brief, what are the steps for changing the habit of subconscious thinking into a conscious one?*

A: The first step is **knowledge**—understanding your subconscious thoughts, feelings, and actions **(TFA)** versus the conscious ones. Then realize the relationship of your inner thoughts, feelings, and actions to the people around you and the external world **(SPR).** This makes the significant difference of being able to observe YOU from outside the box. Change begins with **self-realization** and self-criticism, which can lead to a constructive evolution toward personal growth.

The next step is **practice**. Through the practice of ongoing **self-cognitive therapy**, you will empower your ability to shift focus from subconscious thinking to conscious (fulfilled mainly by the **cingulate gyrus** in the brain).

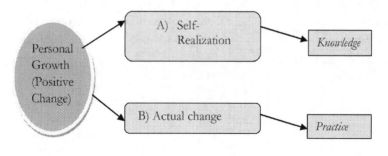

Stages of change

My favorite metaphor is observing a magnificent piece of art through the lens of a zooming camera. If you are too far, you will miss the art in the details, and if you're too close, the overall sense of beauty may be compromised. You want to be able to zoom in when needed to focus on details, and zoom out as desired to feel the big picture.

The same applies to your own mind. **Flexibility** is key to the ability to shift focus on your thoughts. Not only do you want to know what you are *not* aware of (the subconscious thoughts), but you also want to have the capacity to shift to the conscious mind as needed. Over time, practice makes this much easier, to the point where it becomes second nature **(reconditioning).**

Norman Rosenthal said, "Many people see the world the way it is and ask 'why.' I see the world the way it is not and ask 'why not.'" As mentioned in the introduction, the establishment of a **Life Skills Institute** is needed, one that can provide a practical and easy-to-use coaching technique for the average population. It is needed in order to distribute the knowledge and practice tools to recondition the mind and achieve a fundamental change in how we envision the world. Why not? All it takes is *vision, passion,* and a *mission.*

Throughout the globe, there are currently numerous scientists, writers, philosophers, masters, coaches, and gurus who basically convey the same message through different languages and perspectives. They all invite humans to recondition their minds by understanding and accessing the unimaginable powers within their souls and minds. *Collaboration* and *networking* of these leaders and coaches, possibly through a centralized and coordinated facility, may change the path of humanity and Mother Earth forever. Otherwise, I believe, the path human beings have taken collectively will ultimately lead to global disaster, as the signs of crisis are becoming more evident!

CHAPTER 7

"What is necessary to change a person is to change his awareness of himself."
—*Abraham Maslow*

Human Psyche and the Ladder of Personal Growth

The phone rang in the middle of the night. It was about 4 a.m. I jumped out of my bed to grab it. This did not sound good. Phone calls in the middle of the night usually remind me of bad news. It was my uncle from Greece. The shaky tone of his voice made my heart beat faster. "I do not have good news for you, Farsheed," he said (my Persian name is Farsheed). I had a feeling I already knew what he was going to say.

"What happened, Hamid? Is it Dad?" I asked.

"Your dad is in the hospital," he said. "He had a massive heart attack. I'll call you back in a few minutes." He could not talk anymore. I could tell from his voice that he was devastated and could not hold his tears any longer. And you can imagine how I was feeling. I was in total shock. I did not even know for a second how to feel. My father had shown no signs of heart disease to that date, and he was only sixty-two. This was entirely unexpected. I could not help but call my uncle back in a few minutes ... minutes that felt like decades!

"Hamid, tell me the truth; I'm prepared for it," I said, not knowing whether to believe myself or not.

"Farsheed, your dad never made it to the hospital. He passed away immediately after a massive heart attack. We did whatever we could with the paramedics to resuscitate him [he is an anesthesiologist], but unfortunately, he did not make it. I wanted to give you a bit of time to absorb it."

My father had died of a condition called "sudden death." I was devastated. I could not sleep, eat, or work. I could do nothing. For a brief period, I could not continue living. *He was my best friend, my role model, and my hero. How could this happen to me? He was only sixty-two. This in not fair,* I was thinking as a mix of confused feelings flooded my mind and body.

In the next seventy-two hours, I was on the plane back to my home country, Iran, to attend my father's funeral. His body was flown in from Greece the previous day. In our culture, the funeral is held for seven consecutive days after the burial ceremony and finalized on the fortieth day, consistent with the idea that the initial grievance period takes about six weeks.

One night in that first week of the burial ceremony, I had a dream. I dreamt of a poem describing my father and many other fathers. I woke up the next morning and started writing it down word by word. Today, that poem, printed on my father's image, is hanging in a picture frame in my bedroom. Never in my life to this date, apart from that occasion, have I been able to write a poem. In fact, my poetic talent is next to zero. I can hardly memorize more than two lines of a poem. How on earth did that happen?

It made me wonder! Obviously, it is a testimony that somewhere in the depth of my brain, or mind, or soul, or somewhere in the universe, this poem was created. And somehow I had access to it. *I realized that in certain deep emotional and mental states, the gate to a very mysterious, precious, and unlimited resource deep within our psyche opens up. Creative talents and capabilities surface to the world of reality like a volcano erupting from the center of earth.* This is called **transcendence.**

I vowed to pursue the search for this treasure on my trip back to Canada after the funeral was over. This experience was one of the motivations for the book you're reading. You will find the answers in the following chapters!

Now, let us understand the human psyche and correlate it to different parts of the brain functions. Remember, this is a brutally oversimplified description, just for the sake of a better understanding and practical applications of our knowledge.

States of the Human Psyche

Freud developed his **topographical theory,** which divided the mind into *conscious* and *unconscious* (explained in previous chapters). For better clarification, we have proposed a modified scheme that is more concordant scientifically with the development of the human brain. As discussed earlier, this includes the conscious, subconscious, and unconscious (the latter two compose the non-conscious mind).

Over time, Freud incorporated his findings into a new **structural theory**, which consists of three states of the psyche—**id, ego, and super-ego**. These are the main parts of the "psychic apparatus." They are the three theoretical constructs in terms of how one's mental life is described. According to this model, the uncoordinated, instinctual trends are the "id"; the organized, realistic part of the psyche is the "ego"; and the critical and moralizing function is the "super-ego." The ego is the *mediator* between two aspects of the human psyche: the id and the super-ego—the "bad" and the "good."

A fundamental concept in ego psychology is one of conflict among these three areas, as they battle for the expression of instinctual drives on one end, and moralizing conscience on the other (the battle between good and evil since the beginning of humanity). This conflict produces anxiety, signaling to the ego that one or more of its defense mechanisms is required. Even though the model is "structural" and makes reference to an "apparatus," the id, ego, and super-ego are *functions of the mind* rather than physical parts of the brain.

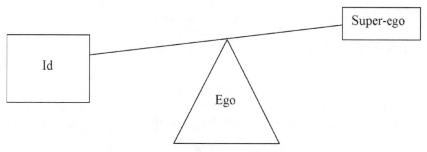

The ego maintains balance between id, superego, and the external world

Id

The id, referred to by some people as the *false ego*, comprises the part of the personality structure that contains the basic drives. It acts based on the *pleasure* principle: it seeks immediate enjoyment. It is focused on selfishness and instant self-gratification. The id is nonconscious by definition. It stands in direct opposition to the super-ego. In philosophical terms, the id is equivalent to a person's "dark side" or "evil side." But after all, you'll see why it is not so evil, since it is designed to ensure *survival*.

Developmentally, the id comes before the ego. The psychic apparatus begins at birth. Thus, the id contains everything that is inherited, that is present at birth—what we know as the *instincts*. The mind of a newborn child is regarded as completely "id-ridden," in the sense that it is a mass of instinctive drives and impulses, and it demands immediate satisfaction. It has not yet learned otherwise.

The id is responsible for our basic drives, such as food, water, sex, and basic impulses. It is amoral and egocentric, ruled by the pleasure-pain principle. It is without a sense of time, completely illogical, primarily sexual, infantile in its emotional development, and will not take "no" for an answer. It is regarded as the reservoir of the libido or "instinctive drive to create."

The id explains the basic personality of the *inner child* of the immature adults in a society who act like children. These individuals have solidified their *immature* defense mechanisms and use them subconsciously in stressful situations. This pattern is often repeated over and over until it becomes a habit and part of the person's personality. This explains why some individuals are more selfish, as opposed to others who are more conscientious.

Super-Ego

The Super-ego works exactly opposite the id. It comprises that part of the personality structure that includes spiritual goals, and the psychic component (commonly called **conscience**) that criticizes and prohibits his/her drives, fantasies, feelings, and actions.

The super-ego acts as the conscience, maintaining our sense of morality. It strives to act in a socially appropriate manner, whereas the id just wants instant self-gratification. The super-ego controls our sense of right and wrong. It helps us fit into a society by making us act in socially acceptable ways. The super-ego's demands oppose the id's, so the ego has a hard time reconciling the two. It exemplifies the *inner wise grandparent* or *inner cop* in you.

Ego

In modern-day society, ego has many meanings. It could mean one's self-esteem, an inflated sense of self-worth, or in philosophical terms, one's self.

In psychological terms, the ego acts as a mediator according to the reality principle. It seeks to please the id's drive as well as the superego's moral demands, in realistic ways that will benefit in the long term rather than bringing grief. *In Freud's theory, the ego mediates among the id, the super-ego, and the external world.* Its task is to find a balance between primitive drives and reality, while satisfying the other two opponents. Its main concern is with the individual's safety, and it allows some of the id's desires to be expressed, but only when consequences of these actions are marginal. It acts like the *inner adult* in you!

Ego **defense mechanisms** are often used when id behavior conflicts with reality or the society's morals, norms, and taboos. Although the id is nonconscious by definition, the ego and the super-ego are both partly conscious and partly subconscious (see Freud's iceberg diagram).

Denial, displacement, intellectualization, fantasy, compensation, projection, rationalization, reaction formation, regression, and sublimation were the defense mechanisms Freud identified. However, his daughter, Anna Freud, clarified and identified the concepts of undoing, suppression, dissociation, idealization, identification, introjection, inversion, somatization, splitting, and substitution. Some of the more common DMs will be explained in depth in the following chapters.

Much of Freud's and other psychiatrists' work remains to be proven or disproved by future technology and scientific research. One of the objectives of this book is to connect the dots between the structural model of Freud, theories of other psychologists and psychiatrists, and somatic correspondence to specific parts of the brain. However, what is important is how to make practical and clinical use of this information in day-to-day life, in a simple language, so that it is accessible to the majority of the people in the world. This leads us to the next major breakthrough in modern psychology—Maslow's pyramid of personal growth!

Maslow's Pyramid

Abraham Harold Maslow (1908–1970) was an American psychologist (10). He is noted for his conceptualization of a "hierarchy of human needs" and is considered the founder of humanistic psychology. He proposed his theory in the 1943 paper, *A Theory of Human Motivation.*

Although a milestone in clinical and behavioral psychology, it is limited in practical use by its complexity and lack of clarification (figure below).

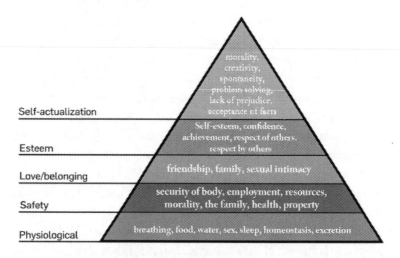

Maslow's pyramid of human development

For better understanding, I will propose a *modified* version of this pyramid, which is more simple and practical (see figure below). The pyramid is divided into three main sections: **basic or physiological needs** (stage 1), **social needs** (stage 2), and **spiritual needs** (stage 3).

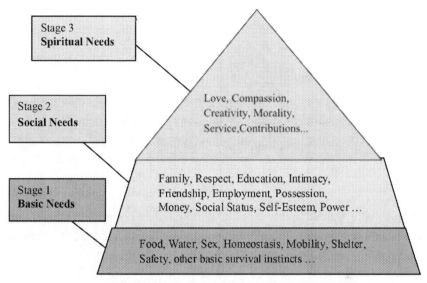

Modified version of Maslow's pyramid

The significance of this modified pyramid is that it has much more practical use and correlates well with the evolution of the brain as a human grows. Putting the pieces of the puzzle together, the diagram in the footnotes demonstrates the correlation of the brain parts and layers to the psychological models of the psyche and mind, and the modified Maslow's pyramid (11).

For thousands of years, the human being has been like a boat in the middle of the ocean, free floating in any direction that may seem appropriate in the context of time and space. Every once in a while, a larger ship would pass by, providing some kind of leadership and guidance. Other times, it would follow where other smaller boats were heading, just to fit in the group. Sometimes with the wind, and other times against it, the free-floating human in the boat has always been in pursuit of happiness and the meaning of life. *This pyramid serves like a compass, giving direction and leading the path to one's destination to happiness and peak personal growth (the third stage)!*

First stage. The first stage corresponds to childhood, and it is born along with the newborn. In fact, this stage is shaped during the gestational period before birth, and the newborn already has some of these needs since day one, such as food, water, and homeostasis. Keep in mind that the needs mentioned above in each stage may not exhibit simultaneously, but develop as a hierarchy within each stage. As the infant develops socially and begins to connect with the outside world, other basic needs, such as mobility and safety, become more explicit. The needs for shelter and sex (in its premature and childish form) show up later during childhood and evolve into early adolescence.

Also remember that the lines in between the stages are not clear cut, but rather demonstrate an overlap period of evolution from one stage into the next. These transitions may last for varied periods of time. In many cases, the distinction between the second and third stage of life may never actually occur. *These two lines correspond to the two major critical evolutionary periods of life*; the first one being the transition from childhood into adulthood (the teen ages), and the second one may be referred to as the "midlife crisis," the period in mid-adulthood when many individuals feel something is missing in their lives and the need to fill that gap. Some people get a wake-up call after the death of a loved one, when they come to realize that the material objects and adult toys they were running for all their lives no longer have the same meaning as they did before the tragedy. While many do creatively and instinctually find their way toward the summit of personal growth and happiness, others unfortunately may not figure it out and end up in a state of confusion, depression, or purposelessness. How many people do you know who worked hard their entire life to build a fortune, and suddenly started giving it away to charities?

What is actually happening is that they are becoming aware of their spiritual needs in the third stage. There is a major push for personal growth, and given the appropriate exposures and guidance, they can follow their pursuit of happiness toward the peak of the pyramid. Following this path, which is a unique experience for every individual, will not only ensure long-lasting happiness, but also awaken the highest human potentials lying within the depth of our nonconscious psyche. Upon entering into the third stage of life, we begin to view the world from a different perspective— what I'll be referring to as the **Third Vision** in this book.

Neurologically, a newborn's brain is obviously different from that of an adult. As discussed previously, the **archipallium,** or **primitive brain,** mainly responsible for the duties of the unconscious mind, has fully evolved in a newborn (first layer in ice cream analogy). Hence, it is fully capable of fulfilling the physiological functions of survival.

I remember delivering a baby, watching one of the many wonders of this beautiful world. As soon as the baby was born and the umbilical cord was cut, we put him on mom's belly with his head close to her breasts. Amazingly, he moved his head around, instinctually found the exact place to put his mouth, on the nipple, and started feeding himself. Where on earth did he learn that from? The unconscious mind had learned through the miracle of genomic evolution to sustain survival!

The biological network of the **paleopallium,** or **intermediate brain (**mainly consisting of the **limbic system),** is also formed in a newborn, but is not yet evolved (second layer in the ice cream). In simple terms, this is the main center for the subconscious mind. *It is extremely important to understand that this part of the brain is molded roughly in the first five years of age, setting the infrastructure of a person's character. Most experts in the field of psychology agree that a person's personality is predominantly formed by age five. This critical period is the biggest opportunity for parents and a caring society to build the future of an individual.*

This is the "acquired" or "environmental" component of one's personality that can be improved. There is no question about the genetic composition of a human, but to this date, we do not have much control in the modification of that component. However, future research in genetics may change the entire path of humanity!

The raw material for the complex neuronal network (the hardware) does exist, but due to lack of exposures and experience (the software), it is not developed yet. The trillions of synapses are waiting to be wired and molded together as newborns receive signals from the world around them, and the synapses form new junctions and patterns as they continue to learn.

The **neopallium,** or **rational brain,** mainly responsible for the conscious mind, is not developed yet in an infant or newborn. The network and development of this part of the brain (the neocortex and mainly the prefrontal cortex) starts forming in early childhood but continues to evolve very slowly throughout the entire life. This explains why "a child is a child," and why many adults are just "big children." Despite having the material for the rational brain, it never develops to full capacity.

According to the Darwinian Theory, since humans appeared on this planet two hundred thousand years ago (the early *hominids* all the way to *homo sapiens*), the "law of jungle" has prevailed. Natural selection would allow the stronger to survive, and the weaker to perish. Humans were not far superior to other inferior animals, and they were "big children" struggling to survive and meet basic needs. Wars and conflicts over food, shelter, and mates have always been part of human history. Some of the social needs, such as family, power, and intimacy, were also experienced by early humans. *But the more complex, mature, and civilized aspects of the human spirit evolved only in the last six or seven thousand years, when human beings formed smaller societies and early civilizations.*

Nevertheless, no one is to blame, since their brain structure was different from that of today's human, and the higher, more rational parts had not yet developed. Archeologists and anthropologists know this fact from comparing the shape and size of the skulls and brains of early humans with the more civilized ones of today. In the past seven million years of human evolution from its ancestors (chimpanzees and gorillas), the size of the prefrontal cortex has increased six-fold.

Similarly, the brain of humans 10,000 years from now is likely to be different and hopefully more mature than that of today. The evolution of the human brain will not stop here, and we have a long way to go to understand our potential and real value as a species. This is what makes us humans so special and unique, different from the rest of the thirty million species on this planet. At the same time we brag about our unique features, we must accept responsibility and take care of our Mother Earth and its inhabitants, simply because we are the only species given the tools and knowledge to do so. Unfortunately, to this date, we have collectively not done a very good job in preserving our global nation. We must not forget that the evolution will continue, and our future generations, hundreds and thousands of years from today, whether on Earth or Mars, will judge us on our actions today. We have a lot of homework to do!

Second stage. The second stage of the modified pyramid corresponds to early adulthood onward, throughout the entire life. In this stage, values and priorities change and have a different meaning. Other needs, such as respect, social relationships, friends, sense of family, possession, and social status, suddenly become more important than the toys we used to play with during childhood. These needs are the motivation leading many to high achievements. The need to achieve and grow is a natural and unique blessing of the **ego**, leading humans to the highest peaks of the ladder of personal growth. As expressed in the introduction, this is one fundamental reason why religions that are based on suppressing the ego have failed to this date.

Consider the brain as a computer. Since birth, the hardware is there in its early forms, and every experience and exposure in life shapes the software as we grow. The difference between the brain and the computer, however, is that the hardware *also* changes as we age, and the brain evolves based on two major factors: *intrinsic factors* (our genetic composition) and *extrinsic factors* (what we *learn,* based on the environment, our exposures, and experiences). What we learn in the first five to six years of age becomes the main software that forms our core personality. Evidence suggests that *major* traumatic events may impact the brain structure, and therefore the future of a person's mental health as early as the first five years (or even in the pregestational period). However, most *minor* events do not have any critical impact. Most criminal minds and social illnesses, such as prostitution and addictions, are rooted in early childhood. To this date, there is no crime gene identified that would automatically turn a newborn into a criminal later on in life. *Every baby is born innocent.* So how on earth can an innocent newborn turn out to be one of the worst criminals, and commit some of the unthinkable acts we see today?

The answer lies in the subconscious mind and the **defense mechanisms of ego**. Make no mistake ... not all defense mechanisms are bad. In fact, they are vital for sustainability of mental health, as explained previously. To date, there are numerous defense mechanisms (DM) identified. Of those, however, the majority are destructive but necessary at different stages of life, and some of them are constructive. These will be explained thoroughly in chapter 9.

The biological network of the **intermediate brain** and the **limbic system** is much more evolved during the second stage of the pyramid. Remember that it is an ongoing process of evolution. This part of the brain is usually solidified by age eighteen, based on intrinsic genetic, familial, and congenital factors, and what the person has learned over time (extrinsic factors). This is why many psychologists believe that one's personality is completely shaped by age eighteen. For centuries, we also used to believe that the brain cannot be changed once it is "hardwired." However, the concept of *neuroplasticity* proved us wrong. We now know that the brain can change itself at any age with proper training. However, the older the brain, and the more solidified it is, the more difficult to change. *The reason is that the 164 trillion connections and synapses that have established very powerful patterns are difficult to undo, but not impossible.*

The development of the **rational brain** is variable among individuals in the second stage. It continues to evolve throughout life, but it does not fully evolve in everyone, and many people may never experience the spiritual stage of their life, remaining in the second stage forever. They may or may not become aware of "something missing" in their lives.

I like the analogy of Google Earth to explain a strategy to find this "missing thing." At higher levels, you get a better sense of the big picture. If you never "zoom out," you will never experience or comprehend what you can potentially see at high levels. On the other hand, you need the flexibility to "zoom in" to observe the details of life around you. As discussed in earlier chapters, it is the cingulate gyrus in the brain that enables this flexibility. Both perspectives are needed to achieve full comprehension of the observation!

Third stage. Finally, a minority group of people at some point in their life are fortunate enough to enter into the realm of third stage. This may happen abruptly with one experience, such as the death of a loved one. In others, it may be a gradual transition over several years. Here is an example to demonstrate the transitions into different stages of life.

Suppose you are six years old, playing soccer with your buddies. Engaged in the activity, you may feel excited, happy, or sometimes angry over losing the game. How do you observe the other kids? How do you feel about them? Probably like themselves—as a child.

Now you are an adult. You get involved in a baseball game with a team of children to have a fun and memorable Sunday. There is again a lot of energy, excitement, feeling, and action going on. How do you observe the kids now? How do you feel about them?

While involved in their activities, you see them from a different perspective. You observe them in a non-judgmental, loving, and caring way and enjoy what they are doing, even though it does not have the same meaning for you as it does for them. You can still feel like a kid but think and observe like an adult at the same time! That's because you are wearing newer glasses and seeing things differently. *The meaning of things has changed, and now you have developed a new "vision." You are in your second stage of life!*

Suppose after a while, you realize there are numerous adults who are struggling and fighting over matters that are meaningless to you. Examples include making a big deal over nothing (such as fighting over a spot in line for pizza), or giving up honorable values in life to acquire a material object like a nice sports car, just to show off to friends and family. *Destructive competition*—as opposed to *constructive competition*—is a habit for many adults. Consumerism and materialism are major preoccupations for many adults today. *There is absolutely nothing wrong with enjoying material achievements and belongings, as long as we view them only as "adult toys" and disposables and do not exchange them with higher values in life.*

You may realize that many adults think, feel, and act differently from you. You begin to view the world from a higher perspective. *Now you have reached your third stage of life.* You may begin to observe such adults as "big children" in a non-critical, non-judgmental way and yet be capable of loving and caring for them. It's just a matter of time that they too, like you, may reach their third stage and view the world from a higher perspective.

Neurologically, the third stage of life becomes evident when the rational brain (the cortical brain and prefrontal cortex) has fully developed. *The conscious and subconscious mind work constantly and very closely together, sometimes in conflict (creating anxiety and depression), and sometimes in peace and resolution (causing happiness and satisfaction).* In this stage, the conscious mind has prevailed and taken leadership in habitual thinking. That's when a new mentality becomes second nature, and the neuronal network is redesigned, configured, and reestablished in the brain. A person in the third stage of life becomes less self-centered and more generous toward others. Higher values become more meaningful and life more purposeful. He/she wears different glasses than the one in second stage. Contribution and service to others become a top priority. Morality becomes a discipline, while creativity reaches its peak. Above all, love for self, other humans, and the rest of the world become highly meaningful and the main motivation for every action in life.

This is the purpose of life: evolution to the maximum capacity of personal growth ... **transformation of the state of awareness!**

At this stage, you are at a higher energy level and more powerful than ever, since you have tapped into your deepest resources of the nonconcious. By removing or minimizing the "viruses" in the subconscious filter, you have managed to bring the deepest levels of your nonconscious mind to conscious awareness, connecting to the universal nonconscious. More than ever, you are aligned with the rest of the world and have the capacity to access the metaphysical powers of the universal matrix through transcendence! *You view yourself united and inseparable from the rest of the universal intelligence in a non-egoistic, selfless form!*

The Dilemma of Insanity

Insane behaviors and thoughts are nothing unusual in today's world. *So why is that?* The answer lies in one word—*survival.*

As mentioned previously, the primary function of the body is to protect us biologically, through the brain, and for the mind to protect us psychologically, through the ego, from any *perceived* threat. The secret lies within the **autonomic nervous system** of the brain, consisting of sympathetic and parasympathetic systems. During distress, the sympathetic system takes control, enabling you to prepare for fight or flight. Two main mechanisms happen in this mode, explaining why it is so challenging to maintain sanity in today's extremely stressful environment.

1. Due to sympathetic over-activity, the blood circulation is redistributed to the organs and body parts more critical for fight or flight—the musculoskeletal system. Your arms and legs are flooded with blood, bringing more oxygen and energy to either protect you or help you run away from

danger. Keep in mind that this takes away blood from other vital organs, such as the kidneys, heart, brain, liver, etc.

2. Similarly in the brain, blood is shifted from the parts that are more critical in *reactive* thinking—the second layer—as opposed to the ones involved in proactive thinking— the third layer. *This is why we are generally less intelligent during distress.* Meanwhile, the ego follows its most basic instincts in attempt to ensure its fundamental responsibility—mental survival.

So, how does the brain perceive, process, and translate messages of survival through evolutionary phenomena in the body and mind? This takes us to the next chapter—the pain-pleasure principle.

CHAPTER 8

"Peace comes from within. Do not seek it without."
—Buddha

The Pain-Pleasure Principle

On a Sunday evening, one of the TV channels caught my attention. It was a documentary about a show called *The Game of Death*. This was a popular reality show in France. About eighty contestants participate as "questioners" in several teams. Each team is composed of eight to ten participants. They will ask a question from an unknown "contestant" who is locked up in an "electric shock room." They cannot see the contestant but can hear his voice and reactions. Taking turns, each questioner is supposed to ask a question from this prisoner, and if he does not answer correctly, an electric shock will be given to him. The shocks start at 20 volts, and escalate in 20-volt increments up to the maximum of 460 volts (which can lead to the prisoner's death!). All the questioners and the contestant sign a document, committing them to obey the order of an "authority" and acknowledging that they are fully responsible for the consequences. They are all aware that these electric shocks will inflict pain. They are told that the chance of a health hazard is low, but there is still a chance of death for the contestant. In each group, the questioners take turns asking the question and administering the shock by pushing a lever. If any of them disobeys, they are considered "rebels," and their entire team loses the chance to win one million euros. If the contestant accumulates enough points through the correct answers, or the questioners reach the maximum of 460 volts, that team *and* the contestant in the shock room will win the one million euros ... that is, if he is still alive!

Interestingly, all of these questioners are ordinary and decent people with jobs and families and no criminal records. The show was amazing. At about 80 volts, you could hear the contestant voicing pain. As the shocks increased in intensity, you could truly sense the contestant suffering inside the shock room. At 240 volts, he would beg the questioners to stop and say that he did not want to play anymore. At 320 volts, there was nothing more heard from the contestant! But the rules and the authority did not allow questioners to stop and would urge them to continue. However, they *did* have a choice; either to stop inflicting pain to a stranger or allow their teammates to lose the chance of winning one million euros. There was intense mental pressure on each questioner when it was his or her turn to push the lever.

The results of this experiment were unbelievable. There were three groups. Only 19 percent of all questioners became "rebels" and quit the show because they could not tolerate inflicting pain on another human being. About 50 percent wanted to give up at some point and would negotiate with the authority to somehow put an end to this dilemma, but after the authority insisted and the audience encouraged the questioner to continue, the questioner went all the way up to 460 volts. The most interesting part to me was that about 30 percent of the "ordinary" questioners did not even challenge or object to the authority and continued to the end!

After the show, each of the questioners was interviewed backstage. It was amazing to hear their experiences and find out what they were thinking or feeling during the experiment. Some of the rebels also met with the contestant to hear what he was experiencing. All of the questioners were suffering for causing pain to someone else, but most of them found a way in their mind to justify their decision and complete the task!

Every day, bombarded by acts of cruelty, we ask ourselves: "How can humans be capable of so much evil?" The story of Abu Ghuraib prison in Iraq exemplifies how young American men and women, who behaved in exemplary fashion in their own small communities back home, ended up behaving like monsters.

In 1971, professors from Stanford University in the United States created a simulated prison in the basement of the psychology department. Using no special criterion, they chose twelve students as guards and another twelve as prisoners, all from the same social background— middle class, strict upbringing, dignified moral values. For two weeks, the "prison guards" would be given total power over the "prisoners."

The experience had to be interrupted after a week. After a few days, the "guards" began to reveal a form of behavior that became increasingly sadistic and abnormal, as they committed barbarities never before suspected. Today, over thirty years later, the two groups still need psychological counseling!

Interpretation of the Results of the TV Show

The result of the first experiment was a surprise to the investigator, who was a psychologist, and viewers such as me. How could 80 percent of a cohort of ordinary people be capable and willing to fulfill such a brutal task? Obviously there was immense struggle between the moral principles and the "legal obligation" they had to obey the authority. But guess who won in 80 percent of cases? The *obedience principle*! The "obedient" participants felt that they had to obey the rules of the game and failed to say no, despite their intense internal conflict and moral turbulence. Other participants simply did not want to "fail" their team and give up the taste of victory and the million euros.

The investigator concluded several points:

- The obedience principle is something that is embedded deeply in our subconscious minds. This comes from birth and early childhood, when we are supposed to follow the orders of authoritative figures, such as our parents, teachers, etc.
- Despite the fact that humans believe they are free and independent beings, we often follow authorities and can easily be dictated. Dictator governments throughout history are testimonials to this fact.
- It takes a significant number of members of a society to say no in order to make a radical change. Saying no is not

easy. It is not improvised, but rather a skill that needs to be learned and practiced.

- The power of media is extreme, perhaps even exceeding that of religions, to influence the people and inflict desired orders.
- Social obedience can be extremely powerful. In this example, more questioners would have presumably rebelled, had it not been because of the audience or their teammates.

In my opinion, in extraordinary circumstances, the human mind has a tendency to regress to the animalistic side (id), and conquer the moral and conscientious principles intellectually, using the defense mechanisms of the subconscious mind. This has been demonstrated repeatedly in war times, where unimaginable crimes are committed by ordinary people.

Before exploring the defense mechanisms of ego in the next chapter, and strategies to evolve them, let us discuss the roots of why the human mind even uses these tools and what happens in the brain as we think subconsciously. This takes us to the concept of pain–pleasure principle.

Pain and Pleasure: The Cognitive Dissonance Theory

Why do humans behave the way they do? What is the motive behind certain contemplated actions? Why do they think the way they do, and why is there so much variability among them?

These questions have haunted me since age eighteen. Of course, there is no simple answer. But over the years, through observation, research, and accumulation of scientific evidence, it began to make sense.

Let us consider more simple behaviors before we can understand complex ones. Why did you go to work yesterday? Why did you go out dining? Why did you yell at your friend? Why are you planning to change your career? Why? Why? Why?

In the conflict between the subconscious and conscious mind, ultimately any action you do has two primary motives only—**either to avoid pain or to incur pleasure! Or both!** When you buy a mobile phone, you either **need** it *(to avoid the pain of the inconvenience without it)* or **want** it *(just for pleasure and fun)*.

When you meet someone new and decide to continue your friendship or relationship, think about the reason behind it. Write down the question and the answer on paper and look at it. Why do I want to continue seeing this person? Is it because I **need** him/her to *avoid loneliness?* Or to fulfill my needs for sex and intimacy *(avoiding the pain of unattended sexual desire)?* Or is it just because he/she is fun to be around *(for pleasure)?* I have challenged myself in the last ten years to find a fundamental reason for what I do—other than these two basic motives—and guess what? There is none.

I challenge you to start thinking about why you do some of the things you do. Don't stop at the first answer that comes to your mind. Continue asking yourself the same question at the next level, and so on. Switch roles between your conscious and subconscious mind and play it like an interview with yourself. Here are some examples:

Scenario 1

Q. *If I am hungry, would I choose a fancy restaurant or go to a fast-food store? Why is that?*
A. Sometimes I'm just hungry and want to *avoid the pain* of hunger. The environment is not a top priority. I may choose a fast-food location. Other times, hunger is not the main issue, and I choose a fancy restaurant for the *pleasure* of the environment and the company of friends.

Scenario 2 (from a politician's perspective)

Q. *Why do I decide to start a war (let's say on terrorism)?*
A. It is either because my nation is being threatened by terrorism (to avoid the *pain* of defeat), or for the *pleasure* associated with expanding my power over certain strategic regions in the world.

Scenario 3 (from a suicide bomber's perspective)

Q. *Why would I be willing to destroy myself and a number of other innocent people in the name of religion?*

A. Bottom line—either because of the *pleasant* thoughts of getting a first-class ticket to heaven by accomplishing this duty, or to avoid the *pain* of injustice in this world!

Think about it ... how on earth can human beings agree to kill hundreds of innocent people, including themselves, and yet believe that they are doing this in *good faith?* Similarly, how can a leader of a civilized nation sleep at night with the thought of destroying other nations, including hundreds of thousands of innocent people ... and yet believe that this is all in *good faith?*

Extraordinary attitudes and behaviors, such as the ones mentioned above, can be explained by the **Cognitive Dissonance Theory**, developed by Leon Festinger in 1957. Cognition, for the purpose of this theory, may be considered as a piece of knowledge or an opinion. In these examples, the perception that the Western world is the root of all problems in the third world is a strong cognition held by many so-called terrorists. On the other hand, the idea that terrorism is a major threat to the Western countries is also a powerful cognition held by many leaders.

Two cognitions are said to be **dissonant** if one is the opposite of another. On the contrary, **cognitive consonance** is defined as the state of harmony and internal consistency among a person's attitudes, behaviors, beliefs, and/or knowledge. In simple words, cognitive dissonance is one of the fundamental roots of anxiety and depression, and cognitive consonance is a major root of happiness!

Cognitive dissonance is central to many forms of persuasion to change beliefs, values, attitudes, and behaviors. In the terrorist example above, he or she likely also has a cognition that killing innocent people is bad. The leader in this example also likely has a cognition that invading other countries and killing their people is not a civilized act. So how do they get to this point? What happens to people when they discover dissonant cognitions?

The answer to this question forms the basic postulate of Festinger's theory. A person who has dissonant cognitions is said to be in a state of **psychological dissonance**, which is experienced as unpleasant psychological *pain, distress, and anxiety.* This is the feeling of uncomfortable tension that comes from holding two conflicting thoughts in the mind at the same time.

Cognitive dissonance is an extremely powerful motivator that can lead us to change any of our conflicting beliefs or actions. **Rationalization** is one of the main defense mechanisms utilized by the distressful mind during cognitive dissonance. The discomfort often feels like a tension between two opposing thoughts. To release the tension, we can take one of three actions: 1) change our behavior; 2) justify our behavior by changing the conflicting cognition (rationalization); or 3) justify our behavior by adding new cognitions (also by rationalizing).

The mind will use all its power and resources (defense mechanisms) to distract from the pain and tension of cognitive dissonance. At some point, the final verdict is reached, and one of the two following situations prevails from the turbulence of *mental cognitive debate*—**to avoid pain or to experience pleasure!**

In brief, every human being forms millions and trillions of cognitions in the mind. As these cognitions become strengthened, they gradually turn into a **belief** and form deep roots in the subconscious as they form strong, solid neuronal networks in the brain. The same thought patterns become deeply seeded in the neurons' memories, and a specific pattern of neurochemical release develops every time this cognition comes to the mind, followed by specific repetitive emotions and actions (TFA principle). Hence, a unique and specific character or personality trait is developed over time.

On the other hand, the mind is constantly and intuitively seeking inner peace (joy) and would like to avoid inner pain and distress. But in this life, with so many conflicting cognitions and thoughts, it becomes very difficult to avoid cognitive dissonance. Hence, the mind subconsciously utilizes all its powerful resources (defense mechanisms), whether destructively or constructively, to distract from the instant distress and to gain relief. Newer cognitions are formed as a result of these defense mechanisms, ultimately leading to the highest level of belief or action. The problem is that the subconscious mind is not designed to think about the long-term consequences of these mechanisms. All that matters to it is instant **biological and psychological survival**! Newer and deeper levels of cognitions are formed, leading to the ultimate thought (belief) and corresponding actions. As discussed in previous chapters, it is the conscious mind that has the ability to consider long-term consequences and utilize more mature and reasonable defense and coping mechanisms to not only eliminate the immediate pain, but also to ensure long-term happiness and cognitive consonance.

Now let us try to understand the mechanisms and processes above from a neuroanatomical and physiological point of view.

The Pain and Pleasure (Reward) Systems in the Brain

The Pleasure System

Researchers have found that the main centers of the brain's **reward circuit** are located along the **medial forebrain bundle (MFB)** in the limbic system. The ventral tegmental area (**VTA**) and the nucleus accumbens (**NA**) are the two major centers in this circuit. However, other centers are also involved, including the septum, amygdala, prefrontal cortex (PFC), and the thalamus.

First described by James Olds and Peter Milner in the early 1960s, the MFB is a bundle of axons that originates in the reticular formation, crosses the VTA, passes through the hypothalamus, and continues into the NA, as well as the amygdala, the septum, and the PFC.

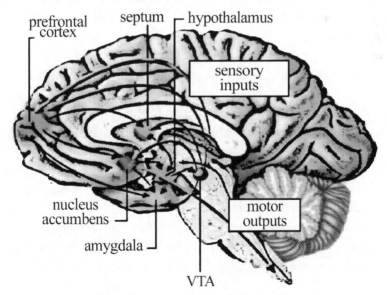

The pleasure pathways in the brain

Four regions of the brain and four neurotransmitters play a significant role and are a major part of the neurological reward pathway:

1. **Dopamine** in the VTA, NA, and the hippocampus
2. **Serotonin** in the hypothalamus
3. **Enkephalins** in the VTA and the NA
4. **GABA**—an inhibitory neurotransmitter—also in the VTA and NA

Out of all these neurotransmitters, dopamine has been singled out as "the primary pleasure neurotransmitter." The **dopaminergic system** has a strong role in addictive behaviors.

When the cortex has received and processed a sensory stimulus indicating a reward, it sends a signal through the MFB, announcing this reward to the VTA, which then releases dopamine not only into the NA, but also into the septum, the amygdala, and the prefrontal cortex. The hypothalamus, which receives signals from different parts of the MFB, then acts not only on the VTA, but also on the autonomic and endocrine functions of the entire body, through the **pituitary gland**. Hence, a number of hormones and neurotransmitters are released into the bloodstream and the brain. These chemical substances act peripherally or centrally through different receptors, applying their effects accordingly.

Collectively, the activation of this medial forebrain bundle (the reward circuit) leads to the repetition of the gratifying action to strengthen the associated pathways in the brain.

The Pain System

Painful stimuli that provoke fight or flight responses activate the brain's **punishment circuit (the periventricular system, or PVS)**, which enables us to cope with unpleasant situations. The PVS was identified by De Molina and Hunsperger in 1962. It involves many of the structures of the limbic system similar to the pleasure system, except the VTA and NA. However, different neuronal pathways are involved through the cholinergic system, with **acetyl choline** being the major neurotransmitter. The punishment circuit functions by means of this protein stimulating the secretion of adrenal cortico-trophic hormone (ACTH). ACTH in turn stimulates the adrenal glands to release adrenalin to prepare the body's organs for fight or flight.

Many brain centers mentioned above are involved in both the pain and pleasure circuits. Although the nerve fibers and neurotransmitters involved in the two networks are generally distinct, in some circumstances they may overlap. **Masochistic** behaviors in the **BDSM** subculture (bonding, discipline, sadism, masochism) are one example. The "bottom" or "submissive" often experiences pain and pleasure at the same time. Watching horror or violent movies may create the same pain/pleasure experience for some viewers. "Disturbing but at the same time exciting" is often how these viewers describe their experience.

So, what is the relevance of all this discussion?

Here is the extremely important point. In brief, the reward circuit (MFB) and the punishment circuit (PVS) can be said to supply most of the primary motivation for our behaviors. Even more clinically important, researchers have proven, through observational experiments, that the mind is often not able to distinguish between an external stimulus in the real world and an imaginary stimulus that is stored in the memory of the nerve cells. An **intense** or **prolonged** external stimulus may produce a specific footprint (or neuronal pattern) deeply embedded in the brain cells. A memory of this stimulus or imagination of a similar one turns on the same neuronal pathway and generates the same outcome. Thus, it becomes more difficult to differentiate between the two. For example, fantasy of a previous pleasurable experience may lead to orgasm. Another example is PTSD (post-traumatic stress disorder), where a situation similar to the original trauma may trigger a flashback of memories associated with that event, leading to unpleasant physical states or actions, such as headaches, anxiety, seizures, syncope, or irrational behaviors.

Why is this important? Knowing this fact, in the absence of a real external stimulus, you can voluntarily choose to alter the *thought* that is creating negative feelings and actions through **self-cognitive therapy**. The "aha" moment is what allows many patients who have been suffering from addictions for years to heal themselves in a short period of time.

Now, the relationship of these complex neurophysiological phenomena and the core psychological principles described previously become more apparent.

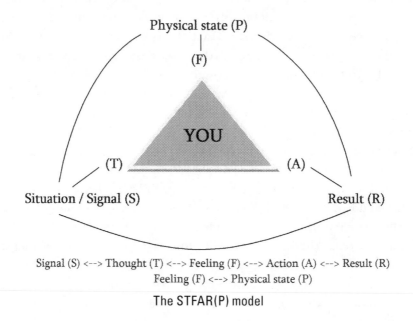

Signal (S) <--> Thought (T) <--> Feeling (F) <--> Action (A) <--> Result (R)
Feeling (F) <--> Physical state (P)

The STFAR(P) model

The signal starts externally (situation) or internally (old memory, thought, or feeling). It is processed in different parts of the brain—let us call it the "evaluating center"—which **interprets** the message in a specific way, talks to the relevant pain or pleasure centers, and elicits responses, resulting in certain physical states or actions, ultimately leading to specific results. With repetition and formation of solid neuronal networks, this process becomes fast, automatic, and conditioned. At this stage, it has become subconscious and may or may not be associated with the initial pain or pleasure motive any more.

Reward Deficiency Syndrome (RDS) and Addictions

In 1954, research psychologist James Olds was running a series of experiments on rats in McGill University. Accidentally, he placed some electrodes inside the rats' limbic system—a part of the brain that is involved in emotions. The brain was wired in a way that this area could be stimulated when the rat pressed on a lever. The rats went back to pressing the connected lever repeatedly—even up to several thousand times per hour. Similar experiments in human subjects created feelings resembling orgasmic sexual arousal by placing electrodes in the hypothalamus. Once other areas of the limbic system were stimulated, negative thoughts were eliminated, and a feeling of pleasant lightheadedness would occur. Thus was born the concept of the brain's reward pathway or pleasure system as described earlier.

The reward system begins with one of several neurotransmitters spreading out to "network" and involve the other neurotransmitters in what resembles a cascade (see diagram below). As a result, one feels secure, calm, comfortable, and satisfied, referred to as the "reward."

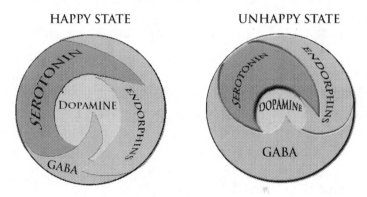

Happy and unhappy brain

In its simplest definition, Reward Deficiency Syndrome is what occurs when such "networking" does *not* occur. In fact, research has shown that a significant amount of human behavior is aimed toward achieving such feelings (12). But why?

Here's the answer: it's all about **survival.** Human beings have learned through genetic evolution, over thousands of years, that at the most basic level, pain is a sign of threat to their existence. Thus, a needle poke to your finger will automatically result in pulling away your hand. At the same time, our brains are wired to ensure that we will repeat life-sustaining activities by associating those with pleasure or reward. The **dopaminergic** and **opioidergic** reward pathways of the brain are critical for survival since they provide the pleasure drives for eating, loving and love making, and reproduction; these are called **natural rewards**.

At the cellular level, many painful processes are in *dissonance*, and pleasurable experiences are in *consonance,* with survival. Over time, physical and emotional experiences (both painful and pleasurable) have become more sophisticated. Whenever this reward circuit is activated, the brain notes that something important is happening that needs to be remembered, and it teaches us to do it again and again, without thinking about it. Because drugs of abuse stimulate the same circuit, we learn to abuse drugs in the same way.

As you can see, the basic principle of pain and pleasure is simple. However, throughout human evolution, it has become sophisticated and influenced by many genetic and environmental factors. The interaction of many neurotransmitters trying to maintain a balanced system is a dynamic process, constantly being affected by internal (thoughts, feelings, etc.) and external stimuli. Thus, it is not possible to make the ultimate "happiness pill" without affecting other neurotransmitters. There are many antidepressant medications being used today. SSRIs, SNRIs, and TCAs are only some of these examples. None of these, however, are without potential risks, and they need to be prescribed with individualized considerations.

Addictions

Addiction is not an expression of bad behavior or a lack of will power. It is a chronic brain disorder. Essentially, addiction is a primary disease, which means it's not necessarily the result of other psychiatric causes. And like cardiovascular illness or diabetes, it must be treated, managed, and monitored over a lifetime, says the American Society of Addiction Medicine, which represents about 3,000 physicians in the United States and Canada involved in the treatment and prevention of all types of addictions.

More than eighty experts spent four years working on ASAM's new definition that takes into account the latest advances in neuroscience. Research now suggests that addiction—whether to alcohol, drugs, gambling, or sex—involves the pleasure system in the limbic system, and the neurocircuitry governing reward, motivation, memory, and impulse control. By shifting the emphasis to biological aspects of the disorder and away from the resulting behavior, ASAM hopes to improve public understanding of a common problem.

The basic science described above explains why it is so complex and challenging to treat addictions. Despite the fact that most addicts are aware of the consequences of their behaviors, why is it that they continue to repeat the same patterns? *It's simply because they cannot stop!*

Most drugs of abuse directly or indirectly target the brain's reward system by flooding the circuit with dopamine (13). When some drugs of abuse are taken, they can release two to ten times the amount of dopamine that natural rewards do. In some cases, this occurs almost immediately (as when drugs are smoked or injected), and the effects can last much longer than those produced by natural rewards. The resulting effect on the brain's pleasure circuit minimizes those produced by naturally rewarding behaviors, such as eating and sex. The effect of such a powerful reward strongly motivates people to take drugs again and again. Theoretically, high dopamine levels associated with the experience of psychoactive substances (alcohol, heroin, cocaine, methamphetamine, marijuana, nicotine, caffeine, glucose, etc.), as well as aberrant behaviors (sex, porn, gambling, internet gaming, masochism and sadism, excessive work, etc.), leaves a long-lasting memory of intense unavoidable pleasure, altering the structural shape of the neuronal networks and forming a "faulty" circuit in the limbic system. The *intensity* and *duration* of exposure are two main factors associated with chances of addiction.

Some drugs, such as marijuana and heroin, can activate neurons because their chemical structure mimics that of the natural neurotransmitters, **the brain's endogenous opioids**. This similarity in structure "fools" receptors and allows the drugs to lock onto and activate the nerve cells, usually in much higher intensity than the endogenous substances. However, these drugs don't activate nerve cells in the same way as a natural neurotransmitter, and they lead to abnormal messages being transmitted through the network. Other drugs, such as amphetamine or cocaine, can cause the nerve cells to release abnormally large amounts of these endogenous opioids, or prevent their normal recycling. Interestingly, refined sugar behaves like psychoactive substances in the brain. Sugar activates the beta endorphin receptors of the brain, which are the same sites stimulated by morphine and heroin. This was documented in a study that was published in the *Journal of Nutrition* by Nicole Avena and colleagues in 2009.

This dysfunction produces a greatly amplified message, ultimately disrupting communication channels. The difference in effect can be described as the difference between someone whispering into your ear and someone shouting into a microphone. Just as we turn down the volume on a radio that is too loud, the brain adjusts to the overwhelming surges in dopamine (and other neurotransmitters) by producing less dopamine or by reducing the number of receptors that can receive signals, a defensive process called **downregulation of receptors**. What the addicts may or may not know is the paradox that the same "relief remedy" they use disrupts the pleasure cascade over time and downregulates the dopamine receptors in the limbic system, resulting in **tolerance.** As a result, dopamine's impact on the reward circuit can become abnormally low, and the ability to experience any pleasure is reduced. This is why the abuser eventually feels flat, lifeless, and depressed, and is unable to enjoy things that previously brought pleasure **(anhedonia)**. This means in order to get the same pleasure, they need more of the substance because a number of dopamine receptors have been depleted or become insensitive.

What happens when addicts try to quit their addiction?

As shown earlier in the diagram, the pain (PVS) and pleasure (MFB) circuits are very closely interconnected. Hence, it would not be a surprise to have an overlap or malfunction in the two systems. A relative deficiency in the reward system (RDS), caused by depletion of dopamine, generates a deficiency in the pleasure feeling. This is associated with negative, unpleasant feelings (both physical and/or emotional pain). Hence, the addict seeks a quick fix to avoid pain, often repeating the same addictive pattern (psychoactive substance or aberrant behavior), which produces a short-term relief and pleasure. *Researchers have shown than long-term drug abuse impairs brain functioning, and this pattern of short-term gain versus long-term pain goes on to the point of total destruction of the person's life, unless at some point, it is interrupted and reversed!*

How does long-term drug taking affect brain circuits?

We know that the same mechanisms involved in the development of tolerance can eventually lead to profound changes in neurons and brain circuits, with the potential to severely compromise the long-term health of the brain. Long-term drug abuse can trigger adaptations in the subconscious memory systems. Conditioning is one example of this type of learning, whereby environmental cues become associated with the drug experience and can trigger uncontrollable *cravings* if the individual is later exposed to these cues, even without the drug itself being available. This learned "reflex" is extremely powerful and can emerge even after many years of abstinence. This explains the high rate of relapse among drug abusers.

So will there ever be a final solution?

Maybe. Maybe not! Currently, many pharmaceutical companies are attempting to find a solution to this cascade malfunction. There will also be numerous attempts to find a final "cure" for depression, anxiety, and other mental disorders. However, as you can imagine, with numerous neurotransmitters and multiple dynamic processes involved, this achievement would be extremely difficult. In order for an external approach to be entirely safe and effective, every factor and interaction needs to be considered as part of the equation. We, as physicians, are using these medications on a daily basis for our patients. However, in my opinion, we will never be able to find the ultimate happiness or addiction pill that is safe, effective, and affordable, without understanding *all* the aspects of the mind and body. While there is no doubt in the value of continued research on the brain and limbic system, humans are far from understanding the full picture! So what do we do?

We have a better chance of success listening to Mother Nature. *The pain and pleasure systems in the limbic system are the foundation of human behavior, and the main motives forming the history of humanity!* As mentioned previously, this forms the basis of our subconscious mind driving our daily lives. We know that our cognitions and thoughts are directly related to feelings (TFA principle). Cognitive therapy (CT) and cognitive-behavioral therapy (CBT) are currently widely accepted therapeutic approaches in modern psychology, and they are effective, safe, affordable, and feasible. However, they too, have their limitations and do not work for everyone and in all circumstances.

In today's complex life and bizarre world, it is impossible to avoid distress. At the same time, there is unlimited exposure to pleasurable experiences. Learning how to manage pain and pleasure is not an easy task. It requires significant knowledge and understanding, a desire for optimal living, and some will power. Mother Nature has done part of the job, equipping us with defense mechanisms that begin to form subconsciously from birth. We have to acquire the rest of the skills through knowledge and practice, to the end of our path! These skills are coping mechanisms to deal with day-to-day distress, which are formed consciously over time.

Both subconscious defense mechanisms and conscious coping mechanisms can be *destructive* or *constructive*. If we don't learn to use the constructive ones, we will likely end up with the destructive and undesired ones. The challenge is how to replace the destructive ones with the more desirable constructive mechanisms. And this takes us to the next chapter on defense mechanisms of the ego, where their different categories will be explained in detail. Being aware of these DMs when they occur, will allow us to utilize them more favorably. Long term practice will enable the conscious mind to take control and drag the ego away from the selfishness of id and team up with super-ego, thus leading us to the summit of personal growth and happiness!

CHAPTER 9

"The ego is like a wild horse. If you make it a friend, you'll get the fastest ride to your destiny. And if not tamed, it can knock you off to the ground. Use the ego to conquer the ego, and grow beyond."

Defense Mechanisms of the Ego

HT grew up in a very poor and harsh neighborhood in Chicago. He was used to street fights and gang violence. The only way to survive was to stay strong. There was a solution for him. Boxing was his escape. He would forget about all the problems in the world during practice. At the same time, boxing kept him strong and gave him satisfaction. He practiced day and night, over and over again, redirecting his emotional pain and frustration. In the ring, the pain of his upbringing helped him conquer every opponent, until he became a champion. Highly admired and respected by his community, he no longer regretted being born poor!

HT may not have been aware that he was subconsciously using a defense mechanism called **sublimation.** In psychology, sublimation is a defense mechanism where undesired or unacceptable impulses and distresses are transformed into behaviors that are accepted by the society. These behaviors usually exceed in excellence and serve a higher cultural or socially useful purpose, as in the creation of arts, sports, or inventions. In Freud's psychoanalytic theories, sublimation is used to describe the spirit as a reflection of the libido (but in fact, it may be triggered by any other emotional distress).

Unveiling the Mystery

As we get into the more exciting parts of this book, bizarre complex human behaviors—having made us scratch our heads for thousands of years—will be more comprehensible. Extraordinary cases presented in this book are examples of such unthinkable complexities of the mind. One of the most profound keys to unlock human behaviors lies within the realm of the psyche and the **defense mechanisms of ego**. There have been more than 400 theories in psychology, and yet this area of the human psyche and brain is poorly understood and underutilized in clinical grounds. Unfolding this secret will unveil many unanswered questions of human behavior and psychology. It can also open up fascinating opportunities for personal growth and improvement of societal, national, and international health.

At times of severe distress in our lives, we may not be able to tolerate reality. This creates significant amount of emotional pain, and we need a way to avoid, minimize, or cope with it. This is when the mind plays tricks on us, distorting the inner or outer world in such a way that the pain becomes tolerable, and we can survive.

There are three main mechanisms that the brain uses to adapt to distress or danger.
1. Involuntary help from within (ego mechanisms of defense used by the subconscious mind)
2. Voluntary help from within (cognitive coping mechanisms used by the conscious mind)
3. Voluntary help from others (social support)

Homeostasis was described as "a body at peace with itself," by physiologist Walter B. Cannon in *The Wisdom of the Body* in the 1930s. The defense mechanisms are designed to ensure psychological survival by maintaining the mental homeostasis. Often, what psychiatrists label as disease is no more than the defenses of the ego to adapt with the "dis-ease." Our mental defense mechanisms creatively rearrange the sources of conflict to make them manageable so that we can carry on with life. *Defense mechanisms of the ego mean to the human psyche what the immune system means to the human body.* Without a healthy immune system, the body will die. Similarly, with the tremendous amount of stress endured in daily living, our mental state would perish, were it not for the ingenious interventions of the ego.

From a mental health standpoint, such emotional and intellectual dishonesty is not only creative, but also healthy and necessary for mental survival. However, from a behavioral and social perspective, some defense mechanisms are *destructive* while others are *constructive*. Therefore, one may appear or behave in a "neurotic," "psychotic," or "odd" manner to the outside observer.

For decades, this crucially important part of the psyche has been less attended to, mainly due to its complex nature. Since Anna Freud's book in 1937, *The Ego and the Mechanisms of Defense,* little has been explored and explained in this area in depth until 1992. Thanks to Professor George Vaillant and his colleagues, modern concepts of defense mechanisms have been developed based on empirical research. This theoretical concept that shaped the core of psychoanalysis was taken to the next level, and its clinical application became more practical to modern psychologists and psychiatrists.

Vaillant's Classification of the Defense Mechanisms

To date, there are over forty defense mechanisms (DM) identified in psychology. Some of these include:

Acting out	Fantasy
Altruism	Humor
Anticipation	Hypochondriasis
Acceptance	Idealization
Asceticism	Identification
Autistic fantasy	Inhibition/Blocking
Controlling	Intellectualization
Counter-transference	Introjection
Denial	Isolation
Devaluation	Objectification
Displacement	Passive-Aggression
Dissociation	Projection
Distortion	Projection (delusional)
Externalization	Projective identification

Rationalization	Splitting
Reaction formation	Sublimation
Regression	Suppression
Repression	Transference
Sexualization	Undoing
Somatization	

Sigmund Freud is known as the father of psychoanalytical theories and the founder of the defense mechanisms in practical psychology. Although highly respected by many colleagues, there is still a lot of controversy about his theories. Some of Freud's main errors include the following:

- He considered all defenses pathological.
- He rooted all pathogenic defenses in childhood.
- He put too much emphasis on sexual drives.
- He put too much focus on internal drives and emotions, and not enough on external relationships.

George E. Vaillant, born in 1934, is an American psychiatrist and professor at Harvard Medical School, director of research for the Department of Psychiatry, and a distinguished speaker and consultant for seminars and workshops throughout the world. He spent his research career charting adult development and the recovery process of schizophrenia, heroin addiction, alcoholism, and personality disorders.

Vaillant took the accepted concepts of modern psychology to the next level. He developed a methodology for systematic review and summarized the latest empirical research, while proposing a universal language and defining a more practical use for the defense mechanisms in clinical psychology. His classification described below is more consistent with the maturity of the human psyche and brain.

The Hierarchy of Defense Mechanisms

Level 1 —*Psychotic* (common in children under five, psychosis, and dreams)

- Denial (of external reality)
- Distortion
- Delusional projection

Level 2—*Immature* (common in adolescence, personality disorders, and severe depression)

- Projection
- Passive-aggressive behavior
- Acting out (compulsive delinquency, perversion)
- Hypochondriasis
- Fantasy (schizoid withdrawal)
- Splitting

Level 3—*Intermediate/Neurotic* (common in everyone)

- Repression
- Reaction formation
- Displacement (conversion, phobias)
- Dissociation
- Intellectualization (isolation, obsessive behavior, undoing, rationalization)

Level 4—*Mature* (common in "healthy" adults)

- Sublimation
- Altruism
- Suppression
- Humor
- Anticipation
- Acceptance

Level 1 DM—Psychotic. These are the most basic mechanisms used by the *primitive* parts of brain and often used by children. Depending on the severity and/or duration of the traumatizing factor(s), these mechanisms may be solidified by the brain as the prominent escape mechanism to avoid or minimize emotional pain. This may grow into adulthood and develop specific neuronal networks, leading to mental disorders, such as schizophrenia (a type of psychosis). The characteristic features of schizophrenics are their "odd" appearance, behaviors, thoughts, and beliefs. In conventional psychiatry, this is categorized as Axis I mental disorder. In simple words, Axis I disorders are those in which there is a disruption in the "hardware" of the brain, either neurophysiologically, chemically, physically, or neuroanatomically. The main solution to this group of mental diseases is pharmacotherapy, but psychoanalytical psychotherapy has also been successful in some conditions.

- *Denial*—the person does not acknowledge or recognize some aspects of external reality that are apparent to others (e.g., children hide their face when scared of something).
- *Distortion*—the person reshapes the external reality to suit his/her inner needs and desires.
- *Delusional projection*—creating a reality in one's mind that is not apparent to others. The person has strong beliefs, often delusional and false, about the external reality (main DM in schizophrenia).

Level II DM—Immature. These defense mechanisms are one step further evolved than the primitive or psychotic ones. They are mainly used by the intermediate parts of the brain, during adolescence. Again, once solidified, these mechanisms may become fixed in a specific pattern and stop maturing. This may often lead to what is known as Axis II psychological disorders in conventional psychiatry, such as personality disorders and various types of addictions. These people usually resort to morally unethical or illegal behaviors, causing significant suffering to the society and outside observers. The best known psychotherapeutic approach to this category is group therapy, such as Alcoholics Anonymous or Narcotics Anonymous, etc. Pharmacotherapy has little value compared to psychotherapy in the treatment of these patients. Many of these DMs are used commonly in a wide variety of mental disorders (or personality traits).

- *Projection*—falsely attributing one's disturbing feelings or thoughts to others (e.g., borderline personality disorder).
- *Passive-aggression*—the person indirectly and ineffectively expresses aggression and hostile feelings toward others or self through passivity and in a non-confrontational manner (e.g., addiction, masochism, borderline personality disorder).
- *Acting out (compulsive delinquency, perversion)*—the person acts without regard for the negative consequences either to self or others (e.g., some teenagers or antisocial characters).
- *Hypochondriasis*—transformation of reproach and hostility toward others, into self-reproach and complaints of pain, somatic illness, and other physical symptoms (e.g., hypochondriacs).
- *Somatization*—the person becomes preoccupied with physical symptoms unrelated or disproportionate to any underlying physical cause (e.g., somatoform disorder).
- *Fantasy (schizoid withdrawal)*—the person uses fantasy and indulges in autistic retreat to avoid interpersonal intimacy, for the purpose of conflict resolution and gratification.
- *Splitting*—the person views external objects as all-good or all-bad, failing to acknowledge their multidimensional aspects. Rapid shifts between these views are also seen without the person being aware of this self-contradiction (e.g., borderline personality disorder).

Level III DM—Neurotic. These are also classified as intermediate defense mechanisms. They are more mature than the previous two and are used predominantly by the intermediate parts of the brain. They are extremely common in "healthy" or "normal" adults. But this does not mean they are necessarily "normal" or "healthy" mechanisms. Take a look around, for instance, and you'll see plenty of day-to-day examples. "Normality" in the Oxford dictionary is defined as "the state of being normal ... the usual, standard, typical, or expected state or level." Considered by many to be the prevailing feature in the *majority* of a group or society, *normality* may be entirely misperceived! Imagine you are living in a village that is struck by an infestation causing massive blindness in the majority of the local population. Over time, the ones who could see would be considered abnormal, and blindness would become the normal phenomenon. This is one of the many sociological confusions and misleading dilemmas today. "Normality" is not necessarily determined by the *majority* of people!

Intermediate or neurotic DMs may not necessarily lead to any specific mental disorder. However, once fixated and solidified, they may lead to specific personality *traits* and subtle characteristics in behaviors, often noticed by other people as an "annoyance." One may or may not have insight (be aware that there is something wrong). Many of these features are referred to as "personality issues" in common terms. This area is where self-management has a prominent role. If you do not realize and acknowledge there's something wrong in your thoughts, feelings, or actions, you may never seek help or do anything to improve it. This is one caveat that may prevent you from further personal growth and maturity. If you are interested in mental and spiritual growth, pay attention to comments made about you. The arrogant side of ego may not allow you to see the red flags within, and that's exactly the challenge—*to pay attention to these signs and try to make subtle changes in thoughts, feelings, and actions.* This change will **undo** the neuronal pathways that are heading toward a disorder! The first and most important step towards self-awareness and personal growth is to *identify* the problem. Once identified, it's much easier to seek help. In this book, some strategies will be discussed to enhance self-management. Psychotherapy also may be useful in many cases. Pharmacotherapy, however, has little or no value in addressing these DMs.

- *Repression*—the person is unable to recall distressful memories, experiences, feelings, or thoughts.
- *Reaction formation*—the person replaces thoughts, feelings, or actions, which are exactly opposite his/her own unacceptable thoughts, feelings, or actions.
- *Displacement (conversion, phobias)*—the person redirects his/her negative feelings about an object or situation, to another

less threatening object or situation (e.g., phobias, or kicking your dog when you are angry).

- *Dissociation*—the person temporarily disconnects with his/her own identity or state of consciousness.
- *Intellectualization*—the person engages in intense abstract thinking to distract from the disturbing feelings (e.g., OCD).
- *Rationalization*—for self-reassurance, the person incorrectly justifies his/her own behaviors.

Level IV DM—Mature. These are the most mature and developed defense mechanisms, utilized by the more sophisticated and higher functioning parts of the brain—the neocortex in the forebrain. They often develop later in adulthood, as the brain matures in structure and function. These *constructive* adaptive systems are much more socially acceptable and bring balance to mental health. Some of these mechanisms, such as humor and sublimation, put you at a high energy level and draw attraction from people and the world around. One of the most profound and yet challenging tasks, which will be discussed further in this book, is to replace the destructive and less mature DMs with these mature and constructive ones. This requires significant understanding and knowledge of the mind and persistent practice of self-management. It requires mastering the task of *shifting focus*. Once achieved, it will take you far up the ladder of personal growth!

- *Sublimation*—the person channels or redirects aggressive and distressful feelings, thoughts, and impulses to modified outlets, often more socially valued ones (e.g., many sports champions).
- *Altruism*—extraordinary but constructive and instinctually gratifying service to others (typical example is Mother Theresa).
- *Suppression*—the person intentionally and consciously avoids thinking about distressful desires, thoughts, feelings, or experiences.

- *Humor*—overt expression of feelings without personal discomfort, and without unpleasant effect on others (e.g., some comedians).
- *Anticipation*—realistic preparation and planning for future inner discomfort.
- *Acceptance* —coming to peace with the inner conflict or distress.

Practical Use of the Defense Mechanisms

We have now learned about the hierarchy of defense mechanisms. So, what is the practical use of this knowledge? How can it be of service in the practice of self–management, specifically **self-cognitive behavioral therapy**?

The concept of the defense mechanisms of ego is one of the most profound, mysterious, and under-attended areas in psychology. It is the root of almost all social problems and diseases, such as crimes, prostitution, and addictions. It is one area that even most psychiatrists and psychologists do not feel comfortable dealing with. It often takes a long time to manage, and it is extremely challenging to undo the destructive defense mechanisms that are already solidified in the brain. It is often much easier to deal with mental conditions that benefit from pharmacotherapy (such as depression, anxiety, and schizophrenia) and see results in a shorter time. However, as mentioned above, many mental problems that utilize the less mature defense mechanism (levels 2 and 3) do not respond easily to pharmacotherapy. They require short- or long-term counseling, cognitive behavioral therapy (CBT), talk therapy, and other forms of psychotherapy.

The good news, however, is that there is a tremendous opportunity to change the paradigm of how we approach and deal with mental health globally. Apart from the less common mental disorders caused by structural brain diseases (such as brain tumors causing depression), in most cases, there is a continuum for mental disorders, resulting from erroneous "software" building up over time. This often happens as a result of cumulative deposition of "viruses" or "dirt layers," due to learned experiences and exposures, and how the brain reacts to those. The analogy of the iceberg below can be used to illustrate this, with the more obvious and severe conditions being apparent at the tip of the iceberg.

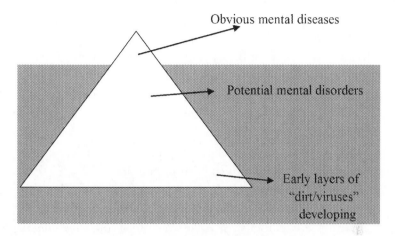

Evolution of mental disorders

If we look at this issue in a broader sense, the available resources in mental health care are dealing with only the tip of the iceberg of the wide spectrum. Even for that small percentage, we do not have enough resources globally. The rest of the potential burden of mental illness remains unattended, which means at some point in the near future, it will blossom to the surface and present as an obvious mental disorder! *So, is there any possible way to address this enormous global burden? Could there be a way to change the direction of humanity in a positive way?*

I believe the only way we could possibly manage the supply and demand balance is to shift focus from the acute care of the mentally ill to **prevention of mental illness and promotion of mental wellness!** That is, to allocate a large portion of our resources to the potential candidates below the surface of the water in the iceberg analogy—to promote self-detection and self-management skills from young ages and to teach parents to look for signs of mental illness.

If you notice a recurrent pattern of illness or infection in yourself or your child, would you not seek medical help and think about the possibility of a problem with the immune system? Remember, the defense mechanisms of the ego mean to the human psyche what the immune system means to the human body. With proper education and knowledge, if we notice signs of repeated red flags in our thoughts, feelings, or behaviors, we are likely using one or more of the destructive defense mechanisms—which means *we need to act fast and seek psychological help. Otherwise, chances are these early traits will solidify in the brain into a more explicit mental disorder!*

In the first five years of life, it is extremely important for parents to be familiar with unusual patterns of defense mechanisms. After that, we can start educating children as young as elementary school to identify some red flags in their thoughts, feelings, or behaviors, and bring it to someone's attention.

So, let us pose the question one more time: how does this knowledge of defense mechanisms help us in clinical practice?

1. By understanding the hierarchy of these DMs, and the relationship with the development of different parts of the brain, we can focus on *early intervention* and *prevention* of mental disorders. The emerging evidence in neuroplasticity has proven the ability of the brain to reshape and reform in any given direction. **Focus** and **intentional distraction** are two extremely powerful features of the prefrontal cortex in the brain. You can actually choose to focus on what you want. Learning how to distract from a distress that triggers your immature defense mechanisms can shift your focus to an alternative *constructive* defense or coping mechanism, which will allow you to grow in a positive direction. This art of *intentional substitution* is not an easy task but definitely a possible one, which can be learned through *knowledge* and *practice*. Repetition of the same thoughts, feelings, and behaviors will establish a new neuronal network in the brain. *Once solidified, you become a different person!*

2. Mental health education about the defense mechanisms of ego can be delivered at three levels.
   • Treating the patient: directly delivered by a variety of mental health care providers. This is the predominant paradigm currently offered in many countries and societies.
   • Training the trainer: by indirectly educating the guides of individuals—parents, teachers, school counselors,

coaches, mentors, etc. This model is also beginning to find a place in many developed and industrialized countries.

- Training the trainee: by directly educating the individuals about self-management skills such as *self-cognitive behavioral therapy (SCBT)*. This area is the least developed, and there is an enormous opportunity for intervention at community, national, and global levels.

3. One of the major criticisms of current therapeutic approaches is that there is not much emphasis on the fundamental principles of the defense mechanisms. These are the leading drives in life, and yet they are under-attended in therapeutic interventions. One main reason is the fact that they have been poorly understood until more recently.

4. There are theories, yet to be proven, that certain DMs from different levels may actually belong to the same "family." For example, passive aggression (level 2) may be the sister DM of reaction formation (level 3) and altruism (level 4). Another example is fantasy and intellectualization. This is based on the observation that certain traits naturally evolve or mature into specific DMs of a higher level. This suggests the possibility of transformation of the lower DMs to the higher levels of "sister DMs." There is little evidence to support this theory, but it is definitely worth contemplating. My guess is that there is one or more specific neuronal pathway for each of these DMs, with overlap among them. No one really knows for sure. If proven at any time in the future, this may explain the rationale behind the theory of "sister DMs." *It may also be the beginning of a potential revolutionary approach to the way we envision and deal with mental health!*

Preventive Mental Health—The Continuum of Mental Disorders

For most of its history, psychology had concerned itself with all that ails the human mind: anxiety, depression, neurosis, obsession, paranoia, and delusion. The goal of practitioners was to bring patients from a negative, ailing state to a neutral normal, or, as University of Pennsylvania psychologist Martin Seligman puts it, "from a minus five to a zero." It was Seligman who on the first day as president of the American Psychological Association (APA) stated, "I realized that my profession was half-baked. It wasn't enough for us to nullify disabling conditions and get to zero. We needed to ask: What are the enabling conditions that make human beings flourish? How do we get from zero to plus five?" He went on to reason, "Mental health should be more than the absence of mental illness."

Today, some of the major challenges in dealing with the mental health spectrum globally include the following:

- The tip of the iceberg—demonstrating the obvious, developed mental diseases—only represents a small percentage of the total population at risk, but unfortunately utilizes almost all resources of mental health professionals in the world.
- There is clearly a significant shortage of physicians and other health care providers to deal with mental problems. With the number of emerging mental disorders, there is absolutely no way the one-to-one health care delivery could meet the balance between supply and demand.
- Once a mental disorder has developed, it is often very difficult to treat. It is much easier and more cost-effective to prevent mental illness than to cure it.
- An individual's mental health is inseparable from the mental status of the society he or she lives in. Look at some of the impoverished or third world countries, where there is no sense of peace or civil rights for their citizens. Utilizing defense mechanisms of the subconscious on a daily basis is essential for survival in these communities. Many studies clearly demonstrate that unhappiness and a prevalence of mental disorders in a society is associated with higher rates of crime, lack of education, higher income gap, and other social determinants of mental health. In other words, the individual's mental health goes hand in hand with that of

the society. This is also true on the larger scale if we see the world as one unit. As the global village is becoming smaller and more interconnected, the impact of less fortunate nations on the rest of the world becomes more apparent.

So, how is it possible to face the challenge of this worldwide increasing burden?

There are several strategies that may make a difference to the collective mental health status:

- One of the solutions to this worldwide problem is to shift focus to *prevention* rather than *cure*. While ongoing treatment strategies are essential for the tip of the iceberg, it makes much more sense to target the "ordinary" suboptimal group for prevention (more than 90 percent of the population) and optimize their mental, emotional, and physical performance.
- Change the current universal model; instead of offering a lot to a small number of people, offer a little to a large number (main investment should be on the body of iceberg, rather than the tip).
- Reassign some of the current mental health care resources to target the potential mental patients below the surface of the water (in the iceberg analogy), or create and train new positions in this specialty to specifically *promote mental health* and *prevent mental illness.*
- "Train the trainer" model. This pyramidal model has been successful in many parts of the world where the supply of health care services does not meet the demand. Through systematic networking, train the trainer at community, national, and international levels. With the technology today, it is possible to take a message to the most remote areas in the world! Short-term focus groups and workshops are needed to teach practical strategies for change. The knowledge and technology are out there. It is time to put the pieces of the puzzle together!

- International organizations, such as the WHO and UN, can collaborate with world leaders to organize more unified events, such as Pangea Day held on May 10, 2008, bringing the global village together. There can be a **Pangea Program** to send a message to the world, enabling global citizens to manage their personal mental challenges.
- Redistribute the mental health care providers to address the needs of underserviced nations. The way to do this is to envision the entire world as **one** nation. In a country, it is the government's responsibility to find ways to deliver health services fairly to all urban, suburban, and rural parts of it—not that this always happens! A nation's collective mental health is crucial for its development and growth, which will inevitably influence the rest of the world as well. In our global village, it is the collective responsibility of all nations to fulfill this task through collaboration of international governing bodies (UN, WHO, etc.) and the world leaders.
- An international fund is needed specifically for this global task.

Let's Get to Work

In my opinion, successful strategies are possible and should be administered at the post-natal level, starting with educational systems for the parents during pregnancy. As mentioned earlier, the most critical period of personality development is the first five to six years of life, when the parents have the most influence in forming the building blocks of their child's future.

After that, as children are influenced more and more by school and the society, the teachers' role becomes more critical in guiding them. Proper age-appropriate programs need to be implemented in the educational systems at the elementary level. Coaching programs for teachers, parents, and the children are invaluable and necessary at this stage to resist the influence of the free-floating society and the powerful media.

As for the individuals themselves, age-appropriate psychology education and self-cognitive therapy techniques may be administered as soon as junior high school, as children and adolescents gain more control and understanding of their "self." These programs need to be adjusted based on age and stage of development all across school into university and adult life. *Coaching is essential all these years, especially during the critical years of adolescence, because of the discrepancy between physical growth (due to a hormonal surge) and mental maturity.*

In an ideal world, it would be tremendously invaluable to have Life Skills Institutes with coaches all across the world. Facing daily distress in different forms is inevitable, and whether we like it or not, we are subconsciously and constantly using defense mechanisms to deal with them. The sooner we become aware of what is going on in our minds and conscious ways of dealing with distress, the more we are able to have control over our destiny and manage the daily challenges in constructive ways!

Understanding how the human brain works is crucial to making a life-long change in our behavioral patterns. For thousands of years, due to this lack of knowledge and understanding, we have collectively "gone with the flow" and allowed our subconscious mind to take control of our lives. We have literally surrendered to the environment and society—in the name of "destiny"!

Maybe it's time for a change. Collectively, we have enough understanding and knowledge to start implementing fundamental changes at individual, community, national, and international levels. A global movement for a global change! What is needed to make this change possible is a worldwide network of individuals with **passion, vision,** and **mission**!

Is this truly possible? Or is it just an idealistic dream? Depends on which half of the glass you look at—the empty or the full part!

CHAPTER 10

"It is a man's own mind, not his enemy or foe, that lures him to evil ways."
—Buddha

Roots of Unhappiness

Have you ever wondered why there is so much discontentment among people today, despite all the capacity for unlimited personal growth? Most people are generally either not happy with their job, their finances, their relationships, their education, or basically just not happy with themselves at all. There always seems to be a reason to complain. There is always a desire for more ... and more ... and more. The question is ... *why?*

Some of the most fundamental roots for unhappiness will be explored here.

1. Ego's most fundamental principle is *survival*. Its primary job is to protect you, not necessarily to make you happy. While the unconscious mind fulfills this task primarily through physiological phenomena, the subconscious mind (primarily the ego) ensures emotional, mental, and psychological survival!

   The defense mechanisms are extremely clever and powerful in order to protect you psychologically, based on the survival mechanism. However, it is not intelligent enough to tell the difference between the true YOU and the apparent you. It confuses your thoughts, emotions, and actions as YOU and continues to protect them as you, your identity, and your self. It is extremely important to understand and be aware of the fact that *YOU are not your thoughts, emotions, or actions, but rather the formless soul behind those. Your mind (TFA) and body are manifestations of YOU, not the actual YOU!* The ego in the subconscious mind uses every resource to acknowledge you and demands all attention and everything for you, the self, your false identity. When this is not achieved, distress occurs, and automatically more defense mechanisms are activated to sustain emotional homeostasis and survive the mental state. As the brain matures with aging through childhood, adolescence, and adulthood, levels of sophistication add on to the primary defense mechanisms. This mental dysfunction is the result of constant inner conflict between the subconscious and the conscious mind. As mentioned previously, the more discordance between these two minds, the more unhappiness. On the contrary, the more concordance between the two, the more inner peace and contentment … the ultimate goal in human life!

2. The ego acts as a mediator between the id, super-ego, and the external world. It has to do its best to suit all three, thus is constantly feeling hemmed by the danger of causing discontent to the two other sides, a major reason for the basic feeling of unhappiness. Many experts believe that the ego tends to be more loyal to the id, while pretending to have a regard for the super-ego. But once developed and solidified, the super-ego is constantly watching every one of ego's moves and punishes it with feelings of guilt, anxiety, and inferiority. To overcome this, the ego employs its powerful defense mechanisms subconsciously.

    What happens if the super-ego is eliminated or under-developed? The ego has a tendency to be dragged by the primitive desires of the id. Therefore, the entire subconscious mind moves toward **selfishness**, which is the universal dilemma of human existence and the root of all man-made problems in the world, today and throughout history. *It is crucially important to understand the difference between the ego and selfishness. They are not exactly the same, but they are identical.* This is one of the most profound confusions in many philosophies, religions, and ideologies, which has failed to lead humanity to ultimate prosperity and happiness. Lack of understanding of the ego, and confusing it with selfishness—which is when the ego and id have teamed up together to conquer the super-ego—is the cornerstone of these ideologies advocating the suppression and dismissal of the ego. This is immensely destructive because the ego is like a baby monster with extremely clever and powerful defense mechanisms that will subdue any resistance and lead to more destructive thoughts, feelings, and behaviors. The solution is to understand the ego—to make friends and live in peace with it. After all, as a tamed horse, it is the very same ego that can team up with the super-ego instead, and lead us toward the third stage of peak personal growth. The art of life is to lead our ego away from id and toward the super-ego, through understanding our subconscious mind and maturing the defense mechanisms. This can be challenging because, by default, there is a tendency for the ego to lean toward the id (which should be respected and acknowledged as part of our psyche, but not empowered). *The reason for this is that there are millions of years toward the evolution and genetic coding of the primitive and intermediate brain, as opposed to only thousands of years of evolution of the superior brain (ice cream analogy).* Thus, it takes much more understanding and effort to direct the ego toward the super-ego. This is doable only by the very same ego, through knowledge and practice—by dis-identifying YOU as your body and mind, but instead identifying it as the awareness, consciousness, or presence beyond all those expressions, the matrix that is above all of those … of the same essence as the universal energy!

3. According to the STFAR(P) model, with every thought, the neuronal network and the combination of 164 trillion synapses fire and shape in a specific manner. As a principle in neuroscience, *neurons that fire together wire together.* Hence, with repeated patterns of thought—negative or positive—the neuronal network solidifies correspondingly. With each emotion **attached** to this thought, certain neuropeptides are released by the hypothalamus in the brain into the bloodstream. They travel to different body parts and find the appropriate receptors sitting on different cells. Once each peptide finds the matching receptor, it forms a complex that acts like a key to unlock the gates of the cell in a certain manner to produce specific results. The overall result is the general feeling of sadness

or happiness, excitement or dullness, etc. Along with that comes the physical state. Therefore, ongoing negative thoughts, feelings, and actions lead to more negative thoughts, feelings, and actions through the turbulence of the defense mechanisms and an overall state of unhappiness. Unless the vicious cycle is broken and reversed, the brain structure forms the basis of a negative personality trait, which can ultimately lead to a disorder.

4. Based on the fundamental laws of survival, the ego is in a constant and essential state of competition. As we grew up, the ego has mistakenly learned from our experiences and exposures, that you have to compete in order to survive. Therefore, it has an immense desire to feel more and want more ... to overcome the core feeling of "not enough." This is also the root of jealousy in humans.

   The ego is constantly giving us the false message, *"If you are not enough, your survival may be at risk, and in order to prove that you are enough, you need to compete with everyone, including yourself. You need to prove to yourself and to everyone else in the world, that you are important and powerful enough, and that you will survive. You need more, and want more ... and more ... and more!"*

   Hence the ego misleads humans to find happiness elsewhere— outside of our own psyche—because it cannot accept that "I" and "my self" are the source of "my problems." It does not understand that the root of unhappiness **and** the way to happiness both lie deep within our minds and psyche! However, the ego is too caught up in its own confusion to sustain the psychological survival for humans, so it needs a different and more mature part of the mind (the conscious mind) and psyche (the super-ego) to clarify the dilemma and lead the path to the inner treasure of happiness.

5. Another major dilemma of the ego is the defense mechanism of *identification*. From the ego's perspective, you are doomed to perish without a sense of identity. One way to define its identity and a sense of self is to seek opposition in order to define its boundaries. Again, it is giving you the message, *"You need to have an identity in order to survive. That means you need a sense of 'self.' Your identity is made up of your thoughts, feelings, actions, belongings, the way you dress, how much money you have, your level of education, your achievements, other people's perception of you ... and all other material and social definitions of*

you. You have to protect these with your life; otherwise you may lose your identity, which means you may not survive!"

As you can see, the ego is very clever and protective of human beings. However, the problem is that it drags us into a constant state of competition with ourselves and the rest of the world. There are *always* people that have more than you do, know more than you, are more respected than you, etc. There's also a very high expectation from your own self to have more, do more, and be more. *How on earth can you ever be at ease with so much pressure?*

Every achievement, possession, and success gives the ego a boost of self-satisfaction and pleasure, but only for a short time! After a while, you'll get used to that and want more.

Alcohol and drugs have similar effects on your mind and body, but much more temporarily and destructively. Make no mistake, while addictive behaviors like alcohol, narcotics, gambling, shopping, food, and porn are unhealthy, the pursuit of success, achievement, and higher education may be considered as healthier and better addictions. They are clearly not to be condemned or discouraged. *The point is that it is the very same needs and desires of the ego that help mature our psyche and lead us toward the third stage of life—the peak personal growth.* It is through the ego that we can perfect the super-ego and our understanding of the psyche. The recommendation is to try not to dismiss, suppress, or resist the desires of the ego, but rather to be *aware* of them and not take them too seriously. Just play the game while realizing that it is only a mind game. Your true identity does not consist of your possessions, achievements, and all of those mentioned above, but the pure eternal consciousness behind the scene, the energy driving all these motives, and the matrix linking YOU to the universal intelligence!

The Science of Happiness

Over the decades, a few psychological researchers have ventured out of the dark realm of mental illness into the sunny land of mental well-being. Perhaps the most eager explorer of this terrain was University of Illinois psychologist Edward Diener, referred to as "Dr. Happiness."

For more than two decades, Diener examined what does and does not make people feel satisfied with life.

There are some surprising results revealed by researchers on happiness. Take wealth, for instance, and all the delightful things that money can buy. Diener's research, among others, has shown that once your basic needs are met, additional income does little to raise your sense of satisfaction with life.

How about a good education? No. Neither education nor a high IQ paves the road to happiness.

What about youth? No. In fact, older people are more consistently satisfied with their lives than the young. They are less prone to dark moods. A recent survey by the Centers for Disease Control and Prevention found that people ages twenty to twenty-four are sad for an average of 3.4 days a month, as opposed to just 2.3 days for people ages sixty-five to seventy-four.

How about marriage? This one is a complicated picture. Married people are generally happier than single people, but studies have not been overall consistent, and more research is needed to find out this dilemma.

Do sunny days bring happiness? No conclusive evidence exists, although there are theories on the sun affecting serotonin and melatonin release by the pineal gland.

What about religion? Not sure. Religious faith seems to genuinely lift the spirit, though it's tough to tell whether it's the God part or the community aspect that does the heavy lifting.

How about friends and a good social life? *A big yes.* A 2002 study conducted at the University of Illinois by Diener and Seligman found that the most salient characteristics shared by the 10 percent of students with the highest levels of happiness and the fewest signs of depression were their strong ties to friends and family and commitment to spending time with them.

"Word needs to be spread," concludes Diener. "It is important to work on social skills, close interpersonal ties, and social support in order to be happy."

Of course, happiness is not a static state. Even the happiest of people feel dull at times. And even the saddest have their moments of joy. *That, along with the simple fact that happiness is inherently subjective, has presented a challenge to social scientists trying to measure happiness.*

In his 2002 book called *Authentic Happiness,* Seligman summarizes his understanding of happiness. As a result of his research, he finds three components of happiness:

1. Pleasure
2. Engagement (the depth of involvement with one's family, work, romance, and hobbies)
3. Meaning (using personal strengths to serve some higher purpose).

Of those three roads to a happy, satisfied life, pleasure is the least consequential. He insists: "This is newsworthy because so many Americans build their lives around pursuing pleasure. It turns out that engagement and meaning are much more important."

Genetic Factors

One of the biggest issues in happiness research is the question of how much our happiness is under our control. In 1996, University of Minnesota researcher David Lykken published a paper looking at the role of genes in determining one's sense of satisfaction in life. Lykken gathered information on 4,000 sets of twins born in Minnesota from 1936 through 1955. After comparing happiness data on identical versus fraternal twins, he came to the conclusion that about 50 percent of one's satisfaction with life comes from genetic programming.

Because of the large influence of our genes, Lykken proposed the idea that each of us has a happiness set point much like our set point for body weight. No matter what happens in our life—good, bad, spectacular, horrific—we tend to return in short order to our set range. But is that true?

When he proposed his set-point theory eight years ago, Lykken came to a drastic conclusion. "It may be that trying to be happier is as futile as trying to be taller," he wrote. He has since come to regret that sentence. "I made a dumb statement in the original article," he tells *Time.* "It's clear that we can change our happiness levels widely—up or down."

Lykken's revised thinking coincides with the view of the positive-psychology movement, which shows you can raise your level of happiness.

There are numerous ways to do that. At the University of California at Riverside, psychologist Sonja Lyubomirsky studies different kinds of happiness boosters.

- *Gratitude journal*—a diary in which subjects write down things for which they are thankful. She found that taking the time to conscientiously count their blessings once a week significantly increased subjects' overall satisfaction with life over a period of six weeks, whereas a control group that did not keep journals had no such gain.
- *Performing acts of altruism or kindness*—visiting a nursing home, helping a friend's child with homework, mowing a neighbor's lawn, writing a letter to a grandparent. Doing five kind acts a week, especially all in a single day, gave a measurable boost to Lyubomirsky's subjects.
- *Gratitude visit*—Seligman has also tested similar interventions in controlled trials in huge experiments conducted over the Internet. He found that the single most effective way to turbocharge one's joy is to make a "gratitude visit"— writing a testimonial thanking a teacher, doctor, pastor, or grandparent, and then visiting that person to read him/her the letter of appreciation.

Summary

As discussed earlier, the root of all motives is either to seek pleasure or to avoid pain! In order to achieve ultimate happiness, this fundamental principle can be followed in all aspects of humanity. For easier understanding, I have summarized all previous research findings in the context of a bio-psycho-socio-spiritual approach, in the following chart.

	Seek Pleasure	Avoid Pain
Biological (Physical)	Things that physically make you feel good, such as eating, sex, exercise, relaxation, physical health	Things that physically make you feel bad, such as physical pain, inactivity, physical addiction, and illness
Psychological	Things that mentally and emotionally make you feel good, such as acts of kindness, gratitude visits, gratitude journaling	Things that mentally and emotionally make you feel bad, such as hatred and cruelty, emotional pain, and mental illness
Social	Things that socially make you feel good, such as socialization and engagement	Things that socially make you feel bad, such as isolation, loneliness, and antisocial behaviors
Spiritual	Things that spiritually make you feel good, such as prayers, meditation, faith, meaningful life, service to others	Things that spiritually make you feel bad, such as lack of meaning in life and emptiness

A bio-psycho-socio-spiritual approach to the pain-pleasure principle

PART FOUR

Spiritual Aspects: The Soul

CHAPTER 11

"All religions, arts, and sciences are branches of the same tree."
—Albert Einstein

The Science of Spirituality

Near-Death Experience

In a devastating day in April 2002, Anita Moorjani's family was shocked to hear from her doctor that she had only hours to live. She was in coma due to a lymphoma—a type of aggressive cancer—and her organs were shutting down. In her book, *Dying to Be Me*, Anita elegantly rewrites her journey from cancer to near death, to true healing.

A near-death experience (NDE) is any experience in which someone close to death perceives events that seem to be impossible, unusual, or supernatural. Dr. Raymond Moody used the term "near-death experience" in his 1975 book, *Life After Life*. While there are many questions about NDEs, one thing is certain—they do exist. Thousands of people have actually perceived similar sensations while close to death. The debate is over whether or not they actually experienced what they perceived.

Anita recalls during this experience, how she began to feel weightless. She was acutely aware of all that was going on around her and could feel the pain of her family members as she lay in her bed. She could strangely hear the conversation that the doctor was having with her husband down the hall forty feet away. The doctor said there was nothing more that they could do because Anita's organs had shut down.

Incredible love filled her soul. She had a talk with her father who had died ten years prior. Time felt different. It felt as if all moments happened at once. There was no sense of time and space. She also realized that the cancer was not some type of bad karma, but rather the result of her many fears to manifest. She manifested this cancer that had overcome her body. During her NDE, Anita initially decided not to come back, but as she went further toward death, her father told her that was as far as she could go before she could not go back. At this point, she realized why this was all happening. She was supposed to come back to help thousands of people understand. She decided to come back and fulfill her purpose.

Thirty hours from the time she was rushed to the hospital, Anita awoke from her coma. Two days later, Anita asked medical personnel to remove the food tube because it bothered her throat, and she wanted to eat real food. Within three days, the tumors had significantly shrunk, and within five days, Anita was transferred from the intensive care unit into a regular room due to miraculous improvement. A few weeks later, the oncologist wanted to do a lymph node biopsy. Anita was sent to radiology for an ultrasound. She smiled when she observed the radiologist and oncologist in shock. They could not find any evidence of cancer! Anita was discharged from the hospital just five weeks after being admitted, and all tests indicated she was cancer-free.

After the NDE, Anita began to recover. Once out of the hospital, she began to live her purpose of allowing more and greater experiences into her life. She had learned to trust her inner guidance and not focus on doing what everyone thought she should do. A great point made by Anita was: "We come into this life knowing our magnificence, but the world erodes our belief in our magnificence over time." Getting rid of cancer was not a result of positive thinking; it was a result of greater awareness and letting go of all thoughts that didn't serve her in a positive manner. All negative beliefs tend to require defense, and anytime you fight something, you get weaker. "We need to believe in our own magnificence, it is as simple as that."

Spirituality

Spirituality has been defined in numerous ways.
- A belief in a power operating in the universe that is greater than oneself.
- Awareness of the purpose and meaning of life, and the development of ultimate personal growth and absolute values.
- An ultimate or alleged immaterial reality.

It's the way you find meaning, hope, comfort, and inner peace in life. It is your view and vision of the world that determine how connected you are to your source, the universal spirit, universal energy, higher intelligence, God, or whatever you wish to name it. *It is the mind that chooses the lens to see the world through!*

In order to understand spirituality, it is critical to understand the difference between truth and reality, as described in chapter 2. Our understanding and perception of life (reality) is what the subconscious mind tells us, which may not necessarily be what the truth of life is. Let's not get too carried away with what we think—it may only be an illusion!

"Life = real life (truth) + what we think is real life (perception of life)"

The point is that each of us live in our own *mental world*, our *reality* about the world. But we may be totally off track. The truth of the world is not necessarily how we perceive it (our reality)! *Understanding this concept allows us to re-define and co-create our reality in such a way that suits us.*

Collectively, we are increasingly used to habitual (subconscious) thinking in the context of *the small picture* surrounding us. Unless we constantly use the brain to think and act outside of the comfort zone, we will lose its unlimited power, capacity, and creativity. These unique features of the human brain are made possible through a connection to the universal intelligence—the cosmos or matrix that is the source of energy for life! However, as mentioned in previous chapters, we are collectively disconnected to this unimaginable resource, due to the "viruses" that have created layers of dirt over our minds and souls. All we have to do is *undo* them in order to reconnect to the source!

Remember the analogy of the light bulb attached to the source of energy, yet unable to glow because it's covered with layers of dirt. The way to remove these layers of negative thoughts and feelings (viruses) is to rearrange the thoughts and learn to master the *conscious thinking* skills as opposed to the *subconscious*, which we are more inclined to use by default. Generally speaking, we have created a bubble in our minds, separating us from the source. Our shortsightedness takes away the opportunity to view life in the context of *the big picture*.

This is why we need to move to a higher perspective—*the Third Vision*—a. bio-psycho-socio-spiritual approach toward humanity. Without understanding humanity, how is it possible to find solutions to the problems created by mankind? **The study of humanity is not complete without understanding the spiritual aspects and addressing the spiritual needs of human beings (third stage of the Modified Maslow's pyramid)!**

The Science of Karma

Karma is one of those words that are difficult to translate literally. However, the concept of karma can be interpreted as the law of moral causation. The theory of karma is a fundamental doctrine in Buddhism. In Indian religions, it is the concept of "action" or "deed," understood as that which causes the entire cycle of *cause and effect* (the cycle called **samsara**). It originated in ancient India and is a common belief in Hindu, Buddhist, and Sikh philosophies. Buddha is the one who explained and formulated this doctrine in the complete form in which we have it today. In Hinduism and Buddhism, karma is considered as the sum of a person's actions in this and previous states of existence, viewed as deciding their fate in future existences. It is the destiny or fate, following as effect from cause.

The simple and short explanation of karma is: you get what you give. In other words, whatever you do intentionally to others, a similar thing will happen to you in the future. Causing suffering to others will cause suffering for you, and causing happiness to others will result in happiness for oneself.

The goal of the spiritual journey is to escape the prison of karma and bring about the true response of our soul, which is **creativity**. *In knowing our true essence beyond time, space, and causality, we become free of the wheel of samsara.*

Although the past determines the circumstances of the present, the choices we make in the present are a function of our state of awareness, which determines the future. The more awake we are, the more unconditioned and creative our responses to those circumstances will be.

These are words and teachings of Deepak Chopra, an Indian medical doctor, public speaker, and writer on subjects such as spirituality, Ayurveda, and mind-body medicine. Chopra began his career as an endocrinologist and later shifted his focus to alternative medicine. Before launching his career in the late 1980s by publishing self-help books on New Age spirituality and alternative medicine, Chopra was a top assistant to Maharishi Mahesh Yogi (1914–2008), who developed the **transcendental meditation** technique and was the leader and guru of the TM movement. The TM technique is based on the ancient Vedic tradition of enlightenment in India. This knowledge has been handed down by Vedic masters from generation to generation for thousands of years. About fifty years ago, Maharishi—the representative in our age of the Vedic tradition—introduced TM to the world, restoring the knowledge and experience of higher states of consciousness at this critical time for humanity. The TM techniques taught today throughout the globe are the same procedures used by teachers thousands of years ago.

More than five million people worldwide have learned this simple, natural technique—people of all ages, cultures, and religions. Over 600 research studies have been conducted at more than 250 universities and research centers in thirty-three countries (including Harvard, UCLA, and Stanford). These studies have been published in more than a hundred journals (14). The scientific research on the transcendental meditation programs is the largest and strongest body of research in the world on any program to develop human potential. This research has demonstrated profound benefits in all fields of life and throughout society—including health, education, defense, business and industry, criminal rehabilitation and crime reduction, and administration in the direction of world peace. Studies have documented that this technology benefits every aspect of life. These benefits are not limited to TM. Although not as extensive, there is also supporting evidence for advantages of other types of meditation. Some of the benefits of the TM programs (both individual and the society) include:

- *Development of total brain functioning and mental potential*
  - Increased use of latent reserves of the brain
  - Greater synchrony and coherence of brain functioning in all cortical areas
  - Increased cerebral blood flow
  - Activation of each brain hemisphere
  - Faster response of the brain in sensory and cognitive processing of stimuli
  - Increased intelligence
  - Increased creativity
  - Increased problem-solving ability
  - Improved academic performance
- *Better physical and mental health*
  - Increased resistance to stress
  - Decreased hospitalization and doctor visits
  - Decreased health expenditures
  - Reduction of psychosomatic health problems
  - Reduction of stress-related biochemicals
  - Reduced substance abuse
  - Reduced anxiety and depression
  - Increased self-development to very high levels
  - Orientation toward more positive values
  - Reduced aggression and hostility
  - Higher levels of moral reasoning
  - Increased tolerance
- *Development of inner peace*
  - Decreased crime
  - Decreased homicide and suicide
  - Improvement in comprehensive quality-of-life indices
- *Reduced regional and international conflict*
  - Improved international relations
  - Reduced regional conflict
  - Decreased wars and related fatalities
  - Improved economic trends

Brainwaves, Sleep, Electromagnetic fields, Karma, Telepathy, and Transcendence

The Brainwaves

It is well known that the brain is an electrochemical organ; researchers have speculated that a fully functioning brain can generate as much as ten watts of electrical power. Other more conservative investigators calculate that if all hundred billion interconnected nerve cells discharged at one time, a single electrode placed on the human scalp would record something like five millionths to fifty millionths of a volt. If you had enough scalps hooked up, you might be able to light a flashlight bulb.

Even though this electrical power is very limited, it does occur in very specific ways that are characteristic of the human brain. Electrical activity emanating from the brain is displayed in the form of brainwaves. There are five categories of these brainwaves—**gamma, beta, alpha, theta,** and **delta—** ranging from the most to the least activity.

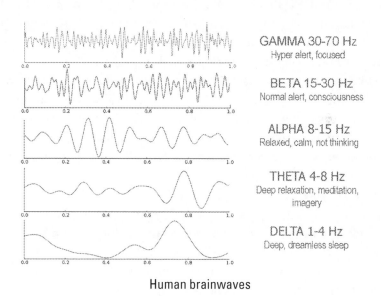

GAMMA 30-70 Hz
Hyper alert, focused

BETA 15-30 Hz
Normal alert, consciousness

ALPHA 8-15 Hz
Relaxed, calm, not thinking

THETA 4-8 Hz
Deep relaxation, meditation, imagery

DELTA 1-4 Hz
Deep, dreamless sleep

Human brainwaves

1. When the brain is aroused and actively engaged in high mental activities, it generates **gamma** waves. These waves are of relatively low amplitude and are the fastest of the five different brainwaves. The

frequency of gamma waves ranges from 30-70 (or even higher) cycles a second (Hz). Gamma waves are characteristics of a strongly focused and engaged mind. During an exam, a person is in gamma. A debater would also be in gamma.

2. The next brainwave category is **beta**, ranging from 15-30 Hz. It represents the active and average thinking state of the brain. A person in active conversation, one making a speech, a teacher, or a talk show host would all be in beta when they are engaged in their work.

3. The next brainwave category in order of frequency is **alpha**. These represent the calm and non-thinking states. Alpha brainwaves are slower and higher in amplitude. Their frequency ranges from 8-15 cycles per second. A person who has completed a task and sits down to rest is often in an alpha state. A person who takes a break from a conference and walks in the garden is often in an alpha state.

4. The next state, **theta** brainwaves, are typically of even greater amplitude and slower frequency. This frequency range is normally between 4-8 cycles per second. A person who has taken time off from a task and begins to daydream is often in a theta brainwave state. During deep relaxation, meditation, or snoozing, the brain is emanating theta waves. The ideation that can take place during the theta state is often free flow, and it is typically a very positive mental state.

5. The final brainwave state is **delta**. Here the brainwaves are of lower amplitude and the slowest frequency. They typically center around a range of 1-4 cycles per second. They never go down to zero because that would mean that you were brain dead. But deep, dreamless sleep would take you down to the lowest frequency—typically, 2-3 cycles a second.

The Sleep Cycle

When we go to bed and read for a few minutes before attempting sleep, we are likely to be in low beta. When we put the book down, turn off the lights, and close our eyes, our brainwaves will descend from beta, to alpha, to theta (light sleep), and finally delta (deep sleep).

When an individual awakes from a deep sleep in preparation for getting up, the brainwave frequencies will increase through the different specific stages of brainwave activity. That is, they will increase from delta to theta and then to alpha, and finally into beta. During focus and high-intensity brain exercises, they will go higher into the gamma range. During this awakening cycle, individuals may stay in the theta state for an extended period of five to fifteen minutes—which would allow them to have a free flow of ideas about yesterday's events or to contemplate the activities of the forthcoming day. This time can be extremely productive and can be a period of very meaningful and creative mental activity.

There are two different types of sleep: **NREM** (non-rapid eye movement), and **REM** (rapid eye movement). As of 2007, the American Academy of Sleep Medicine (AASM) has updated the classification of NREM into three stages: 1, 2 and 3.

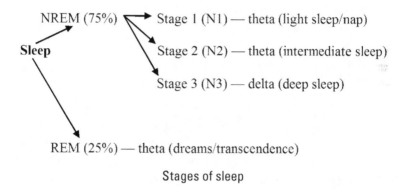

NREM (75%) → Stage 1 (N1) — theta (light sleep/nap)

Sleep → Stage 2 (N2) — theta (intermediate sleep)

Stage 3 (N3) — delta (deep sleep)

REM (25%) — theta (dreams/transcendence)

Stages of sleep

NREM is the type of sleep you enter when you first go to bed. Most of the time asleep is spent here, making up for 75 percent of an adult's sleep. Each stage of NREM takes you deeper and deeper into sleep.

- N1—*(Theta waves)*. This is the first stage of NREM, starting from the moment you first fall asleep. Your brain begins preparing you for the deep sleep ahead. Your body slows down, and your breathing becomes slow and steady. It's a very light sleep. If you wake up at this stage, you might not even know you'd just been sleeping. At this stage, you might experience what's called sleep starts or **hypnic jerks**. It is completely normal and just a sign that your body is slowly shutting down, and sleep will soon be upon you.
- N2—*(Theta waves)*. This is the next stage of sleep. Here you're in a deeper sleep and your body functions slow down even more.

145

- N3—*(Delta waves)*. Also known as **deep sleep**, this is the last stage of sleep. Waking someone from this stage would be pretty difficult, and if you managed it, they would feel very groggy, tired, and disoriented. Brainwaves are now at their slowest. Your body functions slow down to their fullest. Minimal dreaming can happen in this stage (but not like REM), although most of it would not be remembered. This is also the stage in which parasomnias, such as nightmares, nocturnal enuresis, and sleepwalking, mostly happen. *This is where sleep is at its best, deeply nourishing and refreshing. Spending sufficient time in this stage is critical to overall sleep quality.* Many different physiologic processes occur during sleep, but perhaps the most important are the increased secretion of growth hormones, enhanced immune function, and clearance of free radicals (which are destructive to the cells) in the brain. In a disorder called **social dwarfism**, there is failure to grow, and children with this disorder are unusually small. It was called "social" because no biological anomalies could be discovered, but they found that among failure-to-thrive children, there was a high incidence of family dysfunction. There was a lot of stress and tension in the family. It is hypothesized that the children's sleep cycles were disrupted enough so that there was not enough growth hormone being released during deep sleep.

REM is the other type of sleep, which happens after the first cycle of NREM, after about ninety minutes. The brainwaves here are *theta*. This is the stage where most dreaming occurs, with your brain activity much higher than NREM. However, while your brain is active, only your eyes and breathing muscles can move. There are exceptions though; some people can actually fully move in their dreams (sleepwalkers). It is a well-known fact that humans dream in ninety-minute cycles. When the delta brainwave frequencies from deep sleep increase into theta brainwaves, active dreaming takes place and often becomes more experiential to the person. Typically, there is rapid eye movement and paralysis of the muscles. Such paralysis may be necessary to protect one from self-damage through physically acting out scenes from the often vivid dreams that occur during this stage.

The purpose of REM sleep is not fully understood. Studies suggest that REM sleep plays a role in the reorganization and restoration of brain processes that mediate the flow, structure, and storage of information. This includes things like problem-solving, memory consolidation, information processing, and creativity. In other words, it is possible that partial resetting of the brain happens in this stage.

On a psychological level, REM may serve some compensatory process function, as hypothesized by Freud. Personally important experiences may be repressed during the day, and thus you'll see a reciprocal emphasis in dreams at night. More often than not, however, you'll see continuity between pre-sleep experiences and dream experiences of the REM. What you've been thinking about before you go to bed at night, you'll see in the dream of that night.

From an intra-psychic perspective, this level of brain function may be where **transcendence** of the universal energy happens—where the nonconscious mind can connect to the collective or universal nonconscious and transfer digital data and energy from there to the consciousness!

Our bodies cycle between REM and the stages of NREM several times during the night.

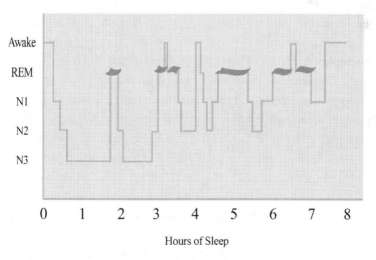

Hours of Sleep

The stages of sleep

Deep sleep is where the party is at in the sleep world. But as you can see, it only happens during the first part of the night. As the night progresses, the amount of time you spend in the deeper stages of NREM sleep decreases, and that spent in REM and the lighter stages of NREM increases. It's natural to wake up a few times in the night after the REM stage. Most of the time, you won't even remember waking up at all.

Being aware of your own sleep cycle can help you effectively plan your sleep schedule. For example, it would be a bad idea to schedule in an hour nap, since you're most likely to be woken by your alarm clock in N3, in deep sleep, where you would no doubt feel much worse than before the nap. A better time for a nap would be around twenty minutes, to make sure you don't go beyond N1, or at least ninety minutes, so that you awake during REM after a complete cycle.

Electromagnetism

Electromagnetic induction was discovered independently by Michael Faraday and Joseph Henry in 1831; however, Faraday was the first to publish the results of his experiments. According to Faraday's Laws: "Any change in the magnetic environment of a coil of wire will cause a voltage (EMF) to be 'induced' in the coil. The change could be produced by changing the magnetic field strength, moving a magnet toward or away from the coil, moving the coil into or out of the magnetic field, rotating the coil relative to the magnet, etc."

In simple terms, every wire through which electricity runs produces an electromagnetic field (EMF) around it (15). The opposite is also true. If you pass an uncharged wire (no electricity running through it) through a magnetic field, electrons move in a specific direction, generating electricity. This discovery formed the fundamental principle of how generators were invented, and we have electricity today.

As mentioned earlier in chapter 2, the brain, consisting of about a hundred billion neurons and 164 trillion synapses, is in a constant state of thinking. Electrical impulses travel as the brainwaves described above, at the speed of a hundred meters per second across the axon. A single nerve can send up to 1,000 impulses per second. These brainwaves have physical properties, such as frequencies and wavelengths, a very important concept in order to understand the connection of our mind to the rest of the world. According to Faraday's laws, the brainwaves collectively produce an electromagnetic field around the scalp and body. However, the voltage is very low, and today, there is limited technology and research capable of measuring it in a meaningful way.

However, the appearance of exciting research from around the world is changing our understanding of this picture. How concepts of "healing energy" have swung from suspicion and ridicule to respectability, is one of the most fascinating and clinically significant stories that can be told. For example, in a few decades, scientists have gone from a conviction that there is no such thing as an energy field around the human body to an absolute certainty that it exists.

Sensitive instruments have been developed that can detect the subtle energy fields around the human body. Of particular importance is the *SQUID magnetometer*, which is capable of detecting subtle biomagnetic fields associated with physiological activities in the body. This is the same field that sensitive individuals have been describing for thousands of years, but scientists have ignored just because there was no objective way to measure it.

In 1963, Gerhard Baule and Richard McFee of the Department of Electrical Engineering at Syracuse University detected the biomagnetic field projected from the human heart. They used two coils, each with two million turns of wire, connected to a sensitive amplifier.

In 1970, David Cohen of MIT, using a SQUID magnetometer, confirmed the heart measurements. By 1972, Cohen had improved the sensitivity of his instrument, enabling him to measure magnetic fields around the head produced by brain activities.

Subsequently, it has been discovered that all tissues and organs produce specific magnetic pulsations, which have come to be known as biomagnetic fields (BMF). The traditional electrical recordings, such as the electrocardiogram (ECG) and electroencephalogram (EEG), are now being complemented by biomagnetic recordings, called *magnetocardiograms (MCG)* and *magnetoencephalograms (MEG)*. Mapping the magnetic fields in the space around the body often provides a more accurate indication of physiology and pathology than traditional electrical measurements.

In the 1920s and 1930s, a distinguished researcher at Yale University School of Medicine, Harold Saxon Burr, suggested that diseases could be detected in the energy field of the body before physical symptoms appear. Moreover, Burr was convinced that diseases could be prevented by altering the energy field.

These concepts were ahead of their time but are now being confirmed in medical research laboratories around the world. Scientists are using SQUID instruments to map the ways diseases alter biomagnetic fields around the body. Others are applying pulsating magnetic fields to stimulate healing. Sensitive individuals have been describing these phenomena for a long time, but there was no logical explanation of how it could happen.

Have you heard of energy healers using their hand to project energy? Is there any logic and science behind that?

In the early 1980s, Dr. John Zimmerman began a series of important studies on therapeutic touch, using a SQUID magnetometer at the University of Colorado School of Medicine in Denver. Zimmerman discovered that a huge, pulsating biomagnetic field emanated from the hands of a TT practitioner. The biomagnetic pulsations from the hands are in the same frequency range as brainwaves.

Confirmation of Zimmerman's findings came in 1992, when Seto and colleagues in Japan studied practitioners of various martial arts and other healing methods. The Qi emission from the hands is so strong that it can be detected with a simple magnetometer consisting of two coils. Since then, a number of studies of QiGong practitioners have extended these investigations to the sound, light, and thermal fields emitted by healers. Specific frequencies stimulate the growth of nerves, bones, skin, capillaries, and ligaments. Of course, Reiki practitioners and their patients have daily experiences of energy healing, and academic medicine is now beginning to accept this therapy as logical and beneficial because of these new scientific findings. Emergence of spiritual medicine as a new specialty in modern medicine is very likely and not too far away.

Some researchers believe that brainwaves are not confined to the brain but actually spread throughout the body via the *perineural system*, the connective tissue sheaths surrounding all of the nerves. Dr. Robert O. Becker has described how this system, more than any other, regulates injury repair processes throughout the body. Hence the entire nervous system acts as an "antenna" for projecting the biomagnetic pulsations that begin in the brain, specifically in the thalamus. Moreover, waves that begin as relatively weak pulsations in the brain appear to gather strength as they flow along the peripheral nerves and into the hands. The mechanism of this amplification probably involves the perineural system and the other connective tissue systems, such as the fascia.

In summary, some of the evidence for the biological and physical basis of energy healing has been demonstrated above. After centuries of neglect, energy therapies can take their appropriate place in clinical medicine, although more evidence-based research is needed to convince the conventional medical society. Our limited science to this date cannot take away the ultimate mystery of life, nor can it detract from the spiritual component of healing. Research on the energy therapies can lead to a much more complete understanding of life, disease, and healing.

Karma, Telepathy, and Transcendence

So, back to the initial question: what is the science of these unexplained concepts?

In order to understand the scientific principles of these poorly understood phenomena, we must explain how the universe may be physically and metaphysically connected to our mind and body. Hence some basic physical principles of communication and telecommunication will be explored here.

Electromagnetic Radiation (EMR) is a form of energy that exhibits wave-like behavior as it travels through the vacuum in space. EMR has both electric and magnetic field components, which oscillate in phase perpendicular to each other. Light consists of **electromagnetic waves**. The **photon**—massless packet of energy that travels at the speed of light—is the basic unit of light and all other forms of electromagnetic radiation, as well as the force carrier for the electromagnetic waves. EMR carries energy and momentum that may be imparted to matter with which it interacts. EM waves can be characterized by any of three properties: **wavelength, frequency,** or **energy.**

EMR is classified according to the frequency of its wave. The **electromagnetic spectrum**, in order of increasing frequency and decreasing wavelength, consists of:

- *Radio waves (RW)*—can penetrate the Earth's atmosphere
- *Microwaves (MW)*
- *Infrared (IR)*
- ***Visible light***—can penetrate the Earth's atmosphere
- *Ultraviolet (UV)*
- *X-rays (XR)*
- *Gamma rays (GR)*

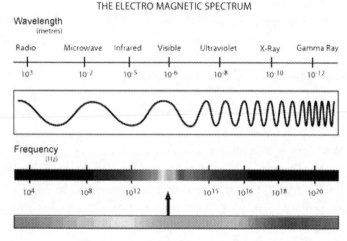

The electromagnetic wave spectrum

The eyes of various organisms sense only a small window of frequencies, called the *visible spectrum*. A typical human eye will respond to frequencies of about 400–800 Hz, and wavelengths of about 400–750 nm. A light-adapted eye generally has its maximum sensitivity at around 540 Hz, in the *green* region of the optical spectrum. Imagine what our world would look like if the visible spectrum was different, let's say 2000–5000 Hz instead of what it is today—just some food for thought!

Only the radio waves and visible radiation can penetrate the Earth's atmosphere. This is important in understanding karma. All other radiation in the electromagnetic spectrum in the space is blocked by the ionosphere.

James Maxwell was the first to predict radio waves through mathematical calculations in 1865. He noticed wavelike properties of light and similarities in electrical and magnetic observations. He then proposed equations that described light waves and radio waves as electromagnetic waves that travel in space. In 1887, Heinrich Hertz confirmed Maxwell's theory of electromagnetic waves by experimentally generating radio waves in his laboratory. Many inventions followed, making practical the use of radio waves to transfer information through space.

Radio waves do more than just bring music to your radio. They also carry signals to your TV and cellular phones. The waves used in cellular phones are much smaller than TV and FM radio waves. If you talked about TV and radio devices 200 years ago, they would probably see that either as magic or as paranormal phenomena coming from the outer world. *While the truth about these waves has always been the same, the reality of people 200 years ago was definitely different from ours.*

Today, however, almost every teenager has a cellular phone, and electronic devices, such as TV, computers, radio, etc., are so integrated in our daily lives that we seem to have forgotten their significance altogether.

So you pick up your phone and call your friend. When you call, radio waves are transmitted through your phone. These waves are sent to the collective pool of energy of radio waves. But how are they received directly by your friend's cell phone? How do they find their way through the unlimited pool of similar waves? This is done by communication of the transmitter and receiver through a mutually understandable language. In the language of physics, these waves connect through a harmony of wavelength, frequency, and energy level—the three physical properties of EM waves mentioned earlier.

So here is the theory: Telecommunication is the remote exchange of information in the form of digital data, as well as energy carried by photons (the basic units of electromagnetic radiation). The brain and body are surrounded by an electromagnetic field at all times—called the biomagnetic field—which can act both as receiver and transmitter.

The unique characteristics of this field, however, vary depending on your overall state of consciousness. This state allows a specific pattern of connectivity to the unlimited resources of data and energy surrounding us at any moment.

*In other words, your collective state of consciousness is determined by two components: your level of **cognitive awake-ness** (state of mental consciousness) defined by the different types of brainwaves, plus your level of **self-awareness** (state of spiritual and psychological consciousness), determined by how much your subconscious and conscious minds are in harmony. How dissonant or consonant are the two minds? Are they in competition or cooperation? This collective state of bio-psycho-socio-spiritual consciousness determines the state of receptiveness of your electromagnetic field to the electromagnetic radiation existing around you in the universe! The same field is also what talks to the universal matrix, by transmitting negative or positive energy to the external world. That is why a negative field attracts negative energies, and a positive field attracts the positive ones!*

Several theorists have proposed that consciousness and karma can be understood as an electromagnetic phenomenon. Susan Pockett, the New Zealand based neurobiologist, and Johnjoe McFadden, professor of molecular genetics from the School of Biomedical and Life Sciences at the University of Surrey in the UK, proposed EM field theories in 2000. What they proposed is that the brain's EM field **is** consciousness.

The conscious electromagnetic information field is, at present, still a theory. But if true, there are many fascinating implications for the concept of free will, the nature of creativity or spirituality, and even the significance of life and death.

CHAPTER 12

"Silence is the language of God, all else is poor translation."
—Rumi

Secrets of the Soul

At age eighteen, like millions of other teenagers, my curiosity led me to the quest of finding answers to some of the most profound questions posed by mankind. *What is life all about? What is the meaning and purpose of life? Who are we? What is our connection to the universe? What is the nature of the universe? Why do people behave the way they do? What is right or wrong, and who determines that?* Overwhelmed by the complexity of these concepts, I became depressed, but somehow found a way toward recovery. I soon realized that the weight of these universal inquiries was too mind-blowing, and the only vehicle that could possibly help feed my curiosity was education. Years later, I finally realized what the problem was at that age, and how I was able to self-treat my depression.

The following analogy demonstrates another one of my life-changing experiences. Imagine you are a fish, let's say Mimo, swimming with millions of other fish near the surface of water. You are happy and playful, but there is always a question on your mind: what is down deep in the water? You begin swimming to the depth of a hundred meters. There, you find a number of other fish, the ones who were thinking like you. You continue swimming deeper down, trying to find out the mysteries of the darkness below. At the level of 1,000 meters, you find a few other fish, but you notice that their number is shrinking. There are fewer fish in deeper levels. You are now lonely and fearful. After all, we have evolved genetically and fundamentally to be social beings.

That's what happened to me at the age of eighteen. I swam to the mid-level but did not know how to continue. It was too much for me at that age. Upon return to the surface, I had not found what I was looking for, but recovered from depression. By joining others, I was able to continue a "normal" life like everyone else.

Years later, you take another deep dive when ready. This time you pass the 1,000 meter level. Hoping to find more answers, the journey continues deep down into the waters. Finally you reach the bottom of the ocean. Wow, there is an entirely different world at this level. Here, the meaning of water and swimming is different. The world is colorful and beautiful. You find many answers here—but not all. Among the pieces of your puzzle is an old box. It's a treasure! Is this what you were looking for? Congratulations—you found it!

In the darkness of deep waters, a shadow is noticed. Wait … you are not alone! There are a few other fish swimming by the treasure. Together, victory is celebrated for finding the answers searched. Soon, the celebration is over, and you are all wondering, *What are we going to do with this treasure now?*

This treasure does not belong to you alone. It belongs to all the other fish, and in fact all the living and non-living creatures in the ocean. You cannot enjoy it without sharing it with everyone else. But wait, it's too heavy. How can you take it up to the surface for the others? After all, not everyone is willing to come to this depth! Oh, so this was only half of the victory! The only way to take this back to the surface is teamwork. All the fish at that level want to share this with the rest of the world—that is, with anyone who is interested. But there are not enough fish to carry it. More recruits are needed, so some of you swim back to the surface to inform others about the discovery, while some stay at that deep level for good.

Back at the surface, everything looks different. You view everything from a new lens! Many previous enjoyable things are now meaningless. Being different, you are seen as an outsider by many previous friends. You feel alone but not lonely! This time though, something very valuable is learned. You took a piece of the treasure along back to the surface: *flexibility.* Having overcome the fear, you now have the capability and choice of swimming down into the deep waters as desired. You also gained the wisdom that we are all social beings and need to be together. There is nothing wrong with being superficial in certain circumstances and profound in others. The choice is yours, and that of course, is very empowering.

You spread the word to the ones swimming at the surface. Many of the fish don't believe you. They simply cannot understand what you are talking about. But many others do. They were not willing to swim alone, but in your leadership, they find the courage to swim with you down to the deep. Once enough recruits are deployed, the treasure is carried and shared with the rest of the world, and your victory is now complete!

Many teenagers either give up their dream of pursuit of the treasure or become deeply ill and can never recover. *Do not give up your dream and pursuit of happiness, but make sure you are ready for the deep dive. We are all in some stage of our spiritual journey.* If you are not ready yet, swim back and wait for the time you *are* ready. There is absolutely nothing wrong with that. *Be flexible.* Just because you have found your treasure, doesn't mean you need to talk about philosophy when everyone is having fun at a party. Just enjoy the environment and other people's company!

The Nature and Essence of the Universe

What is matter? How does it interact with energy? What is the nature of the universe? These are some of the fundamental questions that have puzzled humanity for centuries and millennia. Although modern physics has led to astounding discoveries about the true nature of matter/energy, it seems that it has run into the field of metaphysics. Many physicists will admit that the only way to truly interpret their findings is through a metaphysical explanation.

Albert Einstein, who may have been the greatest thinker of our time, stated that "imagination is more important than knowledge." Yet even he was unable to solve his greatest challenge—formulation of a Grand Unified Field Theory that would explain all the various interactions of matter/energy as the manifestations of a single, supreme force. However, consider that there may be a completely different and astounding theory—that of the vibrational essence of all existence. Unlike many other proposals, this vibrational Grand Unified Field Theory originates not just from multi-billion dollar particle smashers, but from the basic and pure comprehension of the universe shown in the most ancient writings of our ancestors.

Since all of the matter and energy in the universe originated from a single, incredibly hot point at the time of the Big Bang, it would make sense that all those forces were a single force at that specific time. Not only is it feasible that all atomic particles in this microscopic blast-furnace would have been the same type of particle, but also that all the particles would have been the same individual particle. As impossible as it may seem to believe, it is not only just conceivable but highly likely that a single subatomic particle was the cosmic egg that gave rise to the entire universe as we know it today. However, the truth so far is … we don't really know!

The Standard Model and Newer Theories

Our current knowledge about the subatomic composition of the universe is summarized in what is known as the **Standard Model** of particle physics. It describes both the fundamental building blocks out of which the world is made, and the forces through which these blocks interact. About 4.6 percent of the mass and energy of the universe is contained in atoms (protons and neutrons). All of life is made from a portion of this 4.6 percent. The rest is dark matter (23 percent) and dark energy (72 percent).

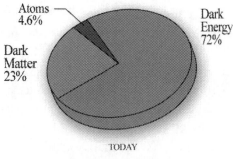

Components of the Universe

Mass—there are twelve basic building blocks within matter, called **quarks** and **leptons**.

Energy —there are **four fundamental forces** in the universe in the form of energy:

1. **Gravity**
2. **Electromagnetism**
3. **Weak nuclear forces**
4. **Strong nuclear forces**

Each of these is produced by fundamental particles that act as carriers of the force. The most familiar of these is the **photon**, a particle of light, which is the mediator of electromagnetic forces. This means that, for instance, a magnet attracts a nail because both objects exchange photons. In 1900, Max Planck suggested that light and all other electromagnetic waves are distributed only in certain discrete packets, called **quanta** (the smallest unit, which is *quantum* of light, is called *photon*). The **graviton** is the particle associated with gravity. The strong force is carried by particles known as **gluons**. Finally, the weak force is transmitted by three particles, **W+**, **W-** , and **Z**.

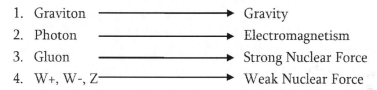

1. Graviton ⟶ Gravity
2. Photon ⟶ Electromagnetism
3. Gluon ⟶ Strong Nuclear Force
4. W+, W-, Z ⟶ Weak Nuclear Force

The four fundamental forces of the universe

The behavior of all of these particles and forces is described with tremendous precision by the Standard Model, with one notable exception—*gravity*. For technical reasons, the gravitational force, the most familiar in our everyday lives, has proven very difficult to describe microscopically. This has been for many years one of the most important problems in theoretical physics—to formulate a **quantum theory of gravity**.

In the last few decades, the **string theory** has emerged as the most promising candidate for a microscopic theory of gravity. And it is infinitely more ambitious than that; it attempts to provide a complete, unified, and consistent description of the fundamental structure of our universe. For this reason, it is sometimes called the *theory of everything*.

The essential idea behind string theory is this: all of the different fundamental particles of the Standard Model are really just different manifestations of one basic object—a string. How can that be? Well, we would ordinarily picture an electron, for instance, as a point with no internal structure. A point cannot do anything but move. But, if string theory is correct, then under an extremely powerful microscope, we would realize that the electron is not really a point, but a tiny loop of string. A string can do something aside from moving—it can *oscillate* in different dimensions. If it oscillates a certain way, then from a distance, we see an electron. But if it oscillates some other way, well, then we call it a photon, or a quark, or a … you get the idea. So, *if string theory is correct, the entire world—including your body, mind and soul—is made of strings!*

String theory, as mentioned above, ran into a problem: another version of the equations was discovered, then another, and then another. Eventually, there were five major "superstring theories". The main differences between each theory were principally the number of dimensions in which the strings developed, and their characteristics. Furthermore, all these theories appeared to be correct. In 1994, a string theorist named Edward Witten, along with other researchers, considered that the five different versions of string theory might be describing the same thing seen from different perspectives. They proposed a unifying theory called **"M-theory"**, which brought all of the superstring theories together. It did this by asserting that strings are really 1-dimensional slices of a 2-dimensional membrane vibrating in *11-dimensional space*.

Quantum Physics and the Nature of the Universe

The success of Isaac Newton's theory of gravity led Marquis de Laplace, at the beginning of the nineteenth century, to argue that the universe was completely **deterministic**. Laplace believed that there should be a set of scientific laws that would allow us to predict everything that would happen in the universe. This was widely accepted until 1926, when German scientist, Werner Heisenberg, formulated his famous *uncertainty principle*.

Contrary to Laplace's belief, the uncertainty theory proposes that nature does not impose limits on our ability to predict the future using scientific laws. This is because, in order to predict the future position and velocity of a particle, one has to be able to measure its initial state (position and velocity) accurately. The obvious way to do this is to shine light on the particle. Some of the waves of light will be scattered by the particle, which can be detected by the observer, indicating the particle's position. However, as soon as you shine light, the position and velocity of the particle will change, according to quantum theory. Even one quantum of light will disturb the particle and change its velocity in a way that cannot be predicted anymore. In other words, the quantum world cannot be perceived directly, but rather through the use of instruments. And, so, there is a problem with the fact that the act of measuring disturbs the energy and position of subatomic particles. This is called the *measurement problem*.

In the diagram below, by the time you observe the particle, develop an image in your visual cortex, and make meaning of it, time has elapsed, and it is not in its original place anymore. The mystery of the *truth* of quantum properties remains unsolved, and all that is left is the *reality* or perception of the observer!

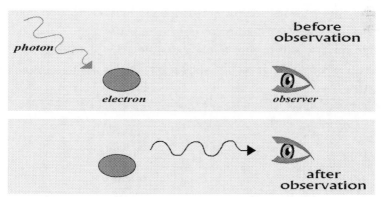

the act of observing effects the position and energy of electron

Measurement problem in Quantum Mechanics

Heisenberg's uncertainty principle is a fundamental property of the world. It has profound implications for the way in which we view the world. Even after more than half a century, these implications have not been fully accepted by many philosophers and are still the subject of controversy. *Many believe what they want to believe, no matter what!* This theory, however, put an end to Laplace's theory and view of a deterministic world. Today, we certainly cannot predict future events exactly, since we cannot even measure the present state of the universe precisely!

One of the most important implications of Heisenberg's uncertainty principle is that particles behave in some circumstances like waves, and sometimes like particles, based on the observation of the observer! In other words, they do not have a definite position but are "smeared out" with a certain probability distribution. The principle, known as *wave-particle duality*, is well demonstrated in the famous **double-slit experiment,** conducted by Thomas Young. This is a demonstration that matter and energy can display characteristics of both waves and particles, depending on the observer's viewpoint.

A light source, such as a laser beam, illuminates a thin plate pierced by two parallel slits, and the light passing through the slits is observed on a screen behind the plate. If light consisted strictly of classical particles, and we illuminated two parallel slits, the expected pattern on the screen would simply be the sum of the two single-slit patterns. In actuality, however, the pattern becomes wider, including a series of light and dark bands. The wave nature of light causes the light waves passing through the two slits to interfere, producing bright and dark bands on the screen—a result that would not be expected if light consisted only of particles.

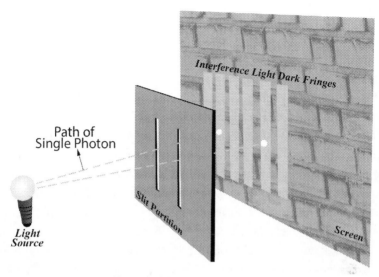

Young's Slit Lamp experiment

However, using a different detector—particle detector—two parallel lines are seen on the screen, indicating that light is found to be absorbed as though it were composed of discrete particles or photons. This establishes the principle known as **wave–particle duality.**

Also known as **Young's experiment,** this phenomenon indicates that light consists of waves, as the distribution of brightness can be explained by the alternately additive and subtractive interference of wave fronts. This single experiment played a vital part in the acceptance of the wave theory of light in the early 1800s, dismissing the theory of light proposed by Isaac Newton, which had been the accepted model of light propagation in the seventeenth and eighteenth centuries. However, the later discovery of the photoelectric effect demonstrated that under different circumstances, light can behave as if it is composed of discrete particles. These contradictory discoveries made it necessary to go beyond classical physics and take the quantum nature of light into account.

*If the physicist looks for a particle—uses particle detectors—then a particle is found (no inference, and only two lines seen on the screen). If the physicist looks for a wave—uses a wave detector—then a wave pattern is found (inference pattern seen as a series of dark and light bands). A quantum entity has a **potential** dual* *wave-particle nature, but its **actual (observed)** nature is one or the other. This is how the observer affects the outcome of the experiment.*

Clearly the two–slit experiment, for the first time in physics, indicates that there is a much deeper relationship between the observer and the phenomenon, at least at the subatomic level. This is an extreme break from the idea of an objective reality or one where the laws of nature have a special, deterministic existence.

The notion of the observer becoming a part of the observed system is fundamentally new in physics. In quantum physics, the observer is no longer external and neutral, but through the act of measurement, *he becomes a part of observed reality.* This marks the end of the neutrality of the experimenter. If in an exact science, such as physics, the outcome of an experiment depends on the view of the observer, then what does this imply for the other fields of human knowledge? It would seem that in any faculty of science, there are different interpretations of the same phenomena. More often, these interpretations are in conflict with each other. *Does this mean that the ultimate truth is unknowable?*

The results of quantum theory, and particularly of Heisenberg's work, left scientists puzzled. Many felt that quantum theory had somehow "missed the point." *Could that be the case? Are we all missing something?*

Try this experiment. Draw a couple 3 dimensional boxes on a piece of paper. Most people can easily do this.

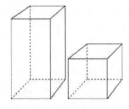

Image of 3D boxes on 2D surface

Now take one of these boxes out and put an apple inside it. I bet you cannot do this. Why?

The reason is that you cannot make a three dimensional box out of a two dimensional image. What you are observing above is not a real box, but an *image* of a box. That is the difference between our real life the way we observe it, and the truth about life. The human mind is so used to the three space dimension (and a fourth dimension of time), that it cannot easily comprehend anything outside of that mental construct. So far, based on the M-Theory, the universe is made up of eleven dimensions. This is what we are missing in the big picture!

The Soul and the Divine Consciousness: Who Are We?

As discussed previously, the subconscious mind creates an *illusion* of who we truly are. The *reality* of you (what you appear to be) is different from the *truth* about YOU. It is not intelligent enough to tell the difference. It confuses your thoughts, emotions, and actions as YOU and continues to protect them as you, your identity, and your self. It is extremely important to understand and be aware of the fact that YOU *are not your thoughts, emotions, or actions, but rather the formless soul behind those. Your mind (TFA) and body are all manifestations of YOU, not the actual YOU! YOU are your soul, the spirit, the pure Consciousness (capital c) that is of the same nature of the divine energy, intelligence, and matrix, of the same essence as the rest of the universe!* Consider a goldsmith who creates pieces of jewelry from gold. He artistically creates a beautiful golden earring of a certain size and shape. He then melts that and creates another piece, this time a fancy ring. Let's say that happens to be the apparent you. What is the apparent you made up of? Gold. What are the properties and characteristics of you? They are the unique features of that specific ring, which no one has control over but the goldsmith, the creator. What is the nature and essence of YOU? It is the matrix and formless substance that gold and all other matter was originated from. The same substance that 4.6 percent of the universe is made from!

But when it comes to humanity, there is one other major difference: *YOU also have a touch of the goldsmith, the creator! In other words, YOU are the co-creator of you and have a major role on how to relate to your past, and shape your present and future. YOU are the created (object) and co-creator (subject) at the same time—the observed and the observer. It depends on how you perceive or view the world.*

That is the whole point of these discussions. To this date, no one has entirely figured out the nature and essence of the goldsmith, the creator and source of the entire universe. Many people call it God (or similar versions in different religions), Source, Universal Intelligence, Universal Energy, Universal Matrix, etc. It may take decades, centuries, or millennia before we can find out the Truth about the source ... or maybe never! *However, we do not need to wait until then to figure out our own role in shaping our destiny and having better control over our lives!*

So let us pose this question again. What is the essence of our soul and spirit?

Deepak Chopra, one of the greatest leaders in spirituality and mind-body medicine, describes the soul or spirit very elegantly in the context of Divine Consciousness. Considering the experiments and scientific concepts explained above, this makes sense from a perspective of quantum physics. Keep in mind, though, not to confuse the Divine Consciousness (capital C) of spirituality with the conscious mind (small c, or conscious level of awareness)—an important concept in psychology discussed in previous chapters. Having said that, the two can become harmonious when you have tapped into the deepest resources of your soul and synchronized with the unlimited powers of the Universal Intelligence.

In Freud's model, the unconscious part of the psyche is the invisible wire attached to the Universal Source, and the subconscious mind entails the layers of dirt covering your light bulb, which has the potential to glow but is obstructed. *The conscious mind is generally obstructed from reaching the unlimited resources of the unconscious because of the subconscious filter.* When the mind becomes reconditioned and you become "aware," the conscious and subconscious mind become one. This is when the obstructing layers vanish, and you begin to glow, tapping into your inner, unlimited capacity for personal growth.

Imagination is one gateway to your inner soul. As Einstein stated, "Imagination is more important than knowledge." While memory is the gateway to the past, imagination is the ticket to your future. Heisenberg's uncertainty principle has proven that through imagination, you can choose your observer lens and alter your path based on *desire* and *intention*. In other words, you can co-create and redesign your destiny!

According to Chopra, everyone has an observer deep inside; everyone is observing based on interpretation, memory, and imagination and is making choices based on desire. Everyone has that common ground that is **infinite possibilities, non-local correlations, uncertainty, procreation,** and **creativity** (the five characteristics of the soul). That's what the soul is.

- Consciousness is awareness of the true nature of existence.
- Divine Consciousness does not exist in space, time, and dimension. It is formless, spaceless, timeless, and beyond dimensionality.
- Consciousness therefore never began and never ends.
- We and everything in the universe are instantly correlated in Consciousness.
- Past, present, and future are correlated in Consciousness. The only way to feel Consciousness is to shut off your brain from the past and the future, and just *be* in the present—just *be*!

The Five Attributes of Divine Consciousness and Soul

1. Field of infinite possibilities
2. Field of entanglement and synchronicity (or correlates non- locally)
3. Embraces uncertainty
4. Infinite source of creativity
5. Co-creates with God and co-creates with the mystery

1—*Infinite possibilities.* At the most basic levels of existence of nature, all is unpredictable. Consciousness is a field of infinite possibilities. Today, quantum physics has well proven this widely accepted concept.

2—*Entanglement.* Consciousness is a field of non-local correlation. In other words, everything in the universe is correlated, entangled with everything else. And the correlation occurs instantly, at the speed of light. All things in the universe are instantly correlated and entangled. The observer is the observed. Consciousness is omnipresence (being everywhere), omniscience (knowing everything), and omnipotence (capable of everything). If you are in touch with your Consciousness, you have intuitive knowledge in which you know everything you need to know when you need to know it. At the deepest part of yourself, you know everything. You don't have to learn anything.

3—*Uncertainty.* Consciousness proliferates in uncertainty. As shown by the uncertainty principle of Heisenberg, nothing as we know or see is certain. We live in an illusion, a world of perceptions. The truth is a field of infinite possibilities. It is the observer's experience that determines what the reality of matter is.

4—*Creativity.* Uncertainty enables creativity. A closed system does not enable creativity. In consciousness, there are *quantum leaps*, infinite realizations, and expressions of creativity. Every single individual on this planet has a hidden source of creativity deep within.

5—*Co-creation with God.* The physical universe does not exist unless there is a Conscious being looking at it. When we exercise Consciousness, the universe comes alive. Otherwise the universe is merely a vibration. Through your Consciousness, infinite possibilities become realities. You also have a say in how to create your world.

To demonstrate the five properties of the Divine Consciousness, consider the following experiment: Imagine you are rotating a round ball attached to a string at a constant rate of one cycle per minute. The observer is asked to look at only one spot: eight o'clock. How often does the observer spot the ball? Obviously, once per minute.

Experiment demonstrating the five attributes of Divine Consciousness

Start rotating it faster, at ten times per minute. Now it is observed ten times per minute at the same location. How many times will the observer spot the ball if you spin at a 1,000 times per minute? If you guessed 1,000 times, the answer is ... wrong. It will be observed at eight o'clock constantly at all times. Depending on the observer's distance from you, at some point, the observer will not see flickering anymore, but instead, a fixed dot. If you ask the observer to look at the center, a full circle (or its shadow) will be observed on the outside. Similarly, look at the light bulb in your room. It is constantly "on." But if you observe lights of a distant city at night, you will see flickering lights: on-off-on-off-on. That is because electrical power in most countries, is generated as an alternating current at a frequency of fifty Hz, which is observed in an interrupted pattern from a distance.

Now instead of eight o'clock, we ask the observer to look at 3 o'clock. He will see a fixed black dot. How about 11 o'clock? Again, a constant dot will be observed. It's an *illusion*. While the *truth* is that the ball is spinning at a very fast pace, what is observed as *reality* is a fixed dot at any *chosen* spot, or a full circle if the center is observed.

Now imagine what will happen if you spin the ball at the speed of light. How about if this is done in many different dimensions? How about if the string theory is true, and the ball is not only spinning in circles, but oscillating in different dimensions. You get the idea?

At any given moment, the ball is observed where the observer *chooses* to see. The ball is everywhere at the same time. The field of existence of the ball has several unique characteristics:

1. Field of infinite possibilities
2. Field of entanglement and synchronicity
3. Uncertainty
4. Infinite source of creativity
5. Co-creativity

In other words, every time the observer is looking at one spot ("on" mode), the ball will be observed at that spot, depending on where the observer *desires* to look. When the observer closes his eyes ("off" mode), the ball is everywhere in the field of existence. Now, guess which one is the truth?

In spirituality, the field of existence is our Soul. The Divine Field of Consciousness is the "off" mode of existence. When we are fully in the present, we are in "off" mode, in harmony with Consciousness. When our subconscious mind (the "noise") takes us to the past or future—which happens almost all the time in most people—we are in "on" mode, viewing and co-creating the world the way we desire to!

There is only one *truth*: the Higher Divine Consciousness, the Universal Energy. The *realities* and perceptions of the world, though, are infinite and uncertain!

From a mathematical perspective, a circle is 360 degrees. So at any *moment*, when you look at one spot, the ball occupies 1/360 of time unit, which translates into 0.3 percent of time. In other words, what you observe is only 0.3 percent of the truth, which is *your* reality. What is in the other 99.7 percent of time? Where is the ball 99.7 percent of the time? *Where you don't see it!*

The point is, the way you observe and interpret the world is only a mental construct called your "reality" and is only a very small part of the Truth. You can co-create your reality the way you desire. If you are not happy with your current life, you can co-create a new one! Our observations consist of only a fraction of the real picture, the Truth. Yet, this illusion becomes our reality in such a way that we often believe in it with no doubts in mind, and act upon it with full heart! *This raises a philosophical question. Could our entire life be only a dream, an illusion? Is it possible that death is the beginning of a new chapter, our true life?*

In my opinion, any person alive is in "on" mode for most of his/her life, except when in deep sleep or in REM, or during deep meditation and other spiritual exercises. Upon death, the *form* of you dissolves into the *formless* and eternal YOU and merges into the "off" mode for good, carrying with it all the digital data and energy it has accumulated over a lifetime. Just like the sugar cube dissolves in hot water, carrying with it the sweet taste!

PART FIVE

Social Aspects: The Outer World

CHAPTER 13

"Love is composed of a single soul inhabiting two bodies."
—Aristotle
"The hunger for love is much more difficult to
remove than the hunger for bread."
—Mother Teresa

Social Aspects of Human Beings

The Love Languages

The *art of loving and being loved* is one of the most fundamental yet sophisticated principles necessary for full achievement of personal growth. This is one of the major steps needed to complete and conquer the summit of peak potentials. *It gives meaning to life and is essential for survival.* Loving and being loved happens before birth to after death! However, the expression and meaning varies at different stages of life.

Dr. Gary Chapman, PhD in Adult Education, is the author of *The 5 Love Languages,* which has been translated into over thirty-six languages. He is a world renowned pastor, speaker, and author.

In his book, Dr. Chapman describes the five love languages as: 1) affirmation and acknowledgment; 2) acts of service; 3) gifts; 4) quality time; and 5) physical touch.

The sixth major love language, which I believe should be added, is *communication and understanding.* Making an effort to understand your partner is an extremely important element of relationships. One powerful way of feeling loved is to be understood.

While many of us have one or more love languages, usually one of these is the predominant expression of love. Remaining subconscious, this fact is often overlooked in couples. Try to find out what your partner's main love language is and bring it to their attention. Bring it to consciousness and confirm it with him or her. They love it, and you will be rewarded for taking the time to acknowledge and recognize that. They may not be aware of it until it is communicated.

Love is a two-sided road. It is not sustainable if only expressed in one direction. Also find out what your own main love language is and let your partner be aware of it. Flood your adored ones with expressions of love, day and night and on special occasions. However, make sure it is meaningful to them. When you say, "I love you," make sure you mean it! Women, in particular, know it when you're not genuine!

The expression of love, whether received or delivered, varies among individuals. *The key to a successful relationship is understanding love exchange from the other person's view!* This is a common mistake observed in relationship counseling. Through years of experience, I have learned that this point is often dismissed in troublesome relationships, being the root of many profound and long-term tensions. What love means to you may not necessarily be the same to your partner, and vice versa. *If we could learn to see through the lens of the other person, and act accordingly, many of our relationship problems would spontaneously resolve.* However, the ego (or to be more precise, the selfishness) often gets in the way. "It's all about me and my desires," not "our relationship." "I liked this, and I didn't like that." This is a common theme in dysfunctional relationships. The problem is this often remains subconscious, and the partner(s) may not be aware of it.

A similar, common scenario in the mental games of ego applies to friendships in our day-to-day life. True friendship is when you love that person as a friend for *him* or *her*, not for *you*! However, the subconscious mind often seeks to know "What's in it for me?" or

"What do I get from this friendship?" That explains why *true* friends are so scarce and hard to find these days.

Other Aspects of Love

A healthy love is the balance between love for self, love for others, and love for our source. In the preceding chapters, the fundamental principles of the human psyche were explained in detail—why and how the ego constantly thinks and acts in favor of self, ultimately to *feel pleasure* and *avoid pain.* However, the ego is not to blame. That is its job—*to serve the id, in order to maintain physical and psychological survival.* It is a universal phenomenon, and there is nothing wrong with that!

Things can go wrong, however, when there is no *balance,* and the bigger picture is overlooked. It becomes a problem when the ego is preoccupied solely by the id, fails to maintain balance, ignores the super-ego, and drives the human psyche to *selfishness. Do not forget that the ego also has another major duty—to serve the super-ego, which as our tool for social conscience functions to ensure survival of the society.* We all have a duty and obligation as human beings to respect the rights of the society we live in, as well as all other inhabitants of this world. Our survival is tied to and ultimately dependent upon the survival of the society—varying from a small community to the entire globe. *We have a duty to respect every right of other creations and maintain the balance between individual and social rights!*

Unfortunately, individual human rights are dismissed in many second and third world countries to this date. Women's and children's rights are ignored. Racial discrimination is pursued, and genocide happens in dismay. What a shame!

On the other hand, in many developed countries, social rights are compromised in the name of a "human charter of rights." For example, the dolphin slaughter in Japan and Denmark (Faroe Islands) clearly demonstrates the dark side of humans. Of course, one cannot expect all humans to be vegetarians, and hunting has been around throughout the entire human history as a way of survival. However, in this day and age of civilization, what is missing is the balance between individual and social rights. Solo or mass hunting should be allowed only in the context of humane and acceptable international rules and regulations—with respect and dignity for the hunted! Not with brutality and massacre, the way it's demonstrated in these real documentaries!

Let us understand the ego and allow it to fulfill its duties as the mediator between the id (protecting benefits of the individual) and super-ego (protecting benefits of the public). If we try to obstruct its duties by suppressing it (as most religions reinforce), the ego will utilize its powerful defense mechanisms to resist that. It will recognize it as a threat to the existence of humanity, and activate its counteractive weapons. The ultimate result—rapidly expanding mental disorders and traits we see today! It's that simple.

The Secrets of Attraction

What are the laws of attraction? Are there any principles of attraction in this universe? How can we become more attractive? Why do we even need to be attractive?

Attraction is a fundamental phenomenon, essential for reproduction and survival of generations, genetically encoded in each of our cells and evolved over billions of years. The key to survival of life over three billion years, since the first protocell (cyanobacteria), has been **reproduction**. The tree of life has evolved through *asexual reproduction* **(agamogenesis)** in the initial protocells (prokaryocytes), to *sexual reproduction* **(gamogenesis)** in the more complex cells (eukaryocytes), which later on evolved to form the fungi, plant, and animal generations. In the basic form, two organisms with complementary reproductive systems are naturally attracted to each other. This results in love making and the reproduction of offspring—and life goes on in the species.

As life became more evolved and sophisticated, so did the apparent laws of attraction. In mammals and human beings, certain physical characteristics, such as appearance, odor, and taste, are more sexually attractive than others. In the humans today, *attraction* has different forms and versions: *physical* (which may be sexual or non-sexual), and *non-physical* (mental, spiritual). In the general population, the latter is often referred to as a person's "energy level" or "karma," which can attract others. Generally speaking, high or positive energy is attractive, and low or negative energy often drives people away.

In humans, attraction seems to be involuntary and unintentional. We often do not know why we are attracted to a certain color, odor, or body figure, etc. It is a *subconscious phenomenon*, until we become aware of it after observing a repetitive pattern. This highly suggests that the related areas in the brain are predominantly subcortical (mainly in the **limbic system**). For example, most psychologists would agree that a child's sexual attractions are formed by the age of ten. *Why and how do these form in our brain? Are there any patterns among the laws of attraction?*

Well, here's the scientific theory of how attractions are formed. The completion of the initial brain structure, capable of comprehending a complex phenomenon, and making a meaningful perception of that, happens around age five. This is, of course, assuming there has been a normal development of the brain, and nothing traumatic happened at earlier ages (which could disfigure the brain pathways). At this age, the hardware is prepared to absorb a tremendous amount of information. The biological network of the midbrain—mainly the limbic system—is formed in a newborn, but not yet evolved. *It is molded gradually over the first five years of age, setting the infrastructure of a person's character. This critical period is the biggest opportunity for parents and a caring society to build the future of an individual.*

Learning, however, starts from day one of birth—or to be more accurate—in the womb. In the first five years, many simple processes are understood, but comprehending complex experiences does not happen because it requires the development of more mature centers in the brain. In addition, most people have no memories at all before the age of four or five, simply because the long-term memory centers in the cortex were not developed at very early ages. Also, this explains why children are generally not ready to start school before the age of five.

The processing and interpretation of experiences in a child in the first five years is different from his view of the world in subsequent years. In this period, a child has different understanding, feelings, thoughts, and defense mechanisms related to the world. At the critical age of five, the structure of the brain is prepared to analyze processes, form and conclude meaningful perceptions, store them in long-term memory, and solidify certain neuronal pathways in the brain. It is similar to building a high rise. Initially, the infrastructure and framework is built. Then it is time to pour the concrete layer by layer, to solidify the structure. If the infrastructure is flawed, chances are that the rest of the building will have problems. The difference is however, the concept of *neuroplasticity*. Unlike a building, the brain has the miraculous and powerful capability of *adaptive transformation*. *At any age, we are able to change our brains with proper training!*

So, what does all this have to do with attractions?

Going back to attractions, the human being is fundamentally attracted to anything that brings pleasure, as discussed previously. With pleasurable experiences and memories, certain neuronal pathways are solidified in the brain, *mainly in the limbic system*. The intensity (in one episode) or duration (in repeated similar episodes) of pleasurable experiences are two main components of how solidly these pathways are formed. This is well demonstrated in addictions. One episode of a heavy narcotic (such as cocaine), or repeated use of a milder toxic agent (such as alcohol), may both be very attractive and addictive to a person. Another equally important factor is *the feeling associated with a specific experience*. For example, if you had a very joyful experience on a speed boat when you were a child, a sports car *may* be an attraction to you in your adult years. The same is true for negative experiences. If you had a fall from a height in early ages, you *may* develop phobia for heights. If your father is tall and powerful, and you had a positive, loving relationship in your childhood, you *may* become attracted to tall men when you are an adult. Similarly, some may be sexually attracted to certain body figures or have racial preferences.

In other words, if the brain is exposed to a highly intense or repeated, similar, pleasurable experiences, it may get fixated on that experience and store it as an "attraction" in the long-term memory centers. Every time that signal or event is re-experienced, a feeling of pleasure and satisfaction ensues, and the individual may constantly seek the same exposure.

This concept has been extremely simplified for the sake of better understanding. These are just simple examples and do not apply to everyone, because how each brain experiences and perceives the world is much more sophisticated. There are numerous other factors that play a role in the building structure of one's brain and character.

These were examples of physical attractions. How about non-physical attractions? What is the secret of being attractive?

How do you feel around a person with a "negative" vibe? How about a "positive" one? Instinctually and subconsciously, all humans seek the notion of "feeling good." Thriving on the positive energy of people around makes you feel good! That is essentially why people with high or positive energy are generally attractive, and vice versa! *The secret of being attractive is to find a way to make others feel good about themselves.* Use the five (or six) love languages. Give compliments to people, entertain them, help them, understand them, teach them something, help them grow, give any sort of positive energy, and they will love you.

In general, there are two ways to be attractive: *passive* or *active*. You are passively (naturally) attractive if you have a beautiful appearance, body, voice, funny or positive character, etc. But do not worry if you don't have any of these. You can still be just as attractive, if not more! *That is by making an effort to attract others.* Just remember a simple secret— find a way to make them feel good! People would do anything to feel good. Remember that the most basic and fundamental human motive is to feel pleasure and to avoid pain. Why do people go to movies? To feel good. Why do people go dancing? To feel good. Why do people eat chocolate? It makes them feel good. Why do people drink alcohol? It makes them feel good. Why do people love celebrities? They make them feel good. Why do people abuse illicit drugs? To feel good. Why do people take revenge? They feel good (even if it's short term, and they may have regrets later on).

So if you want to be attractive, the trick is to do something to make people feel good, and they will love you. Everyone in this world is unique and has something beautiful to be admired. *Find that thing in the person, reflect it to them, and watch their reaction!*

Confidence and Attraction

A person's self-image is extremely important in his/her influence on other people. Self-love and self-confidence subconsciously express strength and create a very powerful way of being attractive. This may be both *passive* (natural from early childhood) or *active* (a learned skill later on in life). The theory behind this is again related to the fundamental principle of survival. The need for survival is deeply embedded in the subcortical layers of our brain, genetically encoded and evolved over millions of years (the primitive and intermediate brain layers in the ice cream analogy). *Any source of strength is a security line and increases the chances of survival during moments of uncertainty. In the more sophisticated species, including humans, there is a fundamental and universal attraction toward anything strong and powerful, expressed in all physical and non-physical forms.*

One of the issues that come up regularly during counseling in Sexual Medicine is challenges of attraction. These are some common themes encountered:

Case 1—"I'm interested in someone. I don't know how to attract her. I'm afraid to approach her."

Case 2—"Do I look good? For some reason, I can't seem to attract others."

Case 3—"No matter how hard I try, the person I'm interested in keeps running away from me!"

Case 4—"My boyfriend is a jerk. He treats me like s— ... But I can't leave him. I don't know what to do."

As discussed earlier, attractiveness is not all about the looks. Non-physical attraction plays a very significant role in human relationships, and confidence is a very powerful non-physical means of attraction.

Case 1. There are a couple issues. In this scenario, we are talking about a one-sided apparent interest from you. The first thing is to let the other person know you're interested. If you don't somehow show her, she simply might not know. The best way is to directly make her aware, either through verbal or non-verbal communication (facial and body gestures).

The second major issue is **fear of rejection**. This shows your lack of confidence. *Do not be afraid of being rejected.* Think about the worst thing that can happen. She may say no! Well thank her for the opportunity to talk, and walk away with no fear. I guarantee there will be plenty of other opportunities. If you are really interested, then don't give up. Try again and again on different occasions. *What you do not* *want to do is sound desperate! This is key to success.* Here's why: the answer lies in the **paradox** of attraction.

Remember, attraction is a subconscious phenomenon. Sexual energy and temptation lies in the limbic system (emotional and immature), not in the neocortex (rational thinking). The subcortical layers of the brain have been genetically coded to be attracted to anything that helps us *survive*. Strength, power, confidence, and beauty are all attractive subconsciously. On the other hand, despair is a sign of weakness and is not attractive—no matter how hard you try. Fear of rejection—which can be easily sensed—is another sign of weakness. On the contrary, repeated effort to express interest *without* despair can be perceived as a sign of determinism and strength, and will increase your chance of success!

Fear of rejection is worth expanding, since it is an extremely common challenge among youngsters. Let us use the TFA model in chapter 3 (see diagram below).

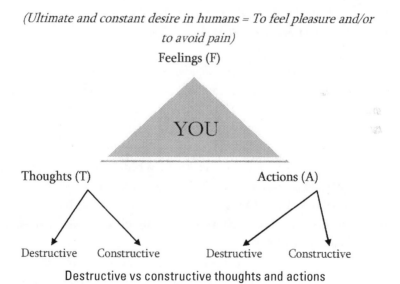

(Ultimate and constant desire in humans = To feel pleasure and/or to avoid pain)

Feelings (F)

YOU

Thoughts (T)　　　　　　　　　　Actions (A)

Destructive　Constructive　　　Destructive　Constructive

Destructive vs constructive thoughts and actions

The feeling (F) associated with being rejected is painful. As a result, the thought (T) of that, which stems from lack of confidence, does not allow one to take any actions (A). The subconscious mind within the ego avoids rejection for reasons discussed in previous chapters. In many individuals, thoughts such as the following find a place in the subconscious mind: *If this person rejects me, that means I'm not worth being loved. I'm not good enough. I will not attract anyone. I cannot find a sex mate. I cannot reproduce. I will not survive.* This misconception may turn into a **false belief** if repeated and solidified. Once turned into a belief, it can significantly damage the self-image, self-confidence, and ability to grow. It turns into a vicious cycle and can further affect future relationships, or even many other aspects of life.

Remember that by changing one arm of the triangle, the other arms will change. As part of cognitive therapy, one extremely powerful way to break this cycle is to use *conscious thinking* as opposed to *subconscious. This requires the skill to see outside the box, to question your own mind (subconscious), using a different lens within your mind (conscious)!*

In this scenario, question your destructive subconscious thoughts and replace them with more constructive, realistic, conscious thoughts, such as: *What am I afraid of? So what if she rejects me? Am I really not worth loving? Am I truly incapable of finding someone who would be interested in me? Maybe not! I haven't even tried approaching her. She may or may not respond. What do I think of myself? I think I am a good person. I think I am worth loving. I have so many friends. I have had partners in the past who were interested in me. Even if she does not like me, that does not necessarily mean that there is something wrong with me. I may simply not be her type. Or maybe she is just not ready now. Maybe she is too shy to respond now. Maybe I should try more. Even if I try, and she still does not respond, I should not take that personally. I have no reason to believe that I cannot find a mate in the future* … and so on!

The whole point is to understand what is initially going on in your subconscious mind. You need to use your conscious mind to realize that! Once you come to that realization, it is much easier to replace them with conscious, more realistic, and rational thoughts!

The concepts above also apply to cases 2, 3, and 4. In case 4, apart from low self-esteem, another very important factor plays a role— **fear of abandonment**. How can anyone be attracted to a jerk? We are not talking about one or two incidences. We are talking about a *character*—about a demeaning habitual behavior and arrogant attitude toward others.

On the contrary, being a gentleman or nice is a positive attractive characteristic. But you may find it surprising that many individuals are "turned off" by nice individuals. *How come? What is going on in the mind?*

Again, the answer lies in the **paradox** of attraction. This becomes clearer when you try to see through their mind. Through that person's lens, being nice may be confused with being naive, and therefore be *misinterpreted* as a sign of weakness. Subconsciously, this may be incompatible with survival! On the other hand, arrogance and lack of regards for others may be misperceived as confidence and needlessness, which can be interpreted as signs of inner strength. *After all, attraction is a subconscious phenomenon.*

CHAPTER 14

"Love is the answer, but while you are waiting for the answer, sex raises some pretty good questions."
—*Unknown*

Sexuality

Case 1

CD is a twenty-three-year-old fitness trainer who has been living with her twenty-nine-year-old boyfriend for two years. They have sex once a week. CD is unhappy with her sex life and angry at her boyfriend. She is not happy with the frequency of sex and believes her boyfriend is not attracted to her, which makes her feel upset and frustrated. She states that everyday sex was the usual in her previous relationship (she only had one other boyfriend in the past and no other experiences). She has lost her confidence and fears their relationship may fall apart due to this problem. She thinks *he* has some kind of sexual problem and needs to seek help. The boyfriend agrees with the frequency of sex, but does not see that as a problem, and does not think he has any sexual problems. He still finds CD very attractive physically and claims his feelings for her have not changed at all. They both agreed that they are spending less quality time together, and other things in life have become more important than sex. Apart from their sexual problems, there are no other conflicts.

After a thorough assessment, psychosexual education and brief sexual counseling was offered. The issue of *sexual dissatisfaction* (rather than *sexual dysfunction*) was clarified, and CD was reassured that her boyfriend does not have any physical abnormalities. Once the traffic light analogy—which will be discussed shortly—was explained, they were able to observe and disclose some minor issues that were interrupting the sex cycle. With minor advice and homework, they were able to come to a common ground (twice a week), and their sex life and relationship noticeably improved within a couple months.

Case 2

EF is a forty-one-year-old anthropologist. His second wife is a thirty-six-year-old nurse. They have been married for five years. In the last year, the frequency of sex has declined to once every one to two months. Their relationship is falling apart, and they are both frustrated at each other. They came to my clinic for help.

EF is polygamous. His idea of male sexuality is interesting and provocative. "It is completely normal for a man to seek multiple sexual partners. This is an ordinary change in human evolution," he mentioned as he gave reference to articles about male polygamy in other animals. He thought it is important to be honest with his wife. In the beginning, they had an open relationship, and as long as they were both honest, each partner was allowed to have other sex mates.

Upon interview, it was revealed that the wife gave in at the beginning but soon found out that she could not be polygamous. She surrendered to her husband's request and allowed him to continue his multiple sexual affairs but gradually became depressed. EF claimed that the only woman he loved was his wife, and all other sexual affairs were purely "physical." His wife became not only less interested, but also aversive toward sex. She was resentful toward EF and was considering separation. "I cannot live like this anymore," she wept hopelessly. On the other hand, EF was angry at her for not understanding his natural right to polygamy—and here I am, wondering where to even begin!

The issue of diverse sexual desire in males is not unique to EF. Throughout my years of medical experience, I was curious to learn about the validity of this theory. Many religions have openly allowed polygamy as the obvious right of men. That aside, the right to polygamy is not an uncommon belief among many males, regardless of culture, nationality, or religion. Many are honestly polygamous through open relationships, or dishonestly through infidelity. On the contrary, another group of men does not think it is fair to their partner once in a committed relationship, even if they do have the desire for multiple sexual partners. Believing in a theory is one thing, acting upon it is another. A third group does not have the desire for diversity at all.

The notion that *a woman seeks many things in one man, while a man seeks one thing in many women* is a very controversial and debatable topic. Anecdotally, based on casual observations, there seems to be some truth to that. However, from a scientific and evidence-based view, I was not able to find sufficient evidence to support this theory in humans.

One may argue, *If this theory is proven to be correct scientifically, and men are biologically evolved to have multiple sex partners, does that mean polygamy is the right of men, and social laws should be changed around that?*

Could this possibly be one of the reasons for sexual disinterest (at least in males) in long-term relationships? Is it possible that suppression of the desire for polygamy may lead to over-inhibition of sexual desire all together, and lead to sexual monotony?

Well, here is my personal opinion about these provocative inquiries. Regardless of the science or philosophy behind this, the question is whether a relationship is "healthy" or "unhealthy." A healthy relationship is tied to a person's mental health and overall personal development. As shown in the proposed modified Maslow's pyramid, a mutually loving relationship is necessary for healthy development of the first and mainly the second stage of personal growth. Sexual desire, whether to one or multiple partners, is part of *id*—the least mature of our psychic apparatus—mainly embedded in the lower functioning parts of our brain. But remember, we also have the higher cortical parts in our brain, and the more conscientious *super-ego* in our psyche. In order to maintain the entirety of a healthy psyche, mind, and brain, we must **balance** the desires of the *id* versus those of the *super-ego*, the needs of the *self* versus those of *others*, the desires of *individual* versus those of the *society*. And that is exactly the responsibility of our *ego*!

Going back to the case of EF, it is not my job to agree or disagree with his ideology. It is my duty, however, to help the couple by reflecting where some of those thoughts and feelings may interrupt the sex response cycle and damage their relationship. That is exactly what I did, which was helpful.

Open relationships are common among many couples, and I personally would not discourage it, as long as both partners are *genuinely* and *honestly* okay with it. The key word is genuinely. If one partner agrees just to please the other, the problem remains unresolved, and resentment will build over time, as was the case with EF. If she disagrees, other means of therapy may be needed, and one or both partners may have to compromise and come to a common ground.

Do not harm others physically, mentally, or emotionally. In this case, EF had to weigh the balance between the pain of emotionally hurting his loved wife and the pleasure of multiple sex partners. As described previously, **cognitive dissonance** was the main force causing internal conflicts within, and external tension between the partners.

This was one of the more challenging cases, which required multiple counseling visits. He finally came to peace with himself (**cognitive consonance**), and they were able to sustain their relationship and revive the sex life.

Case 3

GH is a forty-five-year-old teacher from Afghanistan. His thirty-one-year-old wife is unemployed. They have been married for thirteen years. They have a loving and stable relationship. However, GH has a sexual problem that is hidden from his wife. He learned about my clinic and came in to seek help. He did not want his wife involved in therapy.

GH loved his wife but was not keen on having sex anymore. He was hiding something from her, which he thought was "evil."

"I have these fantasies," he said shamefully. "Well, do you want to share them with me?" I asked to open discussion.

"I am very interested in oral sex and kinky sex," (the technical term is BDSM), "but I cannot do any of that with my wife. I have been thinking of cheating on her lately, but I feel bad. I don't know what to do."

"Kinky sex is a whole range of sexual practices. Is there one specific act you are interested in?" I asked.

"I get really excited when I watch men and women being tied up with a rope and having sex. Especially tying up the woman," he opened up.

"Did you know there are many other men like you who are interested in these sexual activities? Many men and women may have a preferred sexual practice. Help me understand why you cannot practice these fantasies with your wife."

"In my culture, having oral sex is bad. Kinky sex is even worse; my wife would think I'm crazy!"

"How do you know? Have you ever opened a discussion with your wife?"

"It's a cultural thing, especially in my family."

"But do you realize this is your assumption, which may or may not be true? If you have never discussed it with your wife, how could you be sure she thinks the same way you do?"

After many other conversations, I said, "You have choices, and you are responsible for the consequences of the choices you make. You can continue like this and compromise your sex life, or you can choose to cheat on your wife, or you can try to make it work with her. Which one would you like to choose?"

"Well, I'm here because I love my wife and don't want to cheat on her. I'd like to make it work with her," he expressed as his eyes shined with tears.

"I might be able to help you if you are willing to cooperate," I said cautiously.

"Please help me. I'm open to any suggestions," he said eagerly.

"I know it may be a bit challenging for you, but are you open to the idea of involving your wife in therapy?"

"It is very difficult to talk about these things, but I'm willing to give it a try," he replied after a long, thoughtful hesitation.

I provided some brief psychosexual education, which made sense to him, and he left with the hope of inviting his wife to the next session.

In my experience, this theme is more common among less sexually permissive cultures—many from Eastern countries, but also not uncommon in the Western societies. A detailed assessment and interview with GH revealed key points. He had learned through pornography and other sexual tools that there are many other sexual practices outside of his norm, and he had developed fantasies about some of them. However, somewhere in the subconscious mind, it was written that those activities only belonged to porn stars and evil women. He thought of them only as "sex slaves," another subconscious mechanism called *objectification*. His wife was not evil in his mind; therefore, he could not exercise those fantasies with her. This is referred to as "splitting"—black and white with nothing in between, a common defense mechanism in men, especially from sexually prohibited cultures. This was the main *cognitive dissonance*, creating inner tension and conflict. As a result, the subconscious mind used *suppression* as a defense mechanism to dismiss those desires. Over time, this led to the inhibition of sex all together and lack of interest. Many other destructive defense mechanisms may be expressed if a fundamental need or desire is not properly addressed or replaced.

Over several visits, he had extensive sexual counseling. The difference between pornography (destructive) versus erotica (constructive) was explained. Through cognitive therapy, he realized that there was nothing wrong with certain sexual practices, as long as the boundaries are respected and there is no physical, emotional, or mental harm involved, and both partners are in agreement. The negative image was the *feeling* and *thoughts* he attached to the porn stars because of objectification. And that is exactly why certain porn movies, in which the soul and spirit are taken away from the act of sex, can be destructive. Whereas in erotica, the act of sex is often associated with the spirit of love! Once the neuronal pathways were undone, and his cognition was reset, GH was able to combine his fantasies with love and have a fruitful sex life with his wife. His *cognitive dissonance* turned into *cognitive consonance,* and the internal conflicts diminished. Of course, this would not have been possible without the in-depth understanding, love, and cooperation of his wife!

Sexual Disinterest

One of the most common problems encountered in Sexual Medicine is **sexual disinterest** among couples. It is much more common in long-term relationships. A significant number of couples lose sexual interest within six to eighteen months into a long-term relationship.

Undoubtedly, sex is critical not only for reproduction, but also to maintain a healthy long-term relationship. From an individual perspective, our belief system and how we view sex—whether good or bad—plays a significant role in sexual performance. Also, the society we live in, sexual taboos, the media, and other cultural factors have a significant role in determining ideal standards and norms for sexuality.

It is necessary to distinguish between **sexual dysfunction**—which is often within one individual—and **sexual dissatisfaction** between two partners. The issue we are talking about is the latter, often resulting from lack of harmony between the partners' expectations and understanding of sex. There are many couples who have sex once a month or less, and they are both absolutely fine with that. There is no problem here. On the contrary, a couple may have sex every day, but one or both partners may not be happy with its quantity or quality. Here, we do have a problem that is worth exploring.

The following are some "reasons for not having enough sex" offered by couples who seek therapy for the lack of it.

- "He/she just doesn't turn me on."
- "We're too old for sex—it's only natural not to want it after you're forty!"
- "We simply don't have enough time to have sex, with the family and the business and all the pressures we face."
- "Sometimes I think it'd be nice, but it seems like too much effort."
- "Sex is never as good when you've been doing it with the same person for so long."
- "He just doesn't turn me on like he used to when we first met. He was muscular and slim then. Look at him now."
- "She's put on some weight."

Couples in long-term relationships use statements like these to try to explain the absence of sex. And even when they do have sex, it may just be an attempt to make themselves feel better, or to pacify their partner who gives signs of wanting more. All of these reasons, by the way, are okay to be sexually active.

So, here is the million-dollar question. *Why does sexual desire and satisfaction decline in many long-term relationships?*

The simple answer is *no one really knows for sure.* But there appear to be multiple factors involved. The following will outline some of these explanations from a bio-psycho-social perspective.

Sex and the Brain

Alfred Kinsey and his colleagues at Indiana University published two volumes on sexual behavior in the human male and female in 1948 and 1953—known as the Kinsey Reports—both of which had been revolutionary and controversial in their time. Kinsey's work, however, had mainly investigated the frequency with which certain behaviors occurred in the population and was based on personal interviews, not on laboratory observations.

In contrast, the Masters and Johnson research team, composed of William Masters and Virginia Johnson, set about to study the structure, psychology, and physiology of sexual behavior, through observing and measuring masturbation and sexual intercourse in the laboratory. They pioneered research into the nature of human sexual response and the diagnosis and treatment of sexual disorders and dysfunctions from 1957 until the 1990s.

One of the most enduring and important aspects of their work has been the four-stage model of sexual response, which they described as *the human sexual response cycle.* They defined the four stages of this cycle as:

1. **Excitement** phase (initial arousal)
2. **Plateau** phase (at full arousal, but not yet at orgasm)
3. **Orgasm**
4. **Resolution** phase (after orgasm)

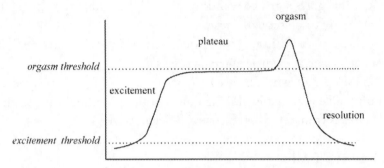

Masters and Johnson's model of the human sexual response cycle

Masters and Johnson's findings also revealed that men undergo a refractory period following orgasm during which they are not able to ejaculate again, whereas there is no refractory period in women: this makes women capable of multiple orgasms. Sexual arousal for most people is a positive experience. When a person fails to be aroused in a situation that would normally produce arousal, and that this remains persistent, it may be due to a **sexual arousal disorder** or **hypoactive sexual desire disorder** (HSDD). There are many reasons why a person fails to be aroused, including mental disorders such as depression, substance abuse, or other physical conditions. The lack of sexual arousal may be due to a general lack of sexual desire or due to a lack of desire for the current partner. A person may always have had low sexual desire (or no desire at all), or this problem may have been acquired sometime during his/her life.

In order to explore the mystery of sexual disinterest, let us go back to the basics and analyze the function of the brain, which is the largest sex organ in the body, and interpret this in the context of sexual function.

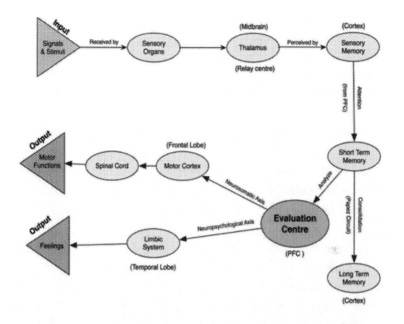

Thought process in the brain

- The sex response cycle starts with *sexual signals* or *stimuli*. These can be *external* or *internal signals*. External signals can be visual (through the eye), auditory (ear), gustatory (taste), olfactory (smell), or tactile (touch). Watching a porn magazine, or the sound of moaning and groaning of the couple having sex next door are some examples. They can also be internal signals, such as previous memories or fantasies.

- As shown in the illustration above, these signals end up in the **evaluation center** of the brain. Here, all the factors related to the past, present, and future are calculated and analyzed in a fraction of a second.

  Any previous belief and negative image of sex, tabboo, or principle may hinder the progression of the sexual response cycle. If you are cuddling with your fiance, but your culture does not permit premarital intercourse, don't expect any magic to happen. Also, all present contexual factors need to be in place. Is this the right person? Is this the right time? Or place? Are there any distractions? And so on. Future factors, such as the prediction of pain during intercourse (if you have had previous painful experiences), may turn you off as well.

• After all these considerations, the virtual evaluating center of the brain announces the final verdict. My favorite analogy is the traffic light. If the light is *red,* the result is a complete turn off, and the signals do not even reach the *excitement threshold (*Masters and Johnson mountain diagram) into the *excitement phase.* If it is *yellow*, the signals will trigger some excitement and pleasure, but fluctuate up and down, and will not progress to the *plateau* and *orgasmic phase.* If the light is *green*, however, a smooth progression all the way to a successful and memorable orgasm is expected to happen.

During the yellow and green lights, the electrical impulses from the evaluation center send weak and strong signals respectively, through the *neurosomatic axis* (shown in the diagram above), all the way down through the spinal cord to the genitals, and stimulates the arousal response (excitement). Concurrently, they send electrochemical messages through the *neuropsychological axis* and the *limbic system* to generate a very pleasant feeling and mood.

In summary, the problem in sexual disinterest is simply the disconnection at the level of the *neurosomatic* and *neuropsychological axis.* It acts like an invisible gate that opens only if the light is green (or weakly when yellow). Keep in mind, however, these are virtual axes, and the specific physical neuronal pathways have yet to be identified with the advancement of technology and science.

So, let us go back to the challenging initial question. *Why does sexual desire and satisfaction decline in many long-term relationships?*

In long-term relationships, there are many factors that do not exist in a new one, turning the "sexual light" red or yellow. Some of these factors include:

- Past contextual factors: cultural taboos, unresolved anger or resentment from the past, previous painful experiences (more common after menopause in women due to vaginal atrophy), suppressed fantasies, etc.
- Present factors: decreased physical attraction to partner (due to natural changes in body), sexual boredom and loss of sexual adventure (*nothing new to be discovered anymore, everything is routine*), current anger or resentment, distractions (*baby sleeping in same room*), lack of attention to sex (*not a priority anymore*), concurrent worries (about many other more important things in life), medical conditions (diabetes, multiple sclerosis, decreased male and female hormones, smoking, etc.).
- Future factors: expected physical pain (due to similar unrewarding experiences), future worries and distractions (finances, mortgages, future of children), etc.

In sexual medicine, one of the most important aspects of diagnosis and treatment is taking a detailed history and understanding the roots of the problem. As demonstrated, sex is a very complex bio-psycho-socio-spiritual phenomenon, and that's exactly the approach that needs to be taken. When the fundamental issue(s) is identified, it is much more manageable, using a variety of medical and psychotherapeutic interventions, including individual psychotherapy (IP), cognitive-behavioral therapy (CBT), group therapy (GT), relationship counseling, pharmacotherapy, and so on. Often times, when the problem is complex and profound, deeply embedded in the subconscious mind, there may be no cure at all, or it may take years of ongoing therapy. If cure is not possible, healing remains the main focus of management.

CHAPTER 15

"We must rapidly begin the shift from a thing-oriented society to a person-oriented society. When machines and computers, profit motives and property rights are considered more important than people, the giant triplets of racism, militarism, and economic exploitation are incapable of being conquered. A nation can flounder as readily in the face of moral and spiritual bankruptcy as it can through financial bankruptcy."
—Dr. Martin Luther King

Money and Mind

History of Money

In the beginning, people bartered. *Barter* is the exchange of a good or service for another good or service, a bag of rice for a bag of beans. However, what if you couldn't agree what something was worth in exchange, or you didn't want what the other person had? To solve that problem, humans developed what is called **commodity money,** which is a basic item used by almost everyone. In the past, salt, rice, tobacco, cattle, and tea were commodities and therefore used as money. However, using commodities as money had other problems. Carrying bags of salt and other commodities was hard, and they were difficult to store or were perishable.

Metal objects were introduced as money around 5000 BC. Metal was used because it was readily available, easy to work with, and could be recycled. Since coins were given a certain value, it became easier to compare the cost of items people wanted.

The history of money then evolved into paper money, dating back to China, where the issue became common from about 960 AD onwards. With the introduction of paper currency and non-precious coinage, commodity money evolved into **representative money**. In other words, what money itself was made of, no longer had to be valuable. Representative money was backed by a government or bank's promise to exchange it for a certain amount of silver or gold. For example, the old British pound bill was once guaranteed to be redeemable for a pound of sterling silver. For most of the nineteenth and twentieth centuries, the majority of currencies were based on representative money through the use of the **gold standard**.

The next stage of financial development was one of the most critical periods of human history, creating wealth for many, while collectively leading humanity toward a major global catastrophe—the invention of the *fractional reserve system* in the Western financial world. This means that major national and global banks are allowed to print bank notes nine times the true value of their clients' deposits. In other words, they can generate 90 percent of their wealth out of nothing—a false value. The fact of the matter—something you may not like to hear—is that despite the common misperception that national banks are governed by the government in protection of the public, that is actually not the case. Major banks, such as the Federal Reserve Bank of America, the European Central Bank, etc., are owned and run by gigantic private corporations and are designed to create wealth for their shareholders. That's it. These banks make their money by lending it to ordinary people and charging interest. Now it's the borrower's problem to come up with principal and interest to repay the loan, whether it's a credit card, loan, or mortgage. On the same token, with the apparently increased buying power of the public—which can falsely appear to be a sign of economic strength—the corporations massively feed on human greed, driving consumerism to its peak and beyond.

A national currency issued by private banks with a capacity of 9:1 "reserve ratio" drives the entire nation toward a debt-based economy, which means there is never enough money among all the borrowers to pay back all the debt. Only through continuous demand for economic growth, and ongoing borrowing, the cycle of economy can function— or rather dysfunction. At some point, however, without the proper economic infrastructure, the domino style collapse of this system is inevitable, and that is in fact what we're observing today as the global financial crisis. Meanwhile, the major banks, protected by the government through taxpayers' money, are the real winners, having accumulated unimaginable wealth.

Consumerism and Greed

The main focus of this chapter is how money and the human psychology around it can impact your life as well as the lives of others.

The discussion of how and when consumerism started is debatable and beyond the scope and purpose of this book. The desire to consume has been around for thousands of years. However, the full-blown, commercialized consumption that most wealthy nations exercise today has only become a trend in the last few centuries. During the seventeenth and eighteenth centuries, there was a gradual emergence of a new ideology, accepting the pursuit of consumer goods as a valid object of human endeavor. During the eighteenth century, the enormous wealth coming from the colonized countries contributed immensely to an industrial revolution in England and other parts of Europe. With this and the growing merchant class, consumerism slowly captivated the culture of many people.

After the Great Depression (1929–1939) and World War II (1939–1945), North America had a major leap in economic growth and consumerism. This was because there was a big jump in money, and low inflation enabled mass population to purchase goods.

To be fair and more accurate, consumerism per se is not the culprit. The major problem is **greed,** as the devastating complication of consumerism. Greed is a social illness, defined as *an **excessive** desire to acquire or possess more than what one needs or deserves, especially with respect to material wealth.* The key word here is *excessive.*

Today, human greed has become a global epidemic and a major threat to the existence of the entire planet. Rapid growth in global population, emerging markets outside North America and Europe, "Westernization" of cultures throughout the world, change in purchasing mechanisms and strategies (such as credit cards), international trade agreements, and many other factors play a role in the exponential growth of global consumerism and greed. The momentum has picked up, and the snowball effect is likely to perish the *limited* global resources, unless a **change** in culture occurs today!

The dilemma is that the rate of exponential growth in greed among the world's population far exceeds its collective mental and cognitive capacity, creating an imbalance between the unlimited desires of human beings and their social conscience.

The Art of Contentment

The source of all mentally created dissatisfactions appears to stem from comparing real-life experiences to what is defined in the mind as "ideal." Many religions believe this was caused by man eating of the forbidden Tree of the Knowledge of Good and Evil. "Man's eyes were opened to know the distinction between good and evil" (Genesis 3:5). The solution is to seek out ways to either make experienced reality conform to the ideal, or to lower expectations to the level of the experienced. *When one can live in the moment with expectations that are in harmony with experiences, one has achieved the greatest mental contentment possible.*

So, what is the ultimate motive in human life?

As mentioned in previous chapters, the most fundamental roots of all human behavior and the motives behind it boil down to two things; *avoid pain* and/or *obtain pleasure,* both of which are genetically designed to ensure *survival* at the most basic level of body and mind as a system! Both pain and pleasure are feelings (F). The TFA triangle demonstrates how they affect our thoughts (T) and actions (A).

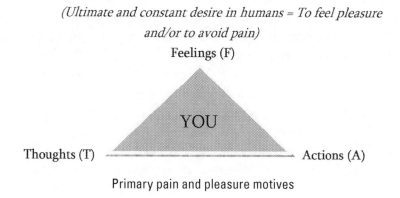

(Ultimate and constant desire in humans = To feel pleasure and/or to avoid pain)
Feelings (F)

YOU

Thoughts (T) ——————————— Actions (A)

Primary pain and pleasure motives

Ultimate happiness is a universal desire. This feeling (F) is what every individual pursues in one way or another. As explained previously, Seligman and like-minded researchers have concluded that happiness has three main components:

1. Getting more pleasure out of life (physically or mentally)
2. Becoming more engaged in what you do
3. Finding ways of making your life more meaningful

Ultimately when you break down all these three components, what they boil down to is the physical or emotional sense of pleasure, which the person attaches to a specific experience.

Taking into account all the external and internal factors, it is the ultimate *feeling of pain or pleasure* within each person that drives him/her to the next step in life, whether short viewed or long. All the thoughts (T) and actions (A) in every single individual on this planet revolve around short-term or long-term avoidance of pain or fulfillment of pleasure. Nevertheless, there is a major difference between **happiness** and **inner tranquility (contentment)**, which is often misunderstood in the general population. Happiness is a state of *mind*, resulting from the balance between the brain's neurotransmitters (dopamine, serotonin, endorphins, etc.). It is often situational and temporary. It may vary daily, weekly, or monthly depending on the circumstances we are in. Good news will make us happy.

Contentment, on the other hand, is a state of the *psyche*, resulting from a balance between our psychic apparatus *(id, ego, and super-ego)*. It is an overview of how satisfied or dissatisfied we are in our life. It is not situational, but rather a long-term and generalized phenomenon. It does not change rapidly. One situation or incident does not change our level of contentment. Owning a Ferrari may make you happy for a while, but will not bring contentment!

An analogy would be the difference between being *wealthy* and being *rich*. By general standards, wealth is determined by how much money or material valuables one possesses. You are wealthy if you own a lot of money or properties, etc. Richness (or abundance), however, is how needless you feel inside, regardless of how much money or valuables you may have. Rich people always have more than they need. A rich person may or may not be wealthy. Similarly, someone who is wealthy may or may not be rich inside. *Wealth is guided by external standards while richness is guided internally. Wealth is measured by what is in your pocket, whereas richness is measured by what is in your heart and mind!* If you always have a pattern of having less than what you need, you will always be poor (even if you become a billionaire), and if you constantly have more than what you need, you will always be rich (even if you do not own a lot of money).

The key point often misunderstood is this: **While wealth can bring you happiness, it is richness that can bring you contentment!**

How many people do you know of that have millions of dollars and are still struggling for more? What is the magic number? When is it enough? On the contrary, many individuals do not have many valuables but have *more than what they need in their mind. They do not feel insecure and financially threatened!* I have chosen to pursue richness in my life, and I'm there already while being far from wealthy. Which one would you choose to pursue?

Today, there is no question that money is a powerful vehicle to help achieve your goals. However, one of the most critical confusions is that *money in itself has become the ultimate goal for many!* That's when one has fallen into the trap of greed, and there is no way out unless there is a change in cognition. Once plagued with greed, there is no finish line, and one is doomed to lifetime struggle and discontentment! Money is not the destination, but *one* of the vehicles in your journey!

Am I suggesting to stop making efforts to grow financially? Or to give up your financial dreams? Absolutely not! *Money does not necessarily bring happiness, but poverty will most likely bring you unhappiness!*

All I'm saying is to learn the art of being content and living in peace. Learn the distinction between *happiness* and *contentment.* Be grateful for what you have and try for more while remaining peaceful inside. *It is the cognition and vision that are key to inner tranquility.* To be able to view material possessions as "toys," as opposed to the goal and destination, while enjoying the journey of achievements without despair. Achievements, financial success, and possessions, are all part of your personal growth—the second stage of modified Maslow's pyramid. *They should not be dismissed (as advised in some religions and beliefs).* Be content and continue to grow into the third level of personal growth, and you will bypass greed to the ultimate source of wealth and happiness!

My father taught me at a young age, "For every one person ahead of you, there are thousands behind you. When you feel unhappy with your financial state, look back, and when you are too confident, look ahead!"

CHAPTER 16

"Where ignorance is our master, there is no possibility of real peace."
—Dalai Lama

Mind and Conflict

Crime and the Mind

In chapter 1, you read the true story of two teenagers receiving the death penalty in Iran in 1997 for committing first-degree murder of a taxi driver. Here's another true story that you may find disturbing and actually happened around the same time in the same place.

I was instructed by my superior officer to attend a criminal investigation. As we were sitting in the backseat of a police patrol truck, he went on to debrief me about what had happened.

A young, premarital lady had a secret affair with a stranger. Premarital relationships are forbidden and highly disgraced in certain cultures around the world, including many rural areas in Iran. To add to this drama, she became pregnant from her boyfriend. While trying hard to secretly have an abortion, her parents found out about it. They had a family meeting, consisting of the parents, the grandmother, and uncle, to decide on the fate of their daughter. The verdict was clear—to murder their daughter. The only question was how. Unfortunately, the young lady was strangled to death, and the grandmother accepted the responsibility of burying her body. We were now on our way to excavate the body for criminal investigation.

With chills in my body, I was told that the grandmother was actually in the front police vehicle, guiding us to the burial site.

Upon arrival, two junior recruits were given shovels to excavate the corpse. I could sense the shock and disturbance in their faces as they hesitantly started shoveling. After a few minutes, the grandmother, who was watching impatiently and was frustrated with the slow pace of the process, grabbed the shovel from one of them and started shoveling fast and furiously, as if her attitude was shouting, "You guys are too timid for this task." I became aware that she had full pride in her act and showed no remorse whatsoever. Soon, parts of the skeleton were unveiled. The most disturbing scene was when several baby bones appeared on the surface!

Why do some people commit crimes regardless of the consequences? Why is crime rate increasing throughout the world? What are the root causes of crime? How can it be reduced or prevented?

Over the last fifty years, almost every country in Western Europe and North America has experienced a significant increase in crime rates. Violence has been recognized as a leading health problem with worldwide impact. Neighborhoods that once were safe at night have become dangerous during the day. Random acts of violence, once almost unknown, have become common.

The United States experienced a dramatic rise in homicides in the late 1980s, which continued into the mid-1990s. The homicide rate is 5.6 per 100,000. Gunshot deaths are the leading cause, accounting for 49 percent of violent deaths. In addition, approximately 4.3 million violent acts are committed in the United States yearly. In excess of 1.8 million emergency department visits yearly are made due to violent injury. The total costs associated with nonfatal injuries and deaths due to violence in 2000 were estimated to be at least $70 billion.

Victims suffer from much more than the immediate wounds inflicted by acts of violence; depression, anxiety, fear, posttraumatic stress syndrome, and substance abuse are other complications. Additionally, adolescent victims are more likely themselves to become perpetrators of violence (17).

Causes and Risk Factors for Crime

Throughout history, people have tried to explain what causes abnormal social behavior, including crime. In the seventeenth century, European colonists in North America considered crime and sin the same thing. They believed evil spirits possessed those who did not conform to social norms or follow rules. To maintain social order in the settlements, persons who exhibited antisocial behavior had to be dealt with harshly.

By the twenty-first century, sociologists and criminologists looked to a wide range of factors to explain why a person would commit a crime. These included biological, psychological, social, and economical factors. Usually a combination of these factors plays a role in the act of crime. Some people decide to commit it and carefully plan everything in advance to increase gain and decrease risk. Some even consider a life of crime better than a regular job—believing crime brings in greater rewards, admiration, and excitement—at least until they are caught. Others get addicted to the adrenaline rush when carrying out a dangerous or illegal act. Others commit crimes on impulse, out of rage or fear. The desire for material gain (money or expensive belongings) leads to property crimes, such as robberies, burglaries, and auto thefts. The desire for control, revenge, or power leads to violent crimes, such as murders, assaults, and rapes. These violent crimes usually occur on impulse or the spur of the moment when emotions run high.

To simplify this complex phenomenon, causes of crime can be categorized into individual and socioeconomic factors.

Individual factors include:
- Age (young)
- Owning a handgun (possible)
- Alcohol and drugs
- Level of education
- Genetic factors (possible)
- Hormonal and other biological factors (possible)

Socioeconomic factors consist of:
- Dysfunctional family
- Unemployment rate

- Socioeconomic status and race
- Societal law enforcement (possible)
- Social media

Individual Factors

Age. Homicide is the second leading cause of death for men aged fifteen to twenty-four in the United States, and the leading cause of death for African Americans in this age group. Mental age is much more important than chronological age.

Handguns. While my personal opinion is that handguns and crime rates have a direct correlation, studies are inconclusive. This issue is debatable and deserves more research. Researchers such as Moody et al. and J. Heichlen have found that handguns have a negligible effect on crime. There may be a rough balance between criminals who use guns in the commission of crime and citizens who use guns to defend themselves and deter crime. Nevertheless, I'd rather live in Canada were guns are prohibited except under strict conditions.

Alcohol and drugs. Numerous studies have shown a high association between substance abuse, such as alcohol and drugs, and criminal activity.

Genetics. Researchers found that identical twins were twice as likely to have similar criminal behavior than fraternal twins who have similar but not identical genes, just like any two siblings. Other research indicated that adopted children had greater similarities of crime rates to their biological parents than to their adoptive parents. These studies suggest a genetic basis for criminal behavior. Having said that, environmental factors play a much more significant role in the likelihood of committing a crime.

Level of education. Empirically, there is a strong inverse correlation between educational attainment and various measures of crime (18). In addition, Lochner and Moretti (2004) estimate that a 1 percent increase in high school graduation rates would save the US economy nearly $2 billion from reduced costs associated with criminal activity.

Neurochemical. With new advances in medical technology, such as CT, MRI, PET scans, and more, researchers probed the inner functions of the brain, searching for links between brain activity and a tendency to commit crime. The role of neurochemicals and hormones in influencing criminal behavior was investigated. Studies indicated that increased levels of some neurochemicals, such as serotonin, decreases aggression. In contrast, higher levels of others, such as dopamine, increased aggression. Researchers expected to find that persons who committed violent crimes had reduced levels of serotonin and higher levels of dopamine.

Hormonal. Neuroscientists also looked at the relationship between hormones, such as testosterone and cortisol, and criminal behavior. Animal studies showed a strong link between high levels of testosterone and aggressive behavior. Testosterone measurements in prison populations also showed relatively high levels in the inmates as compared to the US adult male population in general. Studies of sex offenders in Germany showed that those who were treated to remove testosterone as part of their sentencing became repeat offenders only 3 percent of the time, in contrast to the usual 46 percent. These and similar studies indicate testosterone can have a strong bearing on criminal behavior. Cortisol is another hormone linked to criminal activity. Higher cortisol levels leads to more glucose to the brain for greater energy, such as in times of stress or danger. Researchers found low levels of cortisol were associated with short attention spans, lower activity levels, and often linked to antisocial behavior, including crime.

To this date, there is no single gene, neurochemical, or hormone proven to be directly associated with crime. Instead, it is combination of multiple bio-psycho-socio-spiritual factors that increases the likelihood of criminal activity.

Socioeconomic Factors

Dysfunctional family. Given the facts below, emerging evidence seems to point out that one factor for committing crime overwhelms all the others—*fatherlessness.*

- 85 percent of all children that exhibit behavioral disorders come from fatherless homes (US Center for Disease Control)
- 90 percent of all homeless and runaway children are from fatherless homes (US Bureau of the Census)

- 80 percent of rapists motivated with displaced anger come from fatherless homes (*Criminal Justice & Behavior*, 1978)
- 85 percent of all youths sitting in prisons grew up in a fatherless home (Texas Dept. of Corrections, 1992)

Also, fatherless children are:
- 5 times more likely to commit suicide
- 9 times more likely to end up in a mental institution
- 10 times more likely to abuse chemical substances
- 14 times more likely to commit rape
- 20 times more likely to have behavioral disorders
- 20 times more likely to end up in prison
- 33 times more likely to be abused

Unemployment rate. Normally, as unemployment rises, city revenues decrease because fewer people are paying taxes. This causes cutbacks in city services, including the police force. So a rise in criminal activity may not necessarily be due to fewer police but rather rising unemployment.

Socioeconomic status. A correlation between low family income and antisocial acting out has been repeatedly noted in studies, such as by the National Institute of Mental Health (NIMH).

Law enforcement. Another means of discouraging people from choosing criminal activity is the length of imprisonment. After the 1960s, many believed more prisons and longer sentences would deter crime. Despite the dramatic increase in the number of prisons and imposing mandatory lengthy sentences, however, the number of crimes continued to rise. The number of violent crimes doubled from 1970 to 1998. Property crimes rose from 7.4 million to 11 million, while the number of people placed in state and federal prisons grew from 290,000 in 1977 to over 1.2 million in 1998. Apparently, longer prison sentences had little effect on discouraging criminal behavior.

Social media. Children's television, cartoons, movies, music videos, and video games are potential sources of violent content. Media violence often is perceived as socially acceptable and without consequence. Multiple studies have demonstrated that childhood television viewing is associated with increased risk of subsequent violence. Individual qualities of the viewer and environmental variables interact with the violence that is portrayed to produce a particular outcome in behavior. Adverse effects of increased exposure to media violence may include aggression toward others, increased fearfulness of becoming a victim, with a resultant increase in self-protective behavior, increased desensitization toward actual violence (bystander effect), identification with and acquisition of violent personality traits.

Defense Mechanisms, Personality Disorders, and Crime

The most prominent defense mechanism associated with crime is **acting out**. It is defined as the release of out-of-control aggressive or sexual impulses in order to gain relief from tension or anxiety. Such impulses often result in *antisocial* or *delinquent* behaviors.

Another less intense defense mechanism associated with violence is **displacement**— the person redirects his/her negative feelings about an object or situation to another less threatening object or situation (e.g., kicking your dog when you are angry).

More extreme manifestations of these behaviors are seen in **antisocial personality disorders (APD)**, often leading to criminal activity or **borderline personality disorder (BPD)**, also associated with increased violence.

APD is defined as a pervasive pattern of disregard for and violation of the rights of other people and the normal society. In the general population, sociopath or psychopath is also used to describe these individuals. People with this disorder are not usually patients. They are more often found in courts and prisons and welfare offices. By definition, antisocial personalities are the beginning of APD, and people with these traits are at high risk for committing crime.

There is often evidence of conduct disorders in these individuals before the age of fifteen. In childhood, they typically lie, steal, and fight. They have pervasive difficulties with authority. In adolescence, their sexual behavior may be unusually aggressive. Excessive drinking and drug use are common. By the time they reach adulthood, they are usually unable to hold a job or maintain stable family ties. Alcoholism, unemployment, and social isolation are common among these people.

A substantial number of people with APD commit suicide, and many of them express their anger and frustrations to others.

Surprisingly though, people with antisocial APD can be quite charming. They are often very good at manipulating other people. They can present to the physician or psychiatrist's office in a strikingly normal fashion.

On the other hand, borderline personality disorder (BPD) is defined as a pervasive pattern of instability of interpersonal relationships, self-image, and marked impulsivity beginning by early adulthood. They often demonstrate instability in mood, relationships, and self-image, and a pattern of self-destructive behaviors. Chronic feelings of emptiness and a lack of impulse control, leading to violent activities toward self or others is common. They have a low anger and frustration tolerance. Unstable relationships and repeated self-destructive acts are the most discriminating diagnostic features. These acts include wrist slashing, overdosing, car crashes, drug use, sexual promiscuity, and abrupt changes in jobs. Rather than coping with the resurfacing of negative emotions (i.e., anxiety, fear) associated with past traumatic experiences or a dysfunctional family environment, the child or adolescent acts out these emotions by engaging in externalizing behaviors. These may range from the less serious (i.e., disobedience, moodiness) to the more severe (i.e., suicidal tendencies, violence). Acting out is often associated with rebellious behavior exhibited by children and, especially, adolescents attempting to assert independence.

Fundamental Roots of Crime

So, let us pose these questions again: What are the root causes of crime? How can it be reduced or prevented?

All previous discussions about the complex, multifaceted etiological factors in the commitment of crime can be summarized in the TFA model.

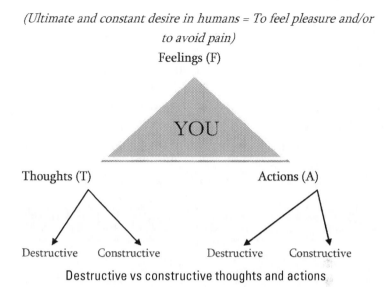

(Ultimate and constant desire in humans = To feel pleasure and/or to avoid pain)

Feelings (F)

YOU

Thoughts (T)   Actions (A)

Destructive   Constructive   Destructive   Constructive

Destructive vs constructive thoughts and actions

Defense mechanisms like the thoughts of acting out and displacement are examples of destructive thoughts (T), often subconscious and out of the person's control. Acts of violence and crime toward self or others, including, murder, physical and sexual assault, promiscuity, suicide, and other antisocial disobedience are examples of the consequent destructive actions (A). As stated previously, the feelings associated with antisocial and borderline personality disorders may include mood swings, lack of anger control, extreme frustration, anxiety, and other negative feelings (F).

According to the STFAR(P) model discussed in previous chapters, the initiation of a criminal activity is often triggered by an unpleasant external stimulus (S), such as an argument, or internal memory of a painful situation (F), such as sexual abuse. In advanced criminals, however, once addicted to the criminal activity, the person does not need any painful triggers to initiate the act anymore. Even the thought of crime, associated with a pleasant feeling of excitement, may be enough to trigger violence.

The fact of the matter is that all infants are born innocent. Despite some evidence of genetic predisposition, it is the persistent negative and distressful circumstances that can potentially turn this child into a sociopath, and ultimately into a criminal at some point. We know from neuroplasticity that the repeated negative impulses create specific neuronal circuits in the brain, slowly transforming it into a potentially criminal one. This process does not happen overnight. It occurs with repeated and persistent exposure to distressful circumstances, ending up in the same thought and action process. A specific negative "antisocial" neuronal circuit is solidified, to the point where it becomes part of the person's character (trait or personality), leading later into a disorder, and ultimately into crime. The spectrum of these progressive brain changes can be demonstrated as:

Healthy Individual	Character/Trait	Personality Disorder	Criminal Activity

This is why prevention at an early stage of antisocial development should be the center of focus and the cornerstone of community programs. One ounce of prevention is much better than a pound of cure. This is consistent with the iceberg analogy of the continuum of mental health, explained in detail previously. It is extremely costly and ineffective to manage these challenging conditions in the later stages of progression.

One of the most fundamental flaws in our educational, health care, and justice systems is that the bulk of available resources are allocated to finding solutions *after the event*—in this case, crime. In the health system, this event can be a heart attack, stroke, or when a mental disorder is diagnosed. The point is that we must do something *before* the occurrence of the event—it may be too late after. *Unfortunately, our collective human resource training and other resources are not directed at the pre-event stage. The key is to redirect our existing resources toward preventive detection and intervention at earlier stages, at a national and international level (19).*

So, what are some of the specific techniques proven effective in reducing crime rates?

The best known psychotherapeutic approach to personality disorders and people using immature defense mechanisms (level II, according to Vaillant's classification), is group therapy, such as Alcoholics Anonymous (AA) and Narcotics Anonymous (NA). Cognitive Behavioral Therapy (CBT) has also proven to be of value in these patients. However, pharmacotherapy has little merit in addressing personality issues. What I'm emphasizing here is *self-cognitive behavioral therapy (SCBT),* where the individual is educated on how the mind and body work, and understands where his thoughts, feelings, and actions are coming from. He/she is then trained on how to intervene to take control of them in very early stages of maladaptive progression, and redirect them toward a healthy pattern. Some studies show the benefits of SCBT in conditions such as depressive and anxiety disorders. However, SCBT by the patient is much less researched compared to CBT by professionals. While more research is needed in this area, from a practical point of view, affordability and accessibility makes SCBT much more advantageous over CBT for the mass population in the iceberg of mental disorders. CBT is only available to the population at the tip of the iceberg, whereas SCBT can be administered to the rest below the water, in a preventive attempt to reduce mental disorders and crime. In an ideal world, these two can be implemented together to optimize the use of available mental health resources.

Another very powerful tool used worldwide is *transcendental meditation (TM).* The scientific research on TM programs is the largest and strongest body of research in the world on any program to develop human potential. This research has demonstrated profound benefits in all fields of life and throughout society—health, education, defense, business and industry, criminal rehabilitation and crime reduction, and administration in the direction of world peace.

Wars of the Minds

Some believe that war is just the manifestation of conflict, and that humans will always be in conflict, if not in war, then in other ways— economic competition between countries, turf wars between gangs, scuffles between siblings, disputes between couples, etc.

War is a state of organized, armed, and often prolonged conflict carried on between states, nations, or other parties. It is often associated with extreme aggression, social disruption, and high mortality. Very similar, organized, warlike behaviors are also found in other primate species, such as chimpanzees, as well as in many ant species.

Even before the dawn of civilization, evidence of war-like activities existed in humans, but on a much smaller scale. One half of the people found in a Nubian cemetery dating to as early as 12,000 years ago had died of violence. Since the rise of the state about five to six thousand years ago, military activity has occurred over much of the globe. The invention of gunpowder and the acceleration of technological advances led to modern warfare. According to Conway Henderson, "One source claims 14,500 wars have taken place between 3500 BC and the late 20th century, costing 3.5 billion lives, leaving only 300 years of peace."

Recent rapid increases in the warfare technologies, and its destructive consequences, have caused widespread public concern. At the end of each of the last two World Wars, popular efforts were made to come to a greater understanding of the underlying dynamics of war and to thereby hopefully reduce or eliminate it altogether. These efforts materialized in the form of **United Nations (UN),** established in 1945 after WW II. The UN is an international organization whose stated objectives are facilitating cooperation in international law, international security, economic development, social progress, human rights, and achievement of world peace. It was founded hoping to stop wars between countries and to provide a platform for dialogue. Shortly after World War II, as a token of support for this concept, most nations joined the UN.

In 1947, in view of the rapidly increasingly destructive consequences of modern warfare, and with a particular concern for the newly developed atomic bomb, the initial developer of the concept, Albert Einstein famously stated, "I know not with what weapons World War III will be fought, but World War IV will be fought with sticks and stones." Fortunately, the anticipated costs of a possible third world war are currently no longer deemed as acceptable by most, thus little motivation currently seems to exist on an international level for such a war.

Why Wars?

If wars have so many negative outcomes, why do they occur in the first place?

War generally involves two or more organized groups or parties. In all cases, at least one participant (group) in the conflict perceives the need to either *psychologically* or *materially* dominate the other participant and is unable or unwilling to accept the possibility of a *true relationship of fundamental equality* to exist between the groups. **The attempt to establish or maintain domination and to avoid equality is a precipitating factor in most wars.** One group wishes to dominate another.

Let's think about it. *Why do humans want or need to dominate one another?* We will come back to this and break it down to its roots even further.

There are different motives for war. A war is either directly **1) offensive,** or **2) defensive,** or indirectly related to **3) a perception of one or the other**.

The occupation of Poland by Hitler in the beginning of WW II is a concrete example of an offensive motive. Saddam Hussein's invasion of Iran in 1980 is another example of an offensive war with the motive to gain more power and economic gain in the Middle East. Iran struck back soon after, exemplifying a defensive war. The war on terrorism initiated by the United States is another example of a defensive war as a result of 9/11.

The third scenario is a bit more complex and sometimes not very clear. The 1948 Arab-Israeli War is another example where both groups feel they are victimized and fighting rightfully to defend their nation. The war started upon the termination of the British Mandate of Palestine and the Israeli declaration of independence on May 15, 1948.

On November 29, 1947, the United Nations General Assembly approved a plan, known as the **UN Partition Plan**, to resolve the Arab-Jewish conflict by partitioning Palestine into two states, one Jewish state (Israel) and a second Arab state (New Palestine). The Jews would get 56 percent of the land, and the Palestinian Arabs would get 42 percent of the land. The Jerusalem area was to become a *corpus separatum*—to be administered by the UN. The Jewish leadership accepted the partition plan. However, arguing that the plan was unfair to the Arabs with regard to the population balance at that time, the representatives of the Palestinian Arabs and the Arab League firmly opposed the UN proposal.

Both sides claim to be in a defensive position, and it is not clear who is right and who is wrong. Each party accuses the other of violation of their rights. To this date, despite significant efforts from worldwide nations, there has clearly been no resolution acceptable to both sides of the conflict.

So, let's pose this question again. *Why do humans want or need to dominate one another?* War-like behaviors are seen in humans, chimpanzees, and ants. What is the common concept among these species than can explain the roots of wars?

To this date, there is absolutely no biological explanation for wars. There is no war gene or war hormone identified to explain the initiation of wars. The roots of wars actually originate within the individual's *mind*.

Let's analyze this from the mind's perspective. Whether for ideological reasons, political power, territorial sovereignty, or financial gains, the *decision to initiate war* is almost always initiated by *one or more individual(s) in charge*. Whether in defense or offense, one individual makes the call after a series of cognitive debate, either solely as a dictator, or in consultation with a number of advisors in democratic states. We are talking about organized warfare activities between two or more parties, not disorganized instinctual behaviors, such as riots. After a series of cognitive debates and challenges, the root of the decision to start a war is one of two things: **either to obtain pleasure or to avoid pain.** *Either for the pleasure of more power, more control, feeling right, acquiring more financial gains, etc., or to avoid the pain associated with defeat, extinction, being overpowered, being wrong, etc.* **At the deepest level of the brain and mind (also a common factor in chimpanzees and ants), it's all about survival!**

The TFA model explains the roots of this decision making in the mind.

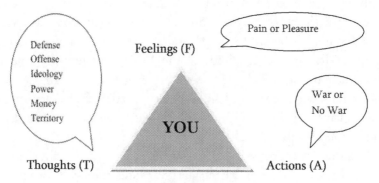

Cognitive dissonance leading to final decision: war or no war

As you can see, it's all about the mind game. The discussion here is not whether a war is right or wrong, reasonable or unreasonable. It's about the psychological roots that originate within the *individual mind* and how we can use this piece of knowledge to alter the end result favorably. Without understanding the core processing of mind, we will never be able to find the etiology of this social disease. Depending on how we define "the enemy"—which is truly nothing but an artificial construct of the subconscious mind—the degree of reaction to a perceived threat can be varied.

The question is *how can we use our knowledge to avoid, eliminate, or minimize wars?*

As illustrated in the STFAR(P) model, the end result (R) is either war or no war, based on the action (A) you choose as a leader of a group. If peace is favored instead of war as the end result (R), appropriate action (A) needs to be taken—for example, diplomatic negotiations instead of military action. To choose the best action possible, one must understand the underlying feelings (F) and thoughts (T) in a rational and mature manner, and analyze the situation (S) in depth before coming to conclusion! *But is that not obvious?*

You may think it is, but I would argue against that. We often fail to understand that the final decision to enter into a war or not is predominantly based on *subconscious thinking* as opposed to *conscious. In other words, the final cognitions are based on a number of other cognitions lying in the deeper levels of our subconscious mind unknowingly.*

Let's take the Arab-Israeli conflict as an example. Apparently, the conflict started between the state of Israel and Palestine. But in fact, it is more complex than that. The distinctive line separating the two groups (Arabs and Israelis) is in fact, religion. Jews versus Muslims, each turning into the enemy for the other. As a matter of fact, both groups in many parts of the area under conflict share similar culture, language, appearances, etc.

Why have they chosen religion to be the distinctive line, and a reason for war? There are many other differences that could have been chosen. Why not the eye color? The green eyes versus the brown eyes. Or their hair color? *Any distinctive line can be chosen to separate two groups and be the reason for their conflict! If that line can be chosen, it can also be un-chosen.* You get the idea?

In ideological conflicts, sometimes and somehow in history, humanity has been fooled by the subconscious mind, and religion has become an important distinctive line, separating the right from wrong! An ideology is a vehicle shared by a specific group, which they believe will lead to their destiny. How can anyone know who is right and who is wrong, when it comes to opinions? Religions exemplify different airlines leading to the same destination! Different languages talking about the same source of creation (with different names)! How on earth did this entity ever gain acceptance as a valid reason for wars? Think about it. It is like saying the English language is right, and the Chinese language is wrong. Or Air France is the right path to a destination as opposed to Air Canada!

It is all about the distinctive or separation line. We have somehow chosen certain boundaries and lines in our minds to justify *defining* our enemies and allies. Geographical borders define national wars. The color of skin initiates racial discrimination. Why was it legitimate for the black to be humiliated and enslaved by the white at some point? Why did this not apply to the eye color? How was the color of skin different from the eyes? Ideology justifies religious crusades. How is an ideology and opinion different from other personal features?

What is the human mind doing to us? Why have we chosen specific distinctive lines as a reason for conflict? The answer is—**ignorance!** In order to understand that, we need to challenge our subconscious thoughts and cognitions over and over again, down to the roots, and rearrange them with the conscious mind. Then you'll see that conflicts over religion and ideology are just as ridiculous and absurd as fighting over the eye color or hair color!

Religions are composed of different components under one umbrella: *spirituality, organization, politics,* and *protocols.* Essentially, the most important and only element common among all religions is **spirituality**—the very concept consistent with the human spirit! It is also the highest purpose of all religions. All other elements are only varieties in expressions or presentations of religion. Spirituality is the music of life. It is a universal language understandable to all humans. It is the *other* elements that misrepresent the main objective of religions, often making them incomprehensible to others.

Let's imagine this scenario for a moment. All inhabitants of the world suddenly become informed that a meteor ten times the size of our planet has escaped its orbit and will collide with Earth in less than a week. We cannot tell where the collision point is, and no place on Earth is immune.

Think about the feelings and thoughts that run through your mind. How would you feel in this context? If you are a Jew, how would you feel about a Muslim or vice versa? Would you still feel the same hatred, or is there now something more important to think about? Would you still think about revenge as a top priority, or instead would you want to team up with all other nations, religions, races, ethnicities, etc. to find a common solution to this new enemy? Suddenly, the definition of *animosity* and *alliance* has changed, and you find yourself on the same side as your previous enemy! You are now an ally to your so-called enemy! War has magically turned into teamwork and collaboration in an instant!

If we are co-creators of our world, and if that is possible in our imagination, then it can also be possible in our reality. The current view and vision of the world does not work. We cannot solve the problems of humanity with the same mind that created them! We need to change our view collectively and envision the entire planet as one nation—all Earthians or Terestrians!! The truth is ... no one is an enemy, but our own ignorance! This takes us to the following chapter, which introduces the next level of civilization!

PART SIX

Connecting the Dots

CHAPTER 17

"Spirit (YOU) + Filter (you) = Identity (perception
of self) + Reality (perception of life)"

The Third Vision

A Shift in Paradigm: A New Civilization

One cannot expect to solve a problem with the same mind that created it!
Humanity has been suffering for thousands of years because of
misunderstandings, misperceptions, and ignorance. Advancements in
science and technology have not diminished any suffering, but only
modernized it. Man-to-man battles have changed to nuclear and
biochemical wars, while swords and spears have upgraded to tanks and
missiles. *What are we collectively missing?*

How much more misery, created by mankind, do we want to
tolerate? Wars and crimes on a daily basis, children dying from hunger
and poverty, discrimination expressing in different ways, disparity at
its peak, and so on? It is time to view the world from a different
perspective—to move on to the next stage of humanity, stop favoring
our self, language, belief, and race as a separate entity, and start defending
our world as one country and its entire people as one nation.

If we could be brothers and sisters in one country, in one religion,
etc., why can we not view this in a larger scale—*in one world!* It is time to
shift from a fragmented view of the world to a congregative one—a world
without artificial borders and enemies. *It is time for a New Civilization!*

Here's a dream: To aim for a better world in harmony and peace. A place where geographic boundaries do not exist, racial varieties are viewed as the colors of the flowers, and differences of opinions and beliefs are tolerated and respected as every human's right. Instead of reasons for crimes and wars, these differences can be viewed as the beauty and strength of creation and employed collectively to build a better future for generations to come! Where we care about children of others as we would for our own, and we treat everyone the way we would like to be treated (the Golden Rule)! Where poverty, hunger, and homelessness become obsolete! Where **ignorance** is recognized as our main enemy and *the root of almost all man-made problems*, hence fought with through raising **global awareness**! Where every non–human species on earth is also considered as part of the equation in major global decision makings! Where the United Nations becomes more democratically involved in the governance and stabilization of all countries, with *equal* representatives from each and every nation in the world. Where we leave behind our shortsightedness and see the bigger picture!

Why does this have to be a permanent dream? What does it take to turn this into reality? After all, we are *co-creators* of this world. Dreams do come true. But for different reasons, the subconscious mind does not want to believe that a major shift is actually possible. However, many individuals in the world think differently. *They materialize their dreams.* These are ordinary people with extraordinary vision, determination, and persistence.

A very interesting quote from an unknown source that sticks in my mind is: "There are four types of people: 1) **Dream Makers**, those who make dreams happen; 2) **Dream Takers**, those who take away your dream; 3) **Dream Fakers**, those who pretend to have a dream but never truly believe in it; and 4) **Dream Undertakers**, those who do have a dream in their thoughts but never act on it and bury it with them."

If we did not have dream makers like Nelson Mandela, there would never be an end to the Apartheid regime and a peaceful democracy in South Africa. If it weren't for determined individuals like Jeremy Gilley, we would never have a Peace Day (September 21). If we did not have visionaries like Barack Obama, there would never be an African American president in the history of the United States. How many more dream makers can *you* think of?

Let's begin by asking this question: *What does it take to make our world a better place to live in?*

The answer is simple but not easy: **change!**

So, a more daring question is: what does it take to initiate a *change* in the world? How is this possible?

Believe it or not, the TFA principle has proven that all it takes is just one individual with a *vision* (thought), *passion* (feeling), and *mission* (action) to make a difference in the world—for the better or worse. Hitler, Buddha, Thomas Edison, and Steve Jobs are only a few of thousands of individuals who have deeply affected the world in a positive or negative way. They believed in themselves and led the world to believe in them. But if we want a big enough change, we need a network of such potential candidates to accomplish the job—networks like Alliance for a New Humanity or the Hay House audience.

A Leap in Time

Rafts and other vessels have been used to cross the seas as far back as five thousand years ago, but it was not until the discovery of the Archimedes Principle by the Greek scientist in 212 BC that marine navigation was taken to the next level. Similarly, invention of the first airplane by Orville and Wilbur Wright in 1903, was made possible through the discovery of Bernoulli's Principle in 1738 by the Swiss scientist, Daniel Bernoulli, leading the aeronautic navigation industry to a new era. Today, unveiling the laws and principles of the entire world as one ecosystem, can lead to another major leap in the history of mankind, creating an opportunity to enter the next level of civilization—*ultra humanity.*

Civilization comes with evolution. Until about five to six thousand years ago, when the early civilizations appeared, "society" and "community" had not established as a clear entity. The perception of a "group" before then was nothing larger than a tribe or a family. With formation of the first human gatherings, communities progressively grew larger with the exponential growth of population, due to surge in food supply after the Agricultural Revolution ten to twelve thousand years ago. Villages, towns, cities, and countries slowly developed, carrying with them a new sense of "societal identity." What had happened was a collective evolutionary change in the mentality of human beings. Their sense of belonging to a specific community, nation, race, etc. grew stronger over time. With that came its advantages and disadvantages. One of the downsides was war.

Now, let us pause for a moment and go back to the modified Maslow's pyramid, but this time view it in the context of *society*, as opposed to the *individual*.

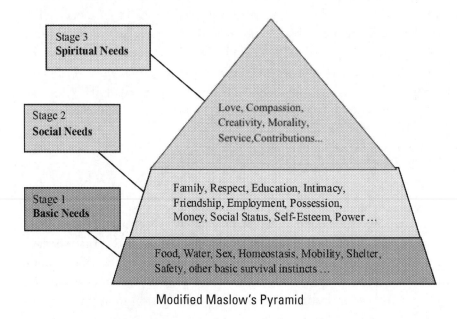

Modified Maslow's Pyramid

For ease of discussion, we can say there are generally three stages of development and psychological evolution in human beings.

- **First stage**—view the individual as one unit
- **Second stage**—view the society as one unit
- **Third stage**—view the world (and rest of the universe) as one unit

If civilization were to have a continuum, can you guess from this diagram what the status of humanity is today?

Yes, you are right. Collectively, we are in the second stage of a societal evolution!

Here's the point: We are missing something critical! We are all struggling with the second stage of civilization—we feel connected to our society, nation, religion, etc. but fail to see our connection to the rest of the world. The current view is "I versus You" and "Us versus Them." We can learn from the cells in our own body. Fifty trillion cells collaborate as one intelligent system, for the benefit of one unit—you. No cells are better than others or work against their mates. In fact, if that happens, the body ends up in a state called **autoimmune disease** and cancer. It's all about the teamwork of the entire system. If we want to see a change in today's world, we need to put on the "spiritual lens" and **collectively** move to the next level of civilization—the **third** level. The only way to survive our own extinction is to view the entire world with over seven billion individuals as one unit—Body of Humanity!

Defining the Third Vision

So what do I mean by the Third Vision, and what are the First and Second Visions?

The First Vision is a purely physical sense with no judgment or interpretation. It exemplifies a camera lens. There is no intelligence, and the "physical eye" is the observer. For example, when you look at a chair using your first vision, all you observe is an image of the chair—that's it.

When intelligence is incorporated to make a judgment or interpretation, you are observing with your Second Vision—"the mental eye." You see the art, craft, and taste of the invisible builder.

The Third Vision allows the observer to see far beyond what we are currently used to. The observer is your "spiritual eye." When you look at a chair with your Third Vision, you see not only a chair and the mastery of its builder, but also wood, trees, forests, oxygen, photosynthesis, Mother Earth, God—*the connection between everything in the universe and the chair is sensed in one snapshot!*

Based on the modified Maslow's pyramid, people who have reached their third stage of life will have the ability to use their Third Vision. The current situation is that we are collectively in the second stage of life, hence the second stage of civilization. For a shift in paradigm, and to evolve to the next civilization, we must begin with self-awareness. As Buddha mentioned, the road to global peace and happiness is through inner peace. The third stage of life would be the ultimate destination for all humans. If enough individuals evolve to this stage, the larval stage of metamorphosis will change the current caterpillar of humanity to the adult butterfly of *ultra-humanity*.

The Butterfly Metaphor

One of my favorite metaphors is the transformation of the caterpillar into the higher state of butterfly, an evolutionary process called *metamorphosis*. This is also seen in other insects, crabs, and rarely in vertebrates. The juvenile form of the animal is significantly different from the mature form. The caterpillar that metamorphoses into a butterfly has been one of the most enduring symbols of human transformation.

Butterflies have four life stages, which include egg, larva (caterpillar), pupa (chrysalis), and adult (butterfly). Metamorphosis is the entire process of how an egg ends up as a butterfly. The butterfly's life begins as an egg that the female lays on the underside of a leaf. It is believed that with the egg come a number of precursor butterfly cells that lie dormant among the caterpillar cells, waiting for the right time to transform. The larva, or caterpillar, hatches from the egg about six days after being laid. These tiny creatures quickly begin to eat away at every leaf in sight. During this time of tremendous growth, the caterpillar sheds its skin several times, becoming stronger and larger with each turn. At the end of this stage, the caterpillar secretes certain hormones, which begin the third stage of metamorphosis. The most amazing part of transformation occurs in this stage in the pupa (chrysalis). When the caterpillar cells die, they become the food for the dormant butterfly cells, which "wake up" and mutate to form the genetic coding for the development of mature butterfly cells. When this happens, the adult butterfly hatches from the pupa, starting the fourth stage of metamorphosis.

Many intellectuals believe that our time is one of accelerated social and individual transformation. Fundamental world views, paradigms of reality, and conceptions of human nature are being questioned and challenged. In a world struggling with economic collapse, fearful of a nuclear holocaust, and on the verge of an ecological catastrophe, we are being challenged to examine ourselves. It seems that two important conclusions are emerging with increasing certainty.

(1) The evolutionary transformation of society and of humanity must take place first in the individual.

(2) The transformation of the individual requires a turning inward, toward the psyche, in the direction of self-realization.

Could we possibly be in the early stages of **transformation** to the ultra-human state? Could human beings be in a kind of larval stage of metamorphosis today? Could we possibly be on the verge of a change that would make us as different from the way we are now as butterflies are from caterpillars? Has the time come for all nations and individuals to unite hand in hand as worldwide brothers and sisters, setting the stage for a **Psychological** and **Cultural Revolution**?

Connecting the Dots

In chapter 2, we explained the two identities of each individual—the true, unconditioned YOU and the false, conditioned you. In fact, you—which is believed to be the real self, is nothing but an illusion of YOU, distorted by the type of lens it is observed through. As discussed earlier, the standard lens in today's civilization is the second vision. In order to observe the true Divine self, we must put a different lens—*the Third Vision.*

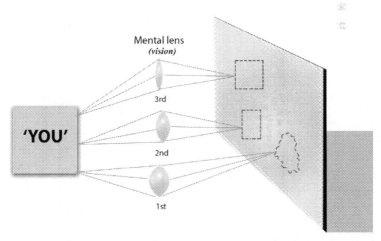

The Third Vision reflecting your true identity—YOU

So let us put the contents of this book into perspective and summarize it by connecting the dots. Using a holistic approach, the diagrams below illustrate how we can observe our true identity through the Third Vision, using a bio-psycho-socio-spiritual lens.

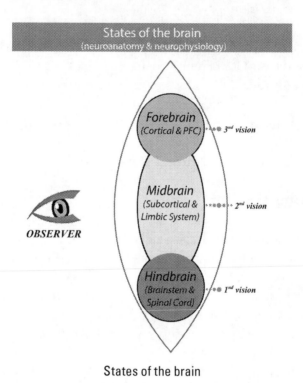

States of the brain

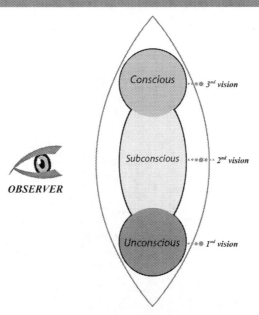

States of the mind

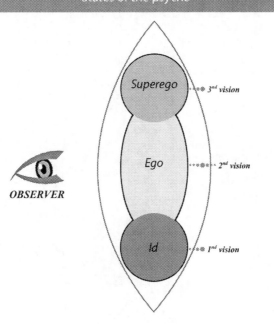

States of the psyche

The Third Vision

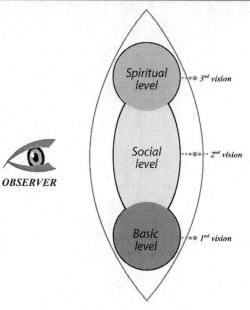

States of personal growth

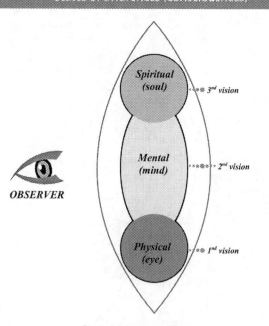

States of awareness

232

In summary, some of the universal dilemmas challenging mankind for thousands of years have been unveiled. Significant emphasis is placed on the connections between what we have learned to date, trying to understand the big picture. In hopes of achieving our peak potentials, and understanding the truth about our self, misperceptions of the collective mind have been clarified. These have been obscuring the lens through which we view the world. *It is now time for a spiritual cataract surgery!* By connecting the dots and placing the final pieces of the puzzle, we hereby propose a new vision—the Third Vision— to view the world differently and to create a better humanity.

STATES	Brain	Mind (TFA)	Psyche	Personal Growth	Awareness (Consciousness)
3	Forebrain	C (thinking)	Superego	Spiritual	Spiritual (Soul)
2	Midbrain	S (thinking)	Ego	Social	Mental (Mind)
1	Behind brain	U (thinking)	Id	Basic level	Physical (eye)

Chart connecting the dots

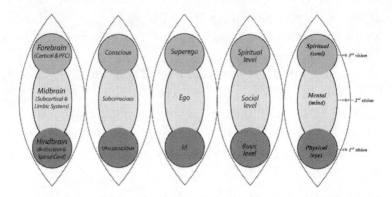

All in one lens

In this chapter, the theoretical principles of the human metamorphosis have been summarized. In the final chapter, practical strategies for a psychological and cultural change will be reviewed.

CHAPTER 18

"If you rule a country, people will respect you. But if
you lead the country, people will follow you."
—*William Wallace*
"And if you empower the people and genuinely make them
feel good about themselves, they will love you."

Conclusion

Change Your Mind, Change Your World

The relationship between the inner and outer world is mutual. For thousands of years, human beings believed that their lives could only be influenced by the outside "reality" of the world, therefore surrendering to "destiny" or "fate." The concept of free will, choice, and the ability to influence the outside world through inside have only been profoundly comprehended in the recent decades, although some ancient philosophers and poets pointed them out centuries ago.

Remember that "if you change the way you see things, the things you see will change."

The conventional understanding so far has been that we are genetically engineered to produce specific outcomes, which may also be influenced by environmental factors. There seems to be little debate on the role of genetics as the primary design. However, the study of **epigenetics** has marked the beginning of an evolutionary phase in our understanding of biology and human life.

At its most basic, epigenetics is the study of changes in gene activity that do not involve alterations to the genetic code but still get passed down to at least one successive generation. These patterns of gene expression are governed by the cellular material—the epigenome—that is above the genome. It is these epigenetic "marks" that tell your genes to switch on or off, to speak loudly or whisper. It is through epigenetic marks that environmental factors like diet, stress, and prenatal nutrition can make an imprint on genes that is passed from one generation to the next!

The Biology of Belief is a groundbreaking work in the field of new biology. Author Dr. Bruce Lipton is a former medical school professor, cellular biologist, and research scientist. His experiments, and those of other leading-edge scientists, have thoroughly examined the processes by which cells receive information. The implications of this research radically change our understanding of life. It shows that genes and DNA do *not* control our biology, that instead we are controlled by signals from outside the cell, including the energetic messages emanating from our positive and negative thoughts.

Dr. Lipton's latest and best research in cell biology and quantum physics is being hailed as a major breakthrough showing that our bodies can be changed as we retrain our thinking. New research reveals that *thoughts* affect genes (20). Groundbreaking scientific studies find that genes can be turned on and off by environmental signals, including thoughts, feelings, and emotions from outside the cell. Dr. Lipton conducted a series of experiments revealing that the cell membrane, the outer layer of a cell, is the organic equivalent of a computer chip, and the cell's equivalent of a brain. Although this view conflicts with the widely held scientific dogma that genes control behavior, papers by other researchers have validated his proposed model.

Traditional cell biology focuses on physical molecules that control life. On the other hand, as a pioneer, Dr. Lipton has been applying the principles of quantum physics to the field of cellular biology. He focuses on the mechanisms through which energy in the form of beliefs can affect our biology, including our genetic code.

In his book *The Biology of Belief*, Dr. Lipton summarizes such leading edge science and explores its implications for our lives. He shows that human beings can control gene activity and even rewrite it by focusing on their beliefs. These beliefs, true or false, positive or negative, creative or destructive, exist not simply in our minds; they are directed downward to the level of the cells of our bodies. He also shows how even our most firmly held beliefs can be changed, which means that we have the power to reshape our lives. Through solid scientific explanations, he demonstrates how environmental signals control cell behavior, gene expression, and adaptation of genes. *The critical point, which can be life-changing, is that these signals may be molecules or energy!*

External energy fields, such as radioactivity, can create a field of energy and have environmental effects similar to physical molecules. Internal energy fields, such as our own thoughts and beliefs, whether negative or positive, may also impact the behavior of our body. This clarifies how the body and mind connect, removing the antagonism between conventional and alternative medicine.

The Continuum of Perception

The continuum of perception and belief is shown in the following diagram. A signal is first *received* through any of the five sensors in the nervous system and *perceived* by the brain to have a specific meaning.

Progression from reception to formation of belief

If you observe a specific ethnicity—a Caucasian, for example—drive dangerously for the first time, this may simply be received as "this was a dangerous driving experience." When a broader meaning or association is attached to the experience, you as the observer perceive it as "this was a Caucasian driving dangerously." If a similar pattern is observed for the second and third time, you begin to establish a cognition: "Caucasians are likely to drive dangerously." Once repeated and solidified, a cognition may turn into a belief, which may express variations in degree of intensity. "I believe Caucasians are dangerous drivers."

This simple yet profound example demonstrates how judgments can lead to prejudice and racial discrimination. Fanatics all around the world will die and kill for their beliefs. Terrorism in the modern world is a testimony to this statement.

Energy, in the form of thoughts and emotions, can therefore act as a signal to control the behavior of cells and the body. It can similarly alter the world and shape our destiny.

As family physicians, every day we see patients presenting with physical symptoms that go through intensive assessments and investigations, and not a single physical cause can be found. These are related to underlying psychosocial problems and are called **psychosomatic symptoms,** manifested through a subconscious defense mechanism called "somatization." These patients are often frustrated by hearing, "It's just in your mind." This does not imply their dishonesty, but rather explains the environmental effect on their cells and the intimate body-mind connection in human beings.

Principles of Change

The first step toward a **positive internal change** is *self-realization (self-awareness)*—realizing that you *need* or *want* to change.

The second step for personal growth is *actual change*, which requires two major components: *knowledge* and *practice*.

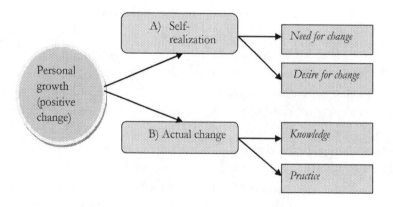

Stages of change

Learning the *knowledge* about the "psychology of change" in previous chapters and understanding all four aspects of humanity—bio-psycho-socio-spiritual—empowers you to implement change and take control of your life. But in fact, the greater challenge is ongoing *practice*. The mere knowledge of the musical alphabet does not enable you to play a song on any musical instrument *without* practice. *In order to master your skills, you need to respect the laws of neuroplasticity and form new neuronal pathways in your brain! It is not possible otherwise.*

Some of the highlights enabling you to gain control over your life, and live it in a much more meaningful, purposeful, and happier way, will be summarized here. However, if you wanted to pick only three take-home messages from this entire book, the following core issues would be suggested.

Core Strategies—Building a Character

1. **Understand who YOU truly are. Discover your inner drive and envision the invisible wire attached to your source!**

   This is extremely important for self-realization. YOU are not who you think you are. YOU are not defined by your labels, possessions, credentials or degrees, social status, clothes, money, etc. YOU are also not your body, mind, thoughts, actions, or feelings. YOU are much higher and more precious than that—the invisible matrix beyond, which holds all those concepts together. YOU are the spirit that lies within each cell, a piece of God, in harmony with the rest of the universal matrix, energy, intelligence, or whatever you want to name it! That spirit was in you as soon as the male and female zygote (egg) combined to form the first fertilized human cell, which then multiplied through a process called **mitosis** to form the rest of the body. Think of that point in time as point A, and your birth as point B. What is driving you and directing that first cell to multiply in a certain way to reach point B? What is it that directs specific cells to shape the eyes, and others to form the heart? Who and what is behind all this miraculous creation? Who or what has designed the genetic coding in the DNA of cells?

   Regardless of what your belief is, that spirit and inner drive is undeniable. It is the same inner drive that leads us miraculously to our ultimate growth potentials (let's say point C).

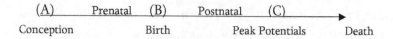

One cannot put enough emphasis on the importance of understanding this inner drive. *It is because of this spirit that every single individual on this planet, regardless of sex, race, religion, nationality, belief, status, etc., deserves to be respected and valued!*

Believe in your self, your spirit, and your soul. It is your soul, through the connection to the Master Engineer, that will lead you to the unlimited—the highest level of personal growth. Your birth (point A to B) is the most solid proof of that!

All it takes is one life-changing "aha" moment to understand and envision this. This is called **realization**. Some people may be fortunate enough to sense this drive naturally. For others, it takes more effort, and they need to discover it. But once they do *envision* the summit of their path—the third level of personal growth—they are already halfway through. The other half is to find out *how to reach* there, which takes us to the next point.

2. **Understand who you are as a filter. Discover the layers of dirt obstructing you from peak potential growth. What are these obstacles blocking your inner light bulb from glowing, despite the connection to the universal source of energy? Once identified, how can they be removed (purification)?**

If, intuitively, we all have the potential to reach from point A to B, and to C, then why is that not happening? What are the obstacles? If you plant a hundred seeds of the same species in the same environment and treat them equally, they will all grow the same height. But this does not apply to humans. You will have one hundred unique individuals with one hundred different levels of growth! Why?

The answer is because human beings are more sophisticated than any other product of creation in this universe. We need a bio-psycho-socio-spiritual approach to consider all aspects of this multidimensional being.

Understand who you are as a filter. This lens—your vision—is what allows your soul to shine through, reflecting your identity (perception of your self), and your reality (perception of life and the rest of the universe).

> "Spirit (YOU) + Filter (you) = Identity (self-image) + Reality (world image)"

Your spirit—'YOU'—is the pure Divine Consciousness attached to the unlimited source of abundance. However, it is your filter—'you'—that may or may not allow that to shine through!

This body-mind filter is what forms your vision, thus requiring a bio-psycho-social approach to fully understand.

The layers of dirt obstructing the glow of your inner potentials are in fact covering your filter. These may develop in different stages of prenatal or postnatal life, in the body, mind, or psyche, and are influenced by internal and external social factors. During the prenatal stage (point A to B), congenital malformations may result from one or more embryological defects. This may be genetic (such as Down syndrome), or environmental (such as Fetal Alcohol Syndrome). Similarly, but in a much more sophisticated way, genetic or environmental (bio-psycho-socio-spiritual) influences after birth may obstruct an individual from reaching the ultimate potential (from B to C). A major difference between the prenatal and postnatal phase is that in the former, *normality* is often the case, with a healthy birth and no defects. In contrast, normality after birth is a defective soul with limited spiritual growth in most cases, and very few people are fortunate enough to reach their peak potential!

The mysterious and beautiful paradox in the human psyche is that *growth* has a unique meaning. Let's use an example to expand on this. When building a tower, growth is defined by *construction* as the major theme. In a society, growth and development is defined by *addition* of the quantity and quality of life of its individuals. Growth implies *construction* and *addition*.

For thousands of years, the same concept has been *erroneously* applied to humans.

Contrary to the examples above, personal growth is all about *reconfiguration* of the human brain! *Deletion* and *undoing* is a crucial element, together with *addition*. It's all about *reconstruction,* rather than just *construction.* All at the same time!

What do I mean by this?

The foundation of one's personality is shaped by about age five, when we still don't have much control over life. We just go with the flow, because the more executive and cognitive layers of the brain—the neocortex and pre-frontal cortex—have not fully developed. And yet the hardware and brain structure—the primitive and limbic system—is in place, ready to incept the software we may be exposed to, through a mechanism called **learning**. Every single experience and exposure is stored in the memory of a newborn from day one. The more these learned processes are repeated, the deeper in the memory they are stored, and the neuronal networks are solidified in a specific pattern pertaining to that memory. These patterns form the basis of one's core "identity" and "reality" by the age of five. By this age, a person establishes an image of self (the "I") through an extremely important process called **identification**, and an understanding of the rest of the world (my "reality") through a process called **realization**, and builds on this image for the rest of his/her life. A child at this age will already have a *cognition*, such as "I am a good person," "I am evil," "I am ugly," or "I am brave, capable, and talented." During this critical period of life, this image and self-cognition is seeded in the child's brain, forming a sense of "who I am." If this "image" is a negative one, the deepest and most important layer of dirt will cover the light bulb of one's spirit. The rest of fate is determined by **cognitive dissonance** and the **defense mechanisms** (DM) utilized by the child. If your image is negative, this is already in dissonance with the innocent nature of the human spirit—which is nothing but "good" and "pure" energy in harmony with the rest of the universe. This leads to profound distress. The child then subconsciously and *unknowingly* uses a series of DMs as a reaction to this distress. The problem is, at this age, most of the DMs available in our "toolbox" are the immature and often destructive ones. The more mature ones are later shaped in the neocortex, which is not yet developed! Do you see the paradox?

As more and more immature DMs are used, other layers of dirt cover the light bulb, and further distress leads to more intense DMs.

This is what I mean by *undoing* and *deleting* these layers. These layers of dirt are the product of numerous bio-psycho-socio-spiritual distresses, followed by destructive defense mechanisms utilized by the subconscious mind to gain temporary relief and escape, at the price of long-term consequences.

From a medical standpoint, there is no magic pill to undo the software. But it is extremely important for the caring people around this child to understand the psychology and apply simple strategies to minimize distress. Also of crucial importance is the person's ability to learn self-management skills later on in life, to delete these "viruses" and replace them with more mature and constructive defense mechanisms.

It is believed that parents have almost 100 percent control over a child up to age five or six, and after that, the parental influence gradually declines. After eighteen to twenty-five years of age in most cases, the parents have no more influence or control, no matter how hard they try. **The parents' biggest obligation is to seed a positive and constructive image in the child's brain by age five!**

Constant repetition of words such as "you are beautiful," "you are strong," "you are capable and talented," "you can achieve anything you want if you put in the effort," and many other positive words are the building blocks of a child's future. To be able to communicate properly in a childish language, and understand their distresses, fears, and frustrations in this phase is extremely important. The idea is not to spoil them and give them whatever they want, but to try to understand their deepest fears and sources of anxiety. *Immense love* combined with *discipline* is key to building a powerful character in your children, and to help them materialize their highest levels of unimaginable potentials!

After age five, the influence of school, society, friends, etc. becomes much more apparent. As the parental control and influence diminishes, so does the window of opportunity! Unfortunately, the collective educational systems in most countries do not offer active programs to build a positive personality. Most of the focus is on learning skills. The current paradigm of learning is designed to help children and adolescents learn basic sciences, without much emphasis on their practicality, and to develop problem solving skills, without much understanding of what the core problems may be. To fill the gaps, it is necessary to implement *age-appropriate psychology* and *self-management courses* from early on.

3. **Broaden your vision, be inquisitive, and think outside the box—learn to see through your Third Vision. Reframe your cognitions and minimize cognitive dissonance.**

   Most people have never learned to think or see 'outside the box'. We often choose the path of least resistance and focus on the first thing that comes to mind. That's how the subconscious mind has learned to think.

   For example, imagine a portrait of a beautiful farm, full of trees and flowers in different colors, a variety of animals, and a big mansion that occupies most of the picture frame. Perhaps, the first thing that grabs our attention is the house, and we can easily get distracted, missing all the other beautiful details of the masterpiece. The subconscious thinker exemplifies one who has his head down, seeing only a few steps in front of him.

   On the contrary, the conscious thinker looks up and around, even sometimes behind, trying to see and absorb everything in the *big picture*. He does not believe or get carried away with every bit of information that enters the realm of his limited senses. He will receive the input, *think about it*, and question it. Is that all there is to the portrait? Is it all about the mansion? What message is the *entire* portrait trying to convey? The wider the scope of our vision, the more developed and mature our conscious thinking centers in the brain will become.

   This center also happens to be our control room for *shifting focus*, enabling us to choose what things in life we want to focus on. In other words, *the knowledge and practice of conscious thinking will grow our prefrontal cortex and higher functioning executive parts of the brain, which empowers us to take control over our life and destiny, as opposed to surrendering to the subconscious mind!*

   Every moment in life and every situation around you is extraordinary. There is no ordinary moment when you look closely. Do not take things for granted and do not cross the moments of life passively. Asking "why" is the key to wisdom. Learn to ask the right questions. Commonly use interrogative adjectives such as *why, why not, what, how, what if, where,* etc. Be better at asking the right question as opposed to finding the right answer. A fundamental flaw in most worldwide educational systems is that they teach how to find answers. *What is not being taught is how to ask the right questions.*

Learn to constantly challenge everything, and know the purpose and reason before accepting it as your reality. You have five powerful senses and a more important resource—your intuition. If something does not make sense, the least you can do is leave a question mark until time clarifies the matter for you. When it comes to critical matters in life, do not just accept anything from anyone without your own research, even if it comes from your parent, leader, doctor, teacher, professor, or most importantly, your own mind!

Do not easily form a belief system without understanding the purpose and roots behind it. Beliefs and deep cognitions can be extremely powerful in forming your destiny, through the process of *identification.* A suicide bomber is an extreme example of this process!

Remember that the subconscious mind can trick you to take control of your life. Constantly challenge and question your *subconscious* thoughts with the *conscious* mind, and reframe your cognitions until they make sense to you. The only place where you have control to alter your destiny is through the conscious mind. This is how you can minimize *cognitive dissonance* and achieve *cognitive consonance*—a state of inner peace between you (your body, mind, psyche, and all other material belongings) and YOU (your formless spirit). This is the key to ultimate long-term happiness and will take you far in life, to the unimaginable realm of unlimited potentials!

General Strategies—Life Skills Training

4. **Think before you judge**.
Everyone's view and perspective of a situation or object is unique. If you show a red car to three different individuals and ask them what color they think it is, you may get three different answers—which may all happen to be true; "light red," "dark red," "burgundy." The key is that every individual has a unique definition of "red" in their mind. It is extremely important to be aware of that when we form a judgment or opinion about something, which may vary individually in the context

of time, person, and place (TPP). An opinion or statement from another person would only make sense if viewed from their perspective. As long as we are aware that each of us views the world from a different lens, we can agree to disagree respectfully. *This simple yet profound fact could have avoided many unnecessary wars over reasons for philosophical disputes, such as religion!*

5. **Be aware of your defense mechanisms during distress.**

Defense mechanisms are the immune system of your psyche. They are vital to mental well-being and crucial to mental survival. We all use them subconsciously in distressful situations, whether we like it or not, and regardless of the long-term consequences they may have. When one or more DM is used predominantly, it becomes a *habitual pattern* and is often used even in much less distressful situations. Hence, it becomes part of your personality. *You cannot eliminate an unwanted DM without providing an alternative.* Learn how to use more mature DMs of ego, and eliminate the less mature ones. This is key to "growing up."

6. **Educate yourself.**

Generally speaking, education stimulates your brain. However, proper education stimulates the specific parts of your brain that help you grow and flourish—the prefrontal cortex. Education about psychology along with proper guidance will help you grow and mature much faster than usual. It will also lead you to the right path—that is, the path that is right for *you*, based on *your* desires, belief systems, values, character, etc. Not one that is dictated by someone else like me, your parent, your teacher, or is designed for the general population. One size does *not* fit all! Throughout history, many disciplines have claimed to lead humanity to ultimate happiness and peace. And yet, we are probably in one of the most un-peaceful eras. In my opinion, there is no perfect or single path to ultimate happiness. Instead, the best discipline is the one(s) that teaches each unique individual the **right tools** to find his/her own path.

7. **Self brain assessment.**

If you notice a specific pattern of negative feelings or thoughts that you need or want to change, try to find out which part of the brain is involved. Do *not* self-diagnose and take medications without the supervision of a medical professional. However, there are plenty of simple, harmless exercises specifically designed to address that area, which may be found in many self-help books. They usually work for mild symptoms, but if they are moderate to severe, medical advice is highly recommended.

8. **Stress management.**

Exercise regular stress management on a daily basis. Choose your method of preference (e.g., physical exercise, yoga, meditation, reading, journaling, music ... or maybe a combination of them). No one is able to avoid regular daily stressors completely, especially in the busy lifestyle today. So it is best to learn how to deal with them in a constructive manner. *Remember that if you are stressed out, it is extremely difficult to think in the right mind*—even if you know the proper techniques and strategies. However, over time, with applying the science and art of "life skills," you will gradually learn to better manage emotions and take control of your life.

9. **Setting goals.**

Setting a goal is the foundation of success, and multidimensional success is key to ultimate happiness. Set long-term and short-term goals. Do not set yourself up for failure. Climb the ladder step by step to boost your confidence and minimize the chances of failure. If you do fail, learn from your mistakes and carry on. **Do not quit!** The sky is the limit, and each mistake is an opportunity for the next success.

Goals take you beyond your limits to a world of unlimited power. The key to evolution and peak performance is to set the bar high enough—yet within reach—*to push you beyond your limits*. Once you are there, set it even higher. The whole point is that *no one* knows what your true potentials are—not even you! So it is up to you to find out. *The only true obstacle to your peak personal growth is your choice to quit.*

10. **Keys to Long-Term Happiness—(BFMP)—Balance, Flexibility, Meaning, Purpose**.

Life is a journey, like a ride to your destination. It starts with a departure and ends in a destination. How do you make it a joyful ride?

Balance and *Flexibility*. At times, you may feel happy driving fast or surpassing other vehicles in the journey of life. These instances can make you happy, but only for a short time. Balance and flexibility are critical to long-term happiness. You may need to drive faster at times, and slow down at other times. Going too fast may lead to unwanted consequences, and going too slowly may prevent you from ever achieving your goal. Another key to a healthy and happy life is flexibility. At times, you may have to turn left, or right, or just take a break. If you pay too much attention to the rules and principles in your life, rigidity becomes the theme, taking away its meaning, defeating its purpose, and making it a less joyful ride.

Meaning and *Purpose*. These are two key elements that make life valuable. Life without meaning is like music without sound. If you cannot find meaning and quality in the ride of life, then revisit your entire journey and the vehicle that needs to be changed to make it more meaningful. Life without a purpose is purposeless! What is the point? What is the destination? What do you want to get out of life, and where do you want to end up? The direction and destination determine the purpose of the ride of your life.

Situational Strategies—Managing Stress and Daily Challenges

11. **Observe your thoughts (T), feelings (F), and actions (A) without judging them.**

    If you want to change one or the other, just look at one step preceding. Be aware of the part of your brain being used. Usually you'd want to change your F. Then change your T or A, and F will automatically change.

12. **Before you act, take action.**

    Learn the skill of proactive thinking as opposed to reactive thinking. Try not to respond to your thoughts immediately (except in dangerous situations). Instead, pause for a moment to think about your action and related consequences. Question your immediate thought. Is it emotional or rational? Is it the best thought? Is it true? Learn how to use your conscious mind rather than the subconscious. *Remember this is not an easy task and does not happen overnight.* It comes with continuous practice and time, but the first step is knowledge—to recognize your thoughts and feelings.

13. Focus and distraction.

Remember life is all about making choices and taking responsible actions. It's up to you to choose what you want to focus on. You can choose to see the empty half or the full half of a glass. Life is like the sky with clouds scattered all over. You can choose to see the clouds or the sky in between the clouds. If you are optimistic enough, you can even see the sunshine through and beyond the clouds.

Focus. Here is one of my favorite examples. You have ten seconds to remember all the red objects around you. Now close your eyes, and wait for ten seconds. Now name all the green objects out loud! *What? I thought you wanted me to name all the red ones,* is what most people would think. But this is just a simple test to show that you will likely remember what you focus on, and not remember what you do not focus on. The simple fact, however, is that you get to **choose** what to focus on in life! Learn to focus on the positive things in life, and distract your thoughts when you have a negative emotion (this is easier said than done, and it is a skill that needs practice).

Distraction. Another simple yet successful technique, which I've used regularly, is what I call the *three-step green approach.* When you are faced with distress:

1. Take a deep breath.
2. Say to yourself, "This too will pass."
3. Find any green object around you and pay attention to its details.

14. Self-cognitive therapy.

Understand your subconscious thoughts and challenge them. Do not believe every thought that comes to your mind. Thought journaling is a powerful and simple exercise to challenge your unwanted thoughts. When you write them down, ask yourself: Is it true? Are you 100 percent sure it is true? If you're not 100 percent certain about its validity, then it may or may not be true. What is the opposite cognition? Is that one true? That may or may not be true as well. But why choose the one that prevents you from reaching your goal over the one that empowers you?

As discussed above, all you have to do is shift focus—from the empty half of the glass to the full half. Here are some examples.

- "I don't have the energy," can be replaced with, "I am part of the universal energy. By connecting to my source, I will have access to all the energy that is needed."
- "I cannot do this. This is not for me," can be replaced with, "There are plenty of people in the world who have achieved the unthinkable. If there is only one person in this world who has done what I want to do, then there is absolutely no reason why anyone else including myself, cannot do it."

SUMMARY

Core Strategies

1. Understand who YOU truly are. Discover your inner drive and envision the invisible wire attached to your source.
2. Aim for your summit of growth—the third level of your personal ladder. Discover the layers of dirt obstructing you from peak potential growth. What are these obstacles, blocking your inner light bulb from glowing, despite the connection to the universal source of energy? Once identified, how can they be removed (purification)?
3. Broaden your vision, be inquisitive, and think *'outside the box'*—learn to see through your **Third Vision**. Reframe your cognitions and minimize cognitive dissonance.

General Strategies

4. Think before you judge.
5. Be aware of your defense mechanisms during distress.
6. Educate yourself.
7. Self-assess your brain.

8. Exercise regular stress management.
9. Set reasonable and realistic goals—both short term and long term.
10. Learn and practice the keys to long-term happiness—balance, flexibility, meaning, purpose (BFMP).

Situational Strategies

11. Observe your thoughts (T), feelings (F), and actions (A) without judging them.
12. Before you act, take action.
13. Focus and distraction—choose the things to focus on that empower you and bring happiness. Distract yourself from distressful thoughts.
14. Learn and practice the skill of self-cognitive therapy.

So why is all this material important … or is it?

I remember assisting an orthopedic surgeon in the operating room in Vancouver, Canada, in 2004. In the midst of a prolonged surgery, I was having a philosophical dialogue with the anesthesiologist about some of the contents mentioned in this book.

"So what is the relevance and importance of the points you are making?" he said in a challenging tone.

"So why are you here in this room? What is your role? What are you trying to do?" I replied with a series of questions. "Umm, well I'm here as part of a team to make a difference—to save a patient and improve his quality of life," he responded while expressing in his eyes something along the lines of "I see where you're going."

"How many years of education and practice did it take you to save one person's life or improve his/her quality of life? Was it worth the hassle?" Knowing his answer, I did not wait for him to reply and continued, "If all these years of education and practice are worth serving one person, how important would it be to try to impact humanity?"

That was the end of discussion for the rest of the operation!

Here are some of the reasons why I believe the contents of this book are so important.

1. Many formulas and patterns of life have been unveiled, demonstrating how the entire universe—and Mother Earth as one element of it—functions as a system with its own rules and mechanisms. Understanding the laws and principles of this ecosystem, creates an opportunity to enter the next level of civilization—*ultra humanity*. We have the choice to impact humanity and the entire planet in a positive or negative way.

2. Map to your destiny—you are not lost in the wilderness of life. Instead, this book acts like a compass, giving you insight to find your way to your desired destiny.

3. It will help you find true happiness in the right place—that is, within yourself, as opposed to the external world.

4. By realizing who YOU truly are and knowing your unlimited potentials, the feeling of love and approval for your self will result in self-gratification, and there is no need for external approval from other individuals or society.

5. Believing in your true spirit and the eternal essence of formless YOU, there is no reason to fear death when you look at the bigger picture of life from a higher perspective.

6. The practical use of the STFAR(P) model has been demonstrated in different scenarios. This principle can be used in any minor or major situation in life.

7. The need for a psychological and cultural revolution was explained.

8. A possible solution and strategy was introduced as the basis for this revolutionary shift in paradigm—the Third Vision—which, in my opinion, can save the future of our planet and its inhabitants from extinction.

9. Prevention of mental illness and promotion of mental wellness was emphasized as the basis of a healthy individual and society.

10. Techniques and strategies were introduced to master your skills of self-cognitive behavioral therapy (SCBT), to empower your conscious thinking and override the subconscious mind.

11. Understanding the self allows self-realization, the first step of a positive change toward peak potential performance. One of the most important principles in evolution is to identify and undo the "viruses" within our "self."

12. Proposal of the modified Maslow's pyramid allows further exploration of the deep roots of the psyche in a more practical way, which helps us understand and control our emotions and behaviors, the basic concepts of self-realization.

13. A scientific and evidence-based approach helps to factualize some of the theories we have been struggling with for thousands of years, such as the biological evolution of the brain, the science of karma, etc.

14. Putting the content into a scientific context is generally more acceptable and appealing to the newer educated generations that are more familiar with the language of science, instead of religion, philosophy, etc. They need to understand, as opposed to blindly accept, why we value certain morals and dismiss other immoralities.

15. And last but not the least, the simple fact of knowledge acquisition satisfies your need and desire for learning—one of the fundamental needs in all three stages of personal growth.

"May God grant me the serenity to accept the things that I cannot change; courage to change the things that I can; and wisdom to know the difference."
—Reinhold Niebuhr

ACKNOWLEDGMENTS

I wish to thank all of the people who supported this book in any way, and offered their encouragement, wisdom, and insight: Farzad Mazarei, Kouhyar Tavakolian, Tom and Leslie Keenan, Fay Arjomandi, John Corey, Kambiz Karbasi, and Saeed Vahidi. Thank you. Thank you. Thank you.

I want to acknowledge Balboa Press and Hay House, outstanding publishers, and their elegant team of editors and designers whose contribution made this dream come true.

Next, my deepest appreciation goes to a number of inspiring teachers, wise coaches, outstanding leaders, and exceptional role models whose contribution to the world brings optimism and hope: Bruce Lipton, Wayne Dyer, Deepak Chopra, Anthony Robbins, George Vaillant, Eckart Tolle, David Suzuki, Oprah Winfrey, Richard Branson, Bill Gates, Norman Doidge, Gary Chapman, Steve Jobs, and Stephen Hawking.

Next, I'd like to express my deepest love to my close family, Parvin, Reza (whose soul is with me), Farhad, Faramarz, Farzad, and Kian, for their undivided love and support.

Most importantly, I want to express my love and appreciation for my beloved wife, Samin, my best friend and life partner. This would not have been possible without your love, support, and encouragement. Thank you for being patient with me. I love you.

ENDNOTES

Chapter 3;

(1) These consist of: medulla, pons, cerebellum, mesencephalon, the oldest basal nuclei. *Medulla Oblongata:* The medulla oblongata functions primarily as a relay station for the crossing of motor tracts between the spinal cord and the brain. It also contains the respiratory, vasomotor and cardiac centers, as well as many mechanisms for controlling reflex activities such as coughing, gagging, swallowing and vomiting. *Pons:* The pons is a bridge-like structure which links different parts of the brain and serves as a relay station from the medulla to the higher cortical structures of the brain. It also contains the respiratory center.

(2) In 1952, Paul Maclean expanded these ideas to include additional structures in a more dispersed "limbic system". The concept of the limbic system has since been further expanded and developed by Nauta, Heimer and others.

(3) The hypothalamus is a small part of the brain located just below the thalamus. It is intimately connected with the pituitary gland. It is one of the busiest parts of the brain, and is mainly concerned with homeostasis. Homeostasis is the process of returning something to a "set point". The hypothalamus is responsible for regulating hunger, thirst, response to pain, levels of pleasure, sexual satisfaction, anger and aggressive behavior, and more. It is also believed to play a role in emotions. However, in general terms, the hypothalamus has more to do with the expression (symptomatic manifestations of the physical states) of emotions than with the formation of the affective states. It also regulates functions like pulse, blood pressure, breathing, and arousal in response to emotional circumstances, through the regulation of the parasympathetic and sympathetic nervous systems (known as the *Autonomic Nervous System*). The hypothalamus sends instructions to the rest of the body in two ways. The first is to the autonomic nervous system. This allows the hypothalamus to have ultimate control of things like blood pressure, heart rate, breathing, digestion, sweating, and all the sympathetic and parasympathetic functions. The other way the hypothalamus controls things is via the pituitary gland. It is neurally and chemically connected to the pituitary, which in turn pumps hormones called releasing factors into the bloodstream.

(4) The hippocampus consists of two "horns" that curve back from the amygdala. It appears to be very important in converting things that are "in your mind" at the moment (in short-term memory) into things that you will remember for the long run (long-term memory). The intact hippocampus allows the animal to compare the conditions of a present threat with similar past experiences, thus enabling it to choose the best option, in order to guarantee its own survival. When both hippocampi (right and left) are destroyed, nothing can be retained in the memory. The subject quickly forgets any recently received message. In other words, the short term memory still works, and the older memories from the time before the damage are untouched. However the conversion of short term memory to older memories is blocked! Thus, a person cannot build new memories, and lives instead in a strange world where everything he experiences just fades away. This very unfortunate situation is elegantly portrayed in the wonderful movie Memento.

(5) The amygdalas are two almond-shaped masses of neurons on either side of the thalamus at the lower end of the hippocampus, connecting with the hippocampus, the thalamus, and other parts of the prefrontal area. These connections make it possible for the amygdala to play its important role on the mediation and control of major affective activities like friendship, love and affection, on the expression of mood and, mainly, on fear, rage and aggression. The amygdala, being the center for identification of danger, is fundamental for self preservation. When triggered, animals respond with aggression. It gives rise to fear and anxiety which lead the animal into a stage of alertness, getting ready to fight or flight. Experimental destruction of both amygdala tames the animal, which becomes sexually non-discriminative, deprived of

affection and indifferent to danger. The electrical stimulus of these structures elicits crises of violent aggression. Humans with marked lesions of the amygdala, lose the affective meaning of outside information, like the sight of a well known person. The subject knows, exactly, who the person is, but is not capable to decide whether he likes or dislikes him/her. Some evidence suggests involvement of the amygdale in regulation of chronic pain through GABA-B neurotransmitters. These can be suppressed by the use of mood stabilizers. On the other hand, the locus coreuleus is involved in acute pain through GABA-A neurotransmitters. In psychiatry, medications such as gabapentin and benzodiazepines have been used in suppressing these nerve activities.

Chapter 4

(6) Shaw, Christopher; McEachern, Jill, eds (2001). *Toward a theory of neuroplasticity*. London, England: Psychology Press.

(7) LeDoux, Joseph E. (2002). *Synaptic self: how our brains become who we are*. New York, United States: Viking. p. 137>>>

Chapter 5

(8) **Alfred Adler** was born in Austria on February 7, 1870. Being a medical doctor and psychologist, he is best known as the founder of Individual Psychology. In addition he is credited, along with Carl Jung and Sigmund Freud, as one of the greatest founding influences of modern psychology. Among Adler's chief contributions are the importance of birth order in the formation of personality, the impact of neglect or pampering on child development, the notion of a "self perfecting" drive within human beings, and the idea that one must study and treat the patient as a "whole person." Other important tenets of Adler's theory are the idea that individuals create a "fiction" or story about themselves in childhood that guides their perceptions and choices throughout life, and that the ability to work with others for a common good was the hallmark of sound mental health. Adler's best known works include *The Practice and Theory of Individual Psychology* (1927) and *Understanding Human Nature* (1927).

Perhaps because his emphasis was so rooted in the daily and real life experience of individuals, in contrast to the sexually obsessed abstractions of Freud and mysticism of Jung, Adler's theory and methodology have found broad acceptance and influence within the mainstream of psychology. Not only does his philosophy remain popular with new students of psychology today, but his influence can also be perceived within the works of Erich Fromm, **Abraham Maslow,** Rollo May, Karen Horney, Julian Rotter, E. C. Tolman, and Carl Rogers. ICASSI and NASAP (North American Society for Adlerian Psychology) both continue to promote his work; in addition a number of schools, dedicated specifically to carry on his philosophy, exist in the the various countries.

(9) Carl Jung, born 26 July 1875, was a Swiss psychiatrist and founder of analytical psychology. He is best known for his theories of the Collective Unconscious, including the concept of archetypes, and the use of synchronicity in psychotherapy. Along with Sigmund Freud, who was his mentor, Jung pioneered modern theories of the relationships between the conscious and unconscious aspects of mind. But while Freud postulated a psychosexual explanation for human behavior, Jung perceived the *primary* motivating force to be spiritual in origin. According to Jung, it was from the soul that the complementary drives of differentiation and integration arose, fueling the processes of growth, development, and healing. Mental illness arose when these processes were thwarted. He was the producer of theory of the Collective Unconscious. His best known works include *The Psychology of the Unconscious* (1912) and *Psychological Types* (1921).

Chapter 7

(10) Abraham Maslow was inspired by, and one of the distinct followers of Alfred Adler. Adler's theory and methodology have found broad acceptance and influence within the mainstream of psychology. Not only does his philosophy remain popular with new students of psychology today, but his influence can also be perceived within the works of Erich Fromm, Abraham Maslow, Rollo May, Karen Horney, Julian Rotter, E. C. Tolman, and Carl Rogers. ICASSI and NASAP (North American Society for Adlerian Psychology) both continue to promote his work; in addition a number of schools, dedicated specifically to carry on his philosophy, exist in the the various countries. Most notable among these in the United States is The Adler School of Professional Psychology, originally founded by Rudolf Dreikurs as The Alfred Adler School of Professional Psychology.

(11) See diagram below for connection of the brain parts and layers to the psychological models of the psyche and mind, and the modified Maslow's Pyramid.

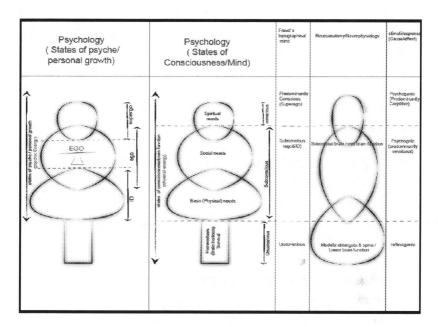

Chapter 8

(12) There are many possible reasons for the dysfunction of the reward system. Genetic abnormalities, exposure to a prolonged stress, and alcohol or other substance abuse leads to a corruption of the "cascade function" of neurotransmitters involved in the reward circuit. Such a disruption results in the opposite of the "reward": feelings of anger, anxiety, and other emotions associated with negativity. It has also been linked with compulsive and impulsive disorders such as alcoholism and attention deficit hyperactivity disorder. Since dopamine has been deemed the most important of all neurotransmitters in the neurological expression of pleasure, some scientists believe that it is a defect in the gene related to this chemical that has been primarily blamed for the reward deficiency syndrome. Among these scientists, is Dr. Kenneth Blum, a researcher on neuropsychopharmacology and genetics. Along with Dr. Ernest Noble, he is often referred to as the co-discoverer of the alcoholism gene due to his study publication in the Journal of the Americal Medical Association in 1990. The dopamine (D2) receptor has been determined the producer of the "reward"-producing neurotransmitters. Other addictions such as the ones related to psychoactive substances (alcohol, heroin, cocaine, methamphetamine, marijuana, nicotine, caffeine, glucose, etc.), as well as aberrant behaviours (sex, porn, gambling, internet gaming, masochism and sadism, excessive work, etc) are also linked to defects in the dopamine receptor genes. However, another notion is that genes are not a direct cause of any such disorder. Defects in genes may distort cell functions and/or processes, which themselves may in turn cause a disorder, but the direct causal relationship between the two has yet to been proven. The mainstream of scientists believe that environmental and social factors definitely play a significant role as well as genetics.

(13) Psychoactive drugs are divided into three groups according to their pharmacological effects:

- Stimulants ("uppers"). This category comprises substances that wake one up, stimulate the mind, and may even cause euphoria, but do not affect perception. Examples: coffee, tea, cacao, ephedra, cocaine, sugar,etc.

- Depressants ("downers"), including sedatives, hypnotics, and narcotics. This category includes all of the calmative, sleep-inducing, anxiety-reducing, anesthetizing substances, which sometimes induce perceptual changes, such as dream images, and also often evoke feelings of euphoria. Examples: opioids (*natural* including opium, codeine, morphine, *semi-synthetic* including heroin, hydromorphone, hydrocodone, oxycodone, oxymorphone, and *fully synthetic* opioids: such as fentanyl, pethidine, methadone). Others include barbiturates, benzodiazepines, and alcohol.

- Hallucinogens, including psychedelics, dissociatives and deliriants. This category encompasses all those substances that produce distinct alterations in perception, sensation of space and time, and emotional states. Examples: THC, and LSD (psychedelics), nitrous oxide (dissociatives), and *Datura*/atropine (a deliriant).

Chapter 11

(14) The research studies below were selected from over 350 peer-reviewed published studies. **Mental Functioning:** –Increased brain coherence *International Journal of Neuroscience* (116: 1519–1538, 2006) –Increased use of brain reserves *Human Physiology* (25: 171–180, 1999) –Increased creativity *Journal of Creative Behavior* (13(3): 169–180, 1979) –Broader comprehension and improved ability to focus *Perceptual and Motor Skills* (39: 1031–1034, 1974) –Increased self-development *Journal of Social Behavior and Personality* (17(1): 93–121, 2005) **Mental Well-Being:** –Increased calmness *Physiology & Behavior* (35: 591–595, 1985) –Increased self-actualization *Journal of Social Behavior and Personality* (6: 189–248, 1991) –Increased strength of self-concept *British Journal of Psychology* (73: 57–68, 1982) –Decreased anxiety *Journal of Clinical Psychology* (45: 957–974, 1989) –Decreased depression *Journal of Counseling and Development* (64: 212–215, 1985)

Physiological Health: –Improved health in university students *Journal of Instructional Psychology* (22: 308–319, 1995) –Reduced illness and medical expenditures *American Journal of Managed Care* (3: 135–144, 1997) –Reduction of high blood pressure *Hypertension* (26: 820–827, 1995) **Workplace:** –Improved job performance *Academy of Management Journal* (17: 362–368, 1974) –Increased job satisfaction *Academy of Management Journal* (17: 362–368, 1974) **Benefits to Society:** –Reduced violent crime in Washington *Social Indicators Research* (47: 153–201, 1999) –Reduced war deaths *Journal of Conflict Resolution* (32: 776–812, 1988) *Journal of Conflict Resolution* (34: 756–768, 1990) –Reduced crime in Washington *Journal of Mind and Behavior* (9: 457–486, 1989) –Reduced crime in U.S. Cities *Journal of Mind and Behavior* (9: 457–486, 1989) –Reduced violent crime *Journal of Mind and Behavior* (8: 67–104, 1987)

Chapter 11

(15) The direction of this field is determined by Fleming's right and left hand rules.

Chapter 16

(17) www.uptodate.com

(18) Freeman (1996) points out that more than two-thirds of all incarcerated men in 1993 had not graduated from high school. In the 1980 wave of the National Longitudinal Survey of Youth (NLSY), 34% of all men ages 20-23 with 11 or 12 years of completed schooling self-reported earning some income from crime, compared with 24% of those with a high school degree, and only 17% of those with more than twelve years of school (Lochner 2004).

(19) A growing body of evidence suggests that early childhood interventions can substantially reduce adult crime rates. The High/Scope Perry Preschool Program for disadvantaged minority children measured lifetime arrests for randomly assigned participants and non-participants. While 55% of all non-participants were arrested 5 or more times through age 40, only 36% of the preschool participants had been arrested that often which is statistically significant (Schweinhart, et al., 2005). The Syracuse Family Development Program also produced large reductions in delinquency (Lally, et al., 1998). These findings lead Donohue and Siegelman (1998) to conclude that small, rigorous early intervention programs may pay for themselves through reduced crime rates alone, if they can be targeted to high-crime groups.

(20) Lipton, Bruce H. (2005). *Biology of Belief.* Hay House Inc.

ABOUT THE AUTHOR

FRANCIS (FARSHEED) H. VALA

is passionate about making a difference in peoples' lives. At 18, his inquisitiveness led to the quest of finding answers to some of the most profound questions posed by mankind ... "what is life all about?", "what is the meaning and purpose of life?", "why do people behave the way they do?", "what is right or wrong, and who determines that?", and so on.

Overwhelmed by the complexity of these concepts, he became depressed, but somehow found a way to self-manage toward recovery. He soon realized that these universal questions are too mind-blowing, and the only vehicle that could possibly help feed his curiosity was education. He decided to postpone the journey to happiness and meaning of life, in order to find some of these answers in a scientific and acceptable way!

He obtained his MD degree at the age of 25. His mission: to promote global education and awareness. His vision: "I am a global citizen, and we are all Earthians! I am not prepared to die without a contribution to the world—change for a better humanity, and a more peaceful planet!"

In 2002, his father's sudden death came as a shock. Emotionally motivated, Francis was determined to resume his journey through a more scientific approach, and attempted to put together the pieces of "the puzzle of life". He started accumulating evidence and research to some of the most profound and unexplained concepts in humanity. By 2009, enough pieces of the puzzle was collected to make sense and view the big picture. He then began writing this book, which was completed in 2012.

Many concepts have been borrowed from outstanding scientists, philosophers, researchers, teachers, and leaders in the past and present, and a few more were added by the author.